The Centre Pompidou
Creation in the heart of Paris

Centre Pompidou

This publication has been supported by

© Éditions du Centre Pompidou,
Paris, 2011
ISBN: 978-2-84426-431-2
Publisher number: 1449
www.centrepompidou.fr
boutique.centrepompidou.fr

Cover: The Centre Pompidou, by night

Photographic Credits

© Archives Archigram: p. 23 b.
© Patrick Bouchain, agence Construire: p. 93
© Bpi [Michaël Levy]: p. 56-59
© Casterman: p. 95
© Collection Centre Pompidou, Dist. RMN-GP: p. 65, 66, [Jacques Faujour] 12 g., [Georges Méguerditchian] 69, 70, [Philippe Migeat] 64 g., 67, 71-73, 94 b., [Jean-Claude Planchet] 68, [Adam Rzepka] 64 dr.
© Centre Pompidou, Paris: p. 17, 20, 30 b., 49, 50 h. g., 92, [Archives] 13, 14 h. dr., [Pierre-Henri Carteron] 16, [Jacques Faujour] 31 h. dr. et b., 53 m. h. (3 ill.) et dr., 78-79, [Georges Méguerditchian] cover and back cover, 4, 6, 8-11, 24-29, 31 h. g., 32, 33 g. et h. dr., 34 g. h. et b., 35, 36 b., 37-39, 40 g. et h. dr., 42-47, 52, 60-61, 74-76, 80 h., 81 b., 82, 83 h., 84-87, [Philippe Migeat] 33 b. dr., 80 b., 81 h., [Jean-Claude Planchet] 48, 62-63, [Bertrand Prévost] 50 dr., [Philippe Prévost] 53 b. m., [Adam Rzepka] 77, [Hervé Véronèse] 50 b. g., 51, 54-55, 83 b., [DR] 18-19, 21
© Centre Pompidou-Metz [Roland Halbe]: p. 88-91
© DHAAP, photographie Lansiaux: p. 22 b. g.
© Robert Doisneau/Rapho: p. 36 h.
© Estate of Billy Klüver and Experiments in Art and Technology: p. 53 b.
© Gilman Paper Company, New York: p. 23 h.
© Jean-Claude Gautrand: p. 15
© Le Figaro / 1970: p. 41 h.dr.
© Le Monde / 1972: p.12
© Alain-Marie Markarian: p. 30 h.
© Photothèque des musées de la Ville de Paris [L. Degraces]: p. 14 g.
© The Hulton Deutsch Collection Limited, Londres: p. 22 h. g.
© Laurent Rousseau/TOP: p. 34 dr.
© Roger-Viollet, Paris: p. 22 h. dr.
All rights reserved: p. 14 b. dr., p. 22 b. dr., 41, 53 g. m. et b.

Copyrights

The Centre Pompidou

Creation in the heart of Paris

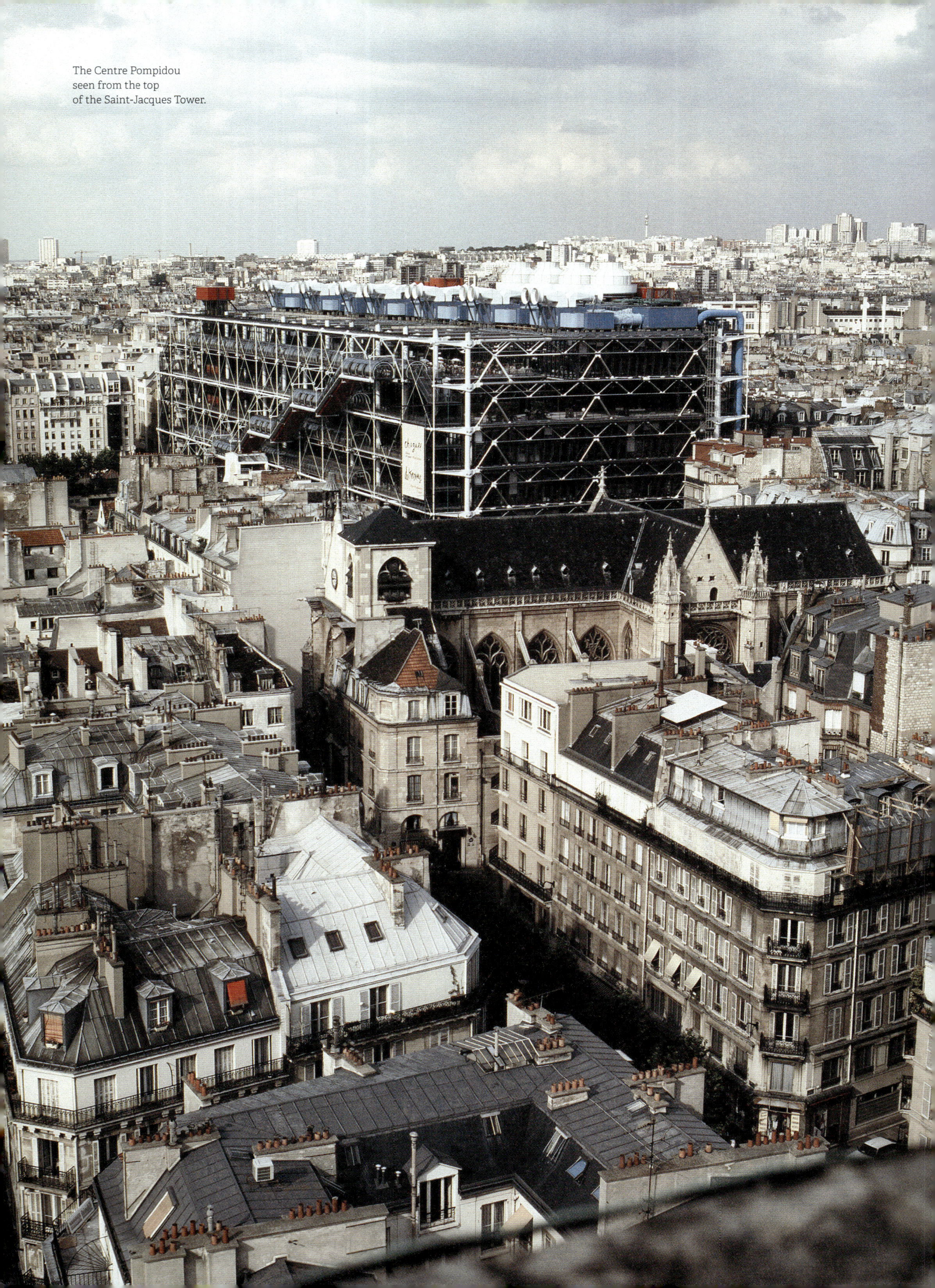
The Centre Pompidou
seen from the top
of the Saint-Jacques Tower.

Contents

The Centre Pompidou seen from the basilica of Sacré-Cœur.

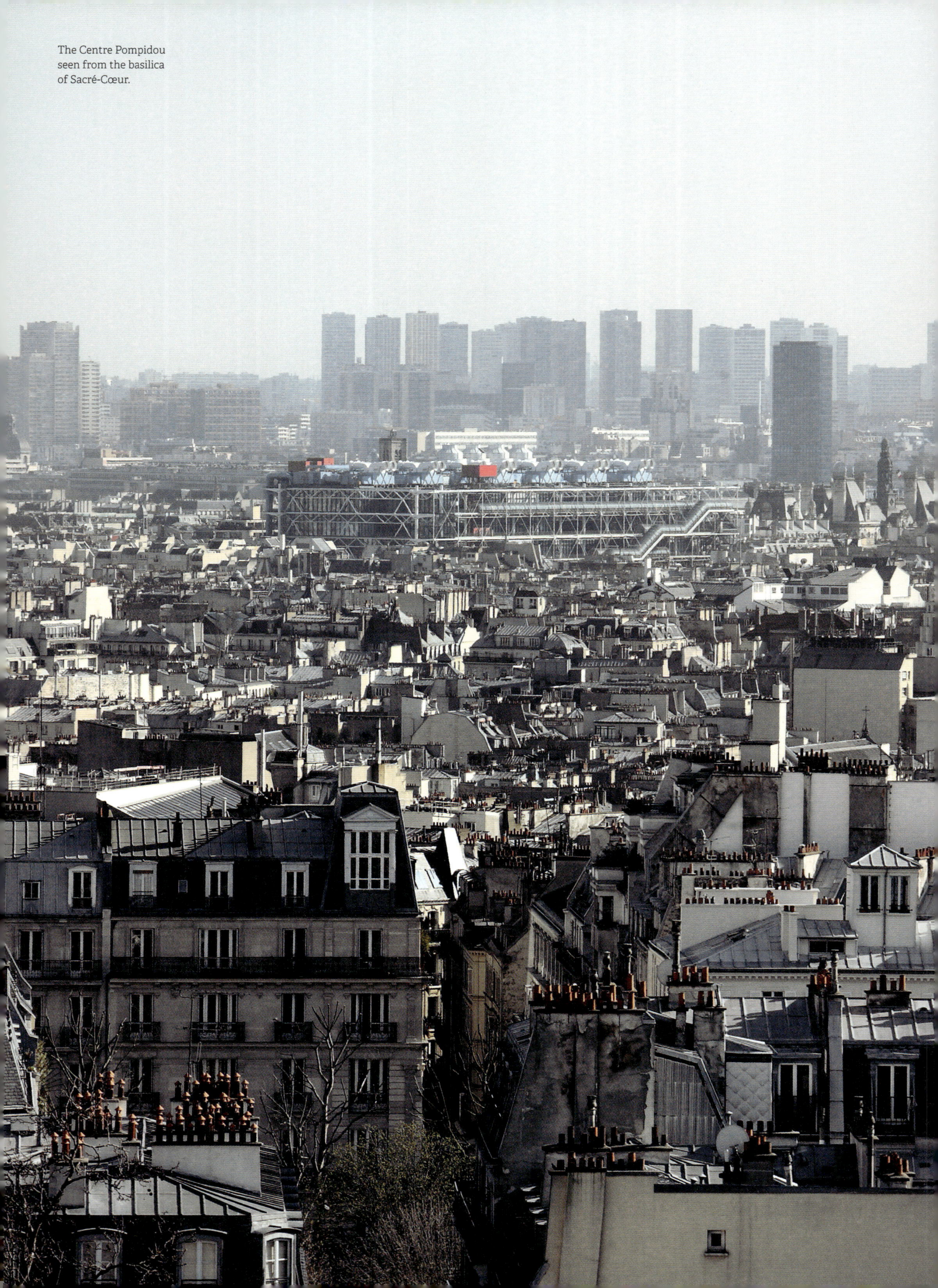

Foreword

Inaugurated in 1977, the Centre Pompidou marked a turning point in thinking about museums and the public's relationship to art. What have its main contributions been?

The Centre Pompidou is the matrix for the contemporary museum. Today, it is impossible to imagine a museum without a media library, an auditorium, temporary exhibitions and other types of events.
One can no longer build a museum that is not a pleasant place to visit or that does not pay special attention to visitors' well-being, both physical and intellectual, through a broad range of services, notably targeting young people and families. The Centre has been a pioneer regarding all these matters, and it continues to be, for example by being the first museum in the world to dedicate an area exclusively to adolescents.
The Centre Pompidou is also a laboratory for developing the modern form of the exhibition, blending two vocabularies since its inception, the one of exhibitions on architecture and society, and the one of exhibitions on art history.
The building has made this possible because it is first and foremost a machine for exhibiting, with its open-plan floors offering the possibility of constantly composing new exhibition designs and of ensuring that each exhibition is a genuine sensorial and intellectual experience.

Is the building's design by Renzo Piano and Richard Rogers one of the keys to the Centre's success?

If it is incontestably revolutionary and in keeping with the contemporary creation of the 1970s, this building is also both the product of a tradition of utopian architectures, such as the Fun Palace, and of the history of cast iron architectures from Paxton to Archigram.
It is the symbol of this other modernity, and perhaps the first post-modern edifice, thanks to an extremely audacious choice and a powerful political act. President Pompidou, who was rather a supporter of an orthodox modernity and whose personal tastes would have pushed him more towards calling on Le Corbusier to build the museum of the 20th century at La Défense, chose not to take part in the selection of its architects. However, it was he who wanted the first major international competition held in France for the Centre. One that was totally open and run by a jury of very strong personalities presided over by Jean Prouvé, the archetypal figure of the architect-engineer and of industrial architecture.
These remarkable circumstances are what enabled this highly unusual project, entrusted to architects barely in their thirties and who had built virtually nothing before, to come into being.

How does the Centre Pompidou, which houses an exceptional collection and hosts renowned modern art exhibitions, remain engaged with the art of its time?

Today the Centre presents the most important collection of modern and contemporary art in Europe, with a very strong multi-disciplinary dimension. A genuine home for artists, it is open to the entire range of artistic scenes around the globe and advocates a global perspective, which is essential for a museum aiming to maintain its mission of universality in the age of artistic globalisation. But the museum is also and especially a storehouse of knowledge, the knowledge developed on the collections and transmitted to the public. Thus, the Centre Pompidou participates in writing the history of art in the disciplines covered by its collections, which include the visual arts, architecture and design. Through its key strategic project, the virtual Centre Pompidou, its entire content is becoming accessible to all on an unprecedented scale.

Alain Seban
President of the Centre Pompidou

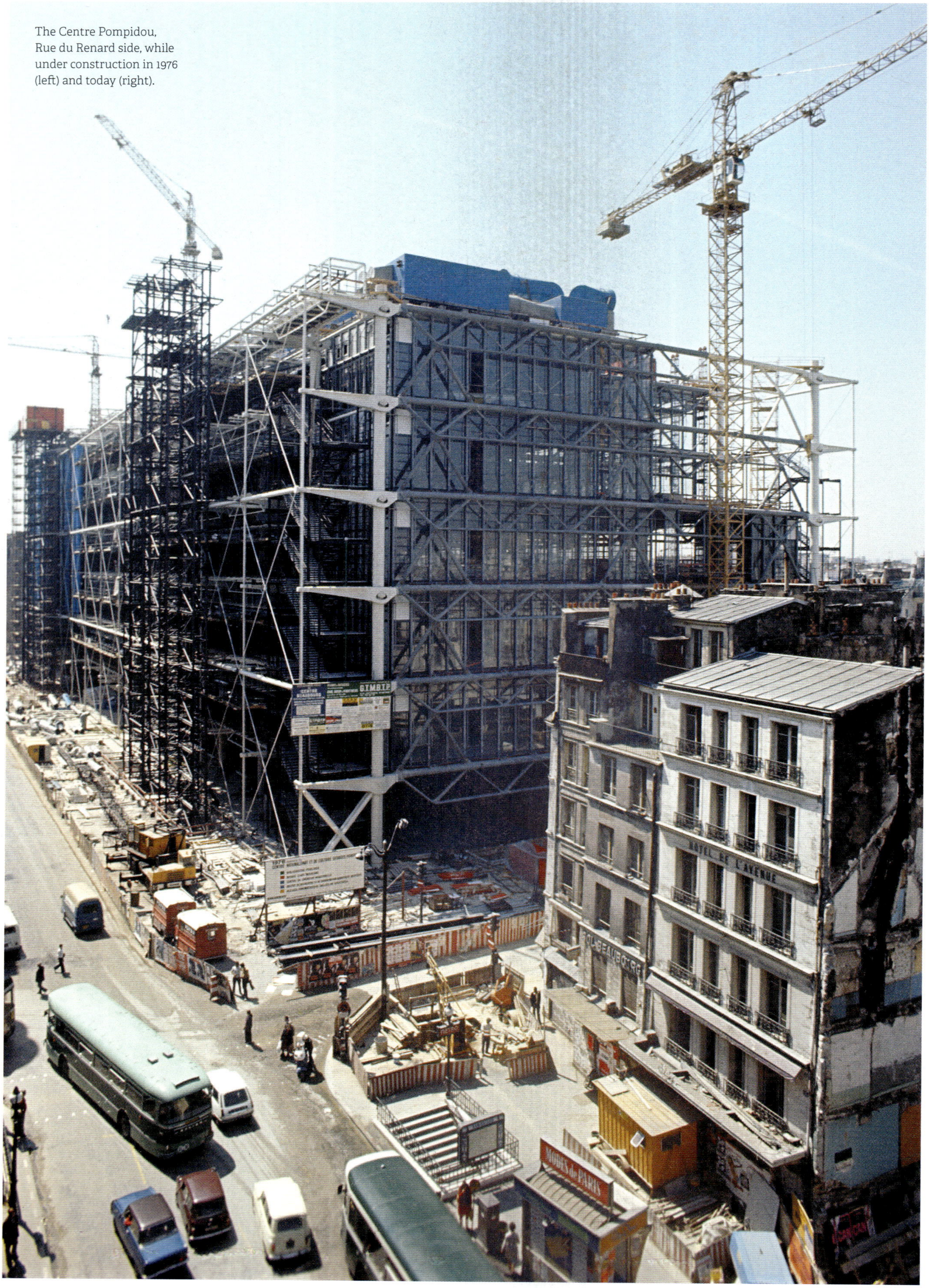

The Centre Pompidou, Rue du Renard side, while under construction in 1976 (left) and today (right).

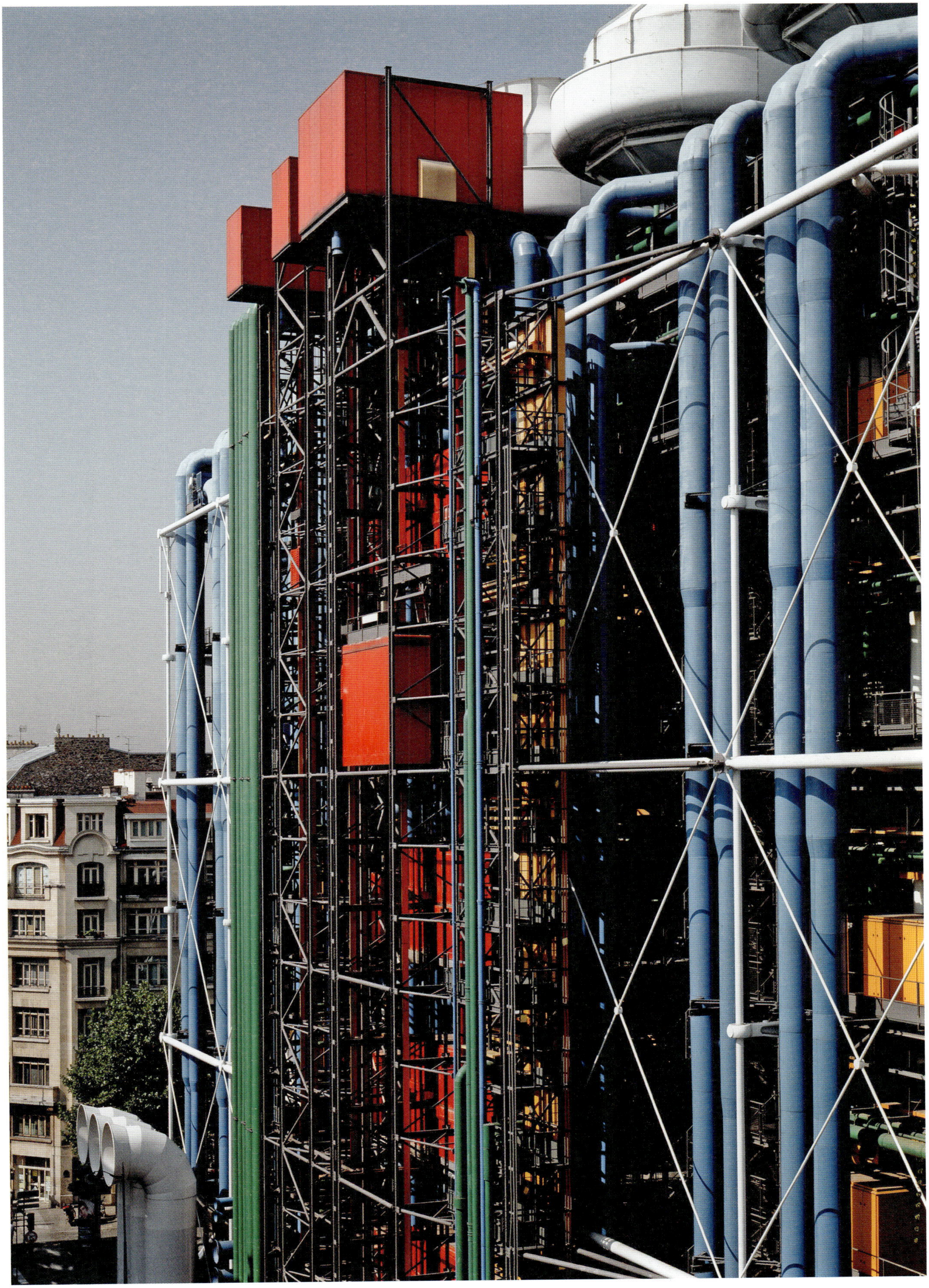

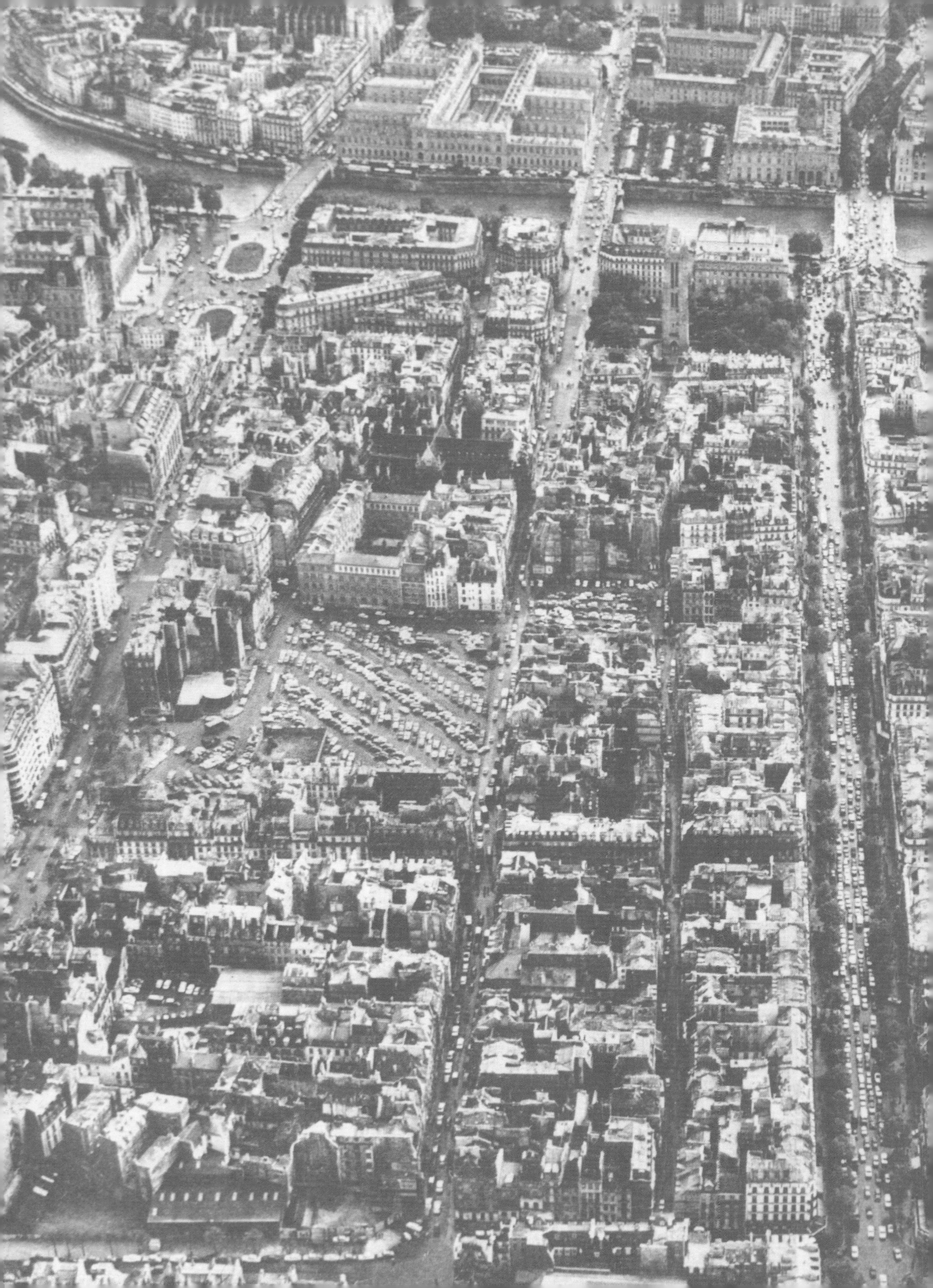

history

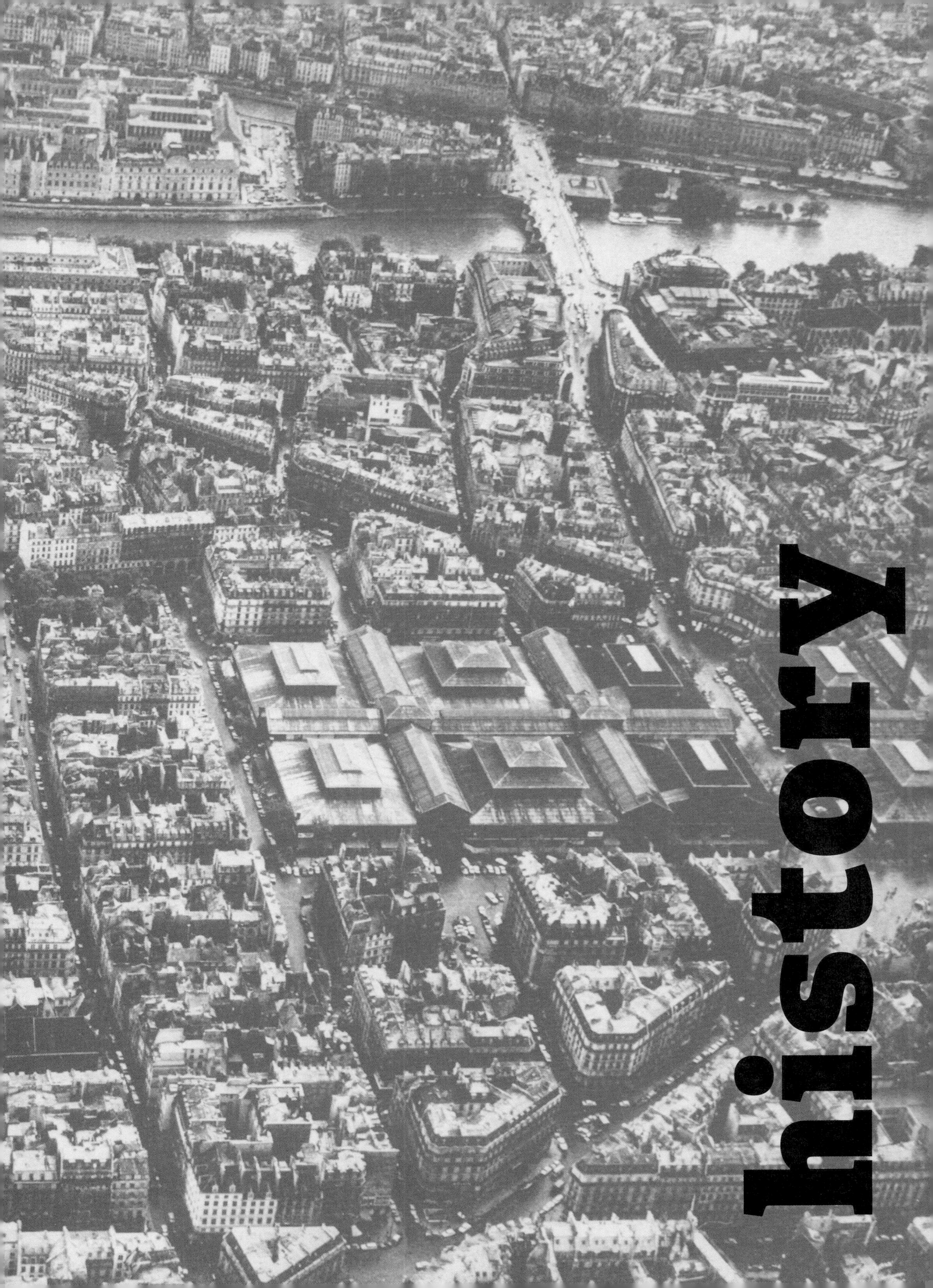

Previous double-page: aerial view of the centre of Paris in the 1960s. On the left, the car park where the Centre Pompidou will stand; on the right, Les Halles by Baltard, before their demolition.

"It is my passionate wish for Paris to have a cultural centre like the ones they have been creating in the United States; with what has thus far been unequalled success. It would be one that is both a museum and a centre of creation where the visual arts take up residence with music, film, books, audiovisual research, etc. The museum can only deal with modern art, since we already have the Louvre. Creation there would obviously be modern and would constantly be evolving. The library would attract the best readers, who would at the same time be placed in contact with arts. The Beaubourg Plateau was only chosen for its location because it was the sole immediately available parcel of land and because I wanted to act swiftly, sure that if I waited, nothing would ever be done."

Georges Pompidou, *Le Monde*, 17 October, 1972

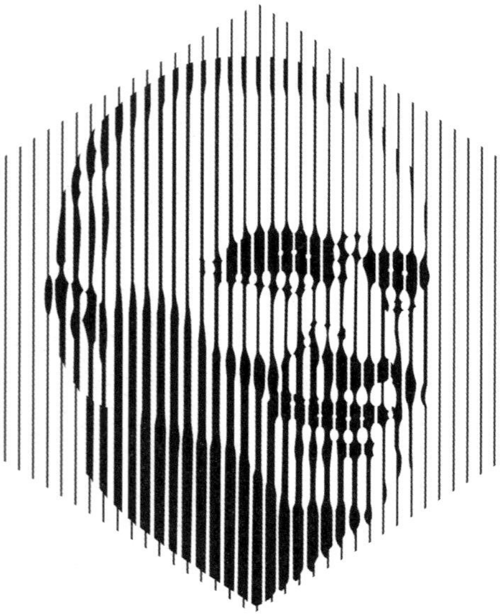

Victor Vasarely (1906-1997), *Homage to Georges Pompidou*, 1976 (left).
For thirty years, the site of the Centre remained a vacant lot transformed into a car park by the neighbours and people working in the nearby Les Halles (right).

Political will

In 1969, just a few short months following his election, President of the Republic Georges Pompidou, took a decision, alone, that would revolutionise the way of thinking about culture. He decided to create a centre open to all, to the public and to artists, blending museum, library and contemporary creation, all disciplines rolled into one location, in the heart of Paris.

Political ambition

This decision was a powerful political act. In the wake of May 19 68, traditional cultural structures no longer seemed adapted to their times. Artists and many professionals in the domain of culture were demanding new places, while the public at large had lost interest in contemporary art, largely because of a lack of comprehension. Something new had to be invented. Very aware of these issues, Georges Pompidou also wished to restore France's place in the concert of cultural nations – proof of its international influence. "Since the 1950s and 1960s, it was generally agreed that Paris had been supplanted by New York. However, it seemed to me that not only had France remained a chosen country for many artists of all nationalities, but that there was a renewal of the arts in France which could be seen emerging in recent creation." But what was the situation? The Musée National d'Art Moderne, housed since 1947 in the Palais de Tokyo and endowed with an exceptional collection of artists' studios,

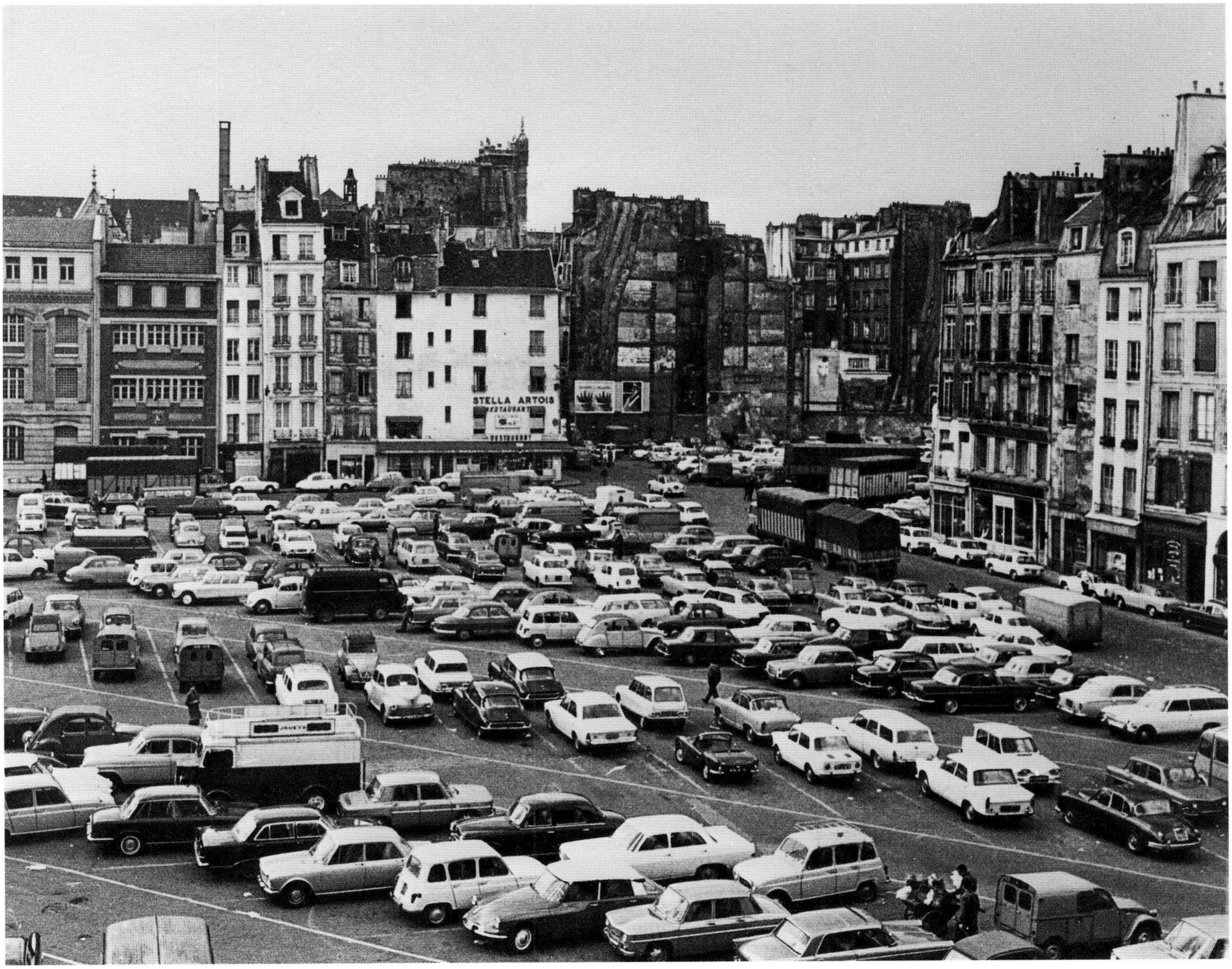

was criticised for not taking into account living artists. In a reaction to this, the Centre National d'Art Contemporain was created in the Rue Berryer, in the former mansion of Salomon de Rothschild, as well as the Centre de Création Industrielle, which offered a place for design within the Musée des Arts Décoratifs. A connoisseur of modern art, familiar with galleries and attentive to the young generation of artists (notably the New Realists), Georges Pompidou was well aware of France's institutional shortcomings. Taking the initiative, and counter to the sensitivities of a significant part of the French intelligentsia of the day, he imagined a new tool for disseminating culture, one for which there was no model to look to abroad.

Multi-disciplinary approach and contemporary creation

He outlined his idea in a letter addressed to the Minister of Cultural Affairs, Edmond Michelet, in December 1969: "The architectural ensemble will not only have to include a vast museum of painting and sculpture, but special facilities for music, record albums, eventually cinema and theatrical research. It would be desirable for it to also include a library, at the very least a library offering books dedicated to the arts and their most recent developments."

This unique multi-disciplinary vision formed the identity of the Centre that would become the home of the Musée National d'Art Moderne (MNAM), the Public Information Library, the Centre de Création Industrielle, cinemas, live performances – notably dance through the creation of the Festival d'Automne – and the IRCAM, whose acronym is better known than its name (Institut de Recherche et Coordination Acoustique / Musique), with contemporary creation providing the link between the institution's various components.

Thus the traditional academic compartmentalisation was shattered. To ensure success of this project, which aroused fierce opposition, an original administrative status was devised which granted the future institution a great deal of independence.

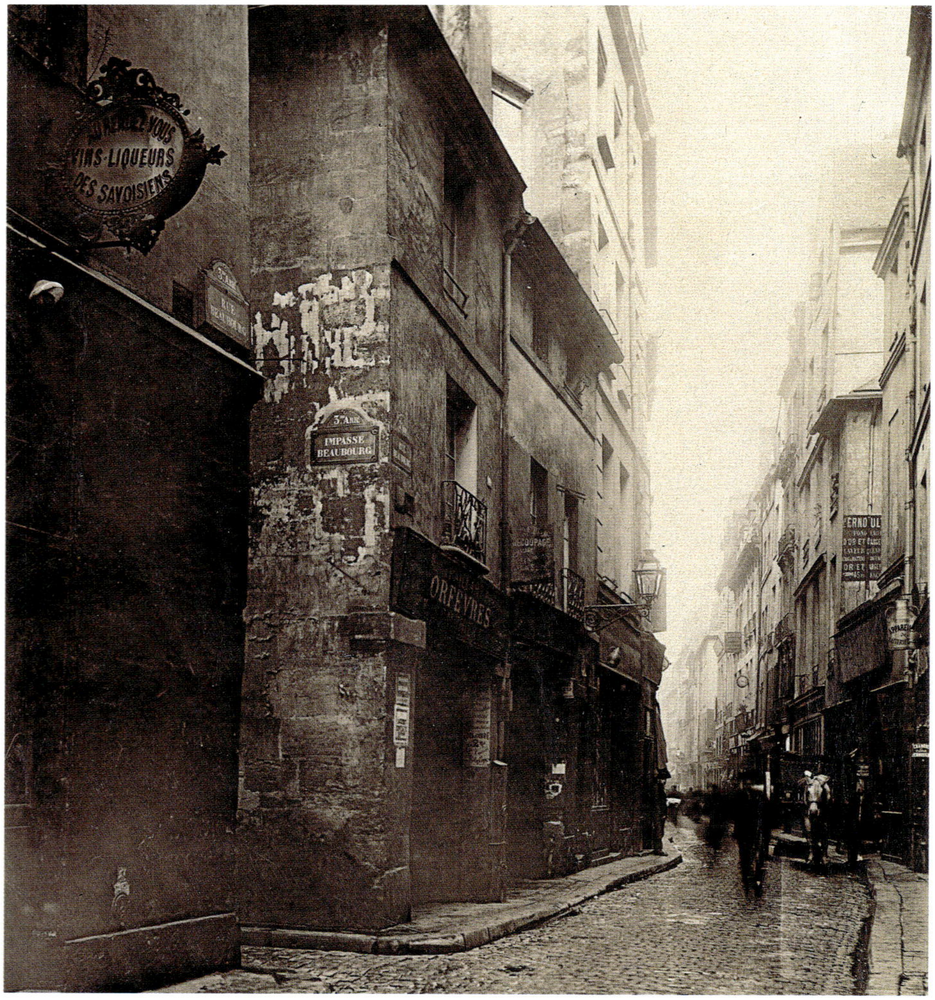

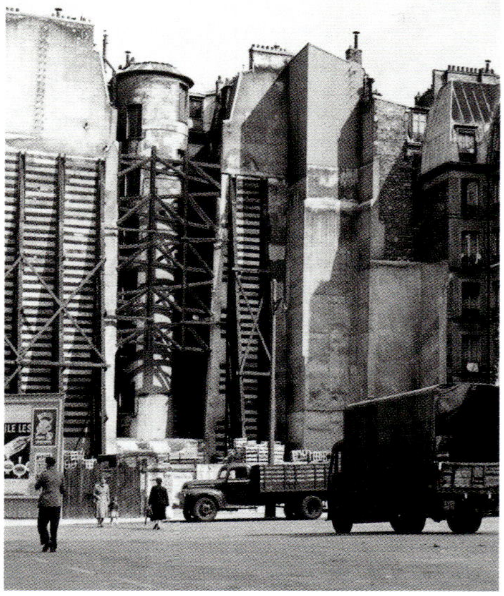

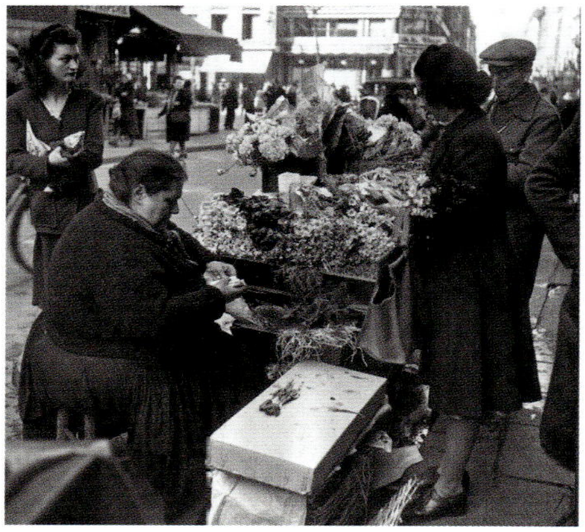

The Beaubourg neighbourhood, before the Centre Pompidou (above, from top to bottom and left to right):
the Rue Beaubourg circa 1900, shoring of dilapidated buildings in what is now the Quartier de l'Horloge, a florist in the Rue Saint-Martin, circa 1950.
Jean-Claude Gautrand, *Chute d'un toit (Falling Roof)*, "Assassination of Baltard" series, 1971 (right page).

The Beaubourg Plateau

Georges Pompidou chose an amazingly available site right in the centre of Paris for the location of the future cultural facility: the "Beaubourg Plateau." Lying between the Cathedral of Notre-Dame, the medieval tower of the gothic Church of Saint-Jacques (destroyed during the Revolution) and the mansions of the aristocracy in the Marais, lay a vast empty space transformed into a car park by inhabitants of the neighbourhood and the workers and clients of the nearby Les Halles food market.

Historic neighbourhood

However, the neighbourhood is one of the oldest in the capital with the Rue Saint-Martin, now running along the Piazza, following the original route of the ancient Roman road. Later, the city wall built by King Philippe Auguste at the end of the 12th century encompassed the area. Close to the river port, the Place de Grève and the grounds of Champeaux Market, it is the beating heart of Paris. Somehow it managed to escape all the major urban renewal projects while acquiring the reputation of a dodgy (the 15th-century alchemist Nicolas Flamel lived there), seamy and unhealthy neighbourhood, owing to its houses of ill repute and the crooks who found refuge in its dark and narrow streets. Populous, commercial, comprised of a maze of alleys, its name "Beau Bourg" (beautiful town) was almost certainly meant to be ironic. Since the Middle Ages, it has been a favourite neighbourhood of poets and musicians, as attested in the verses of

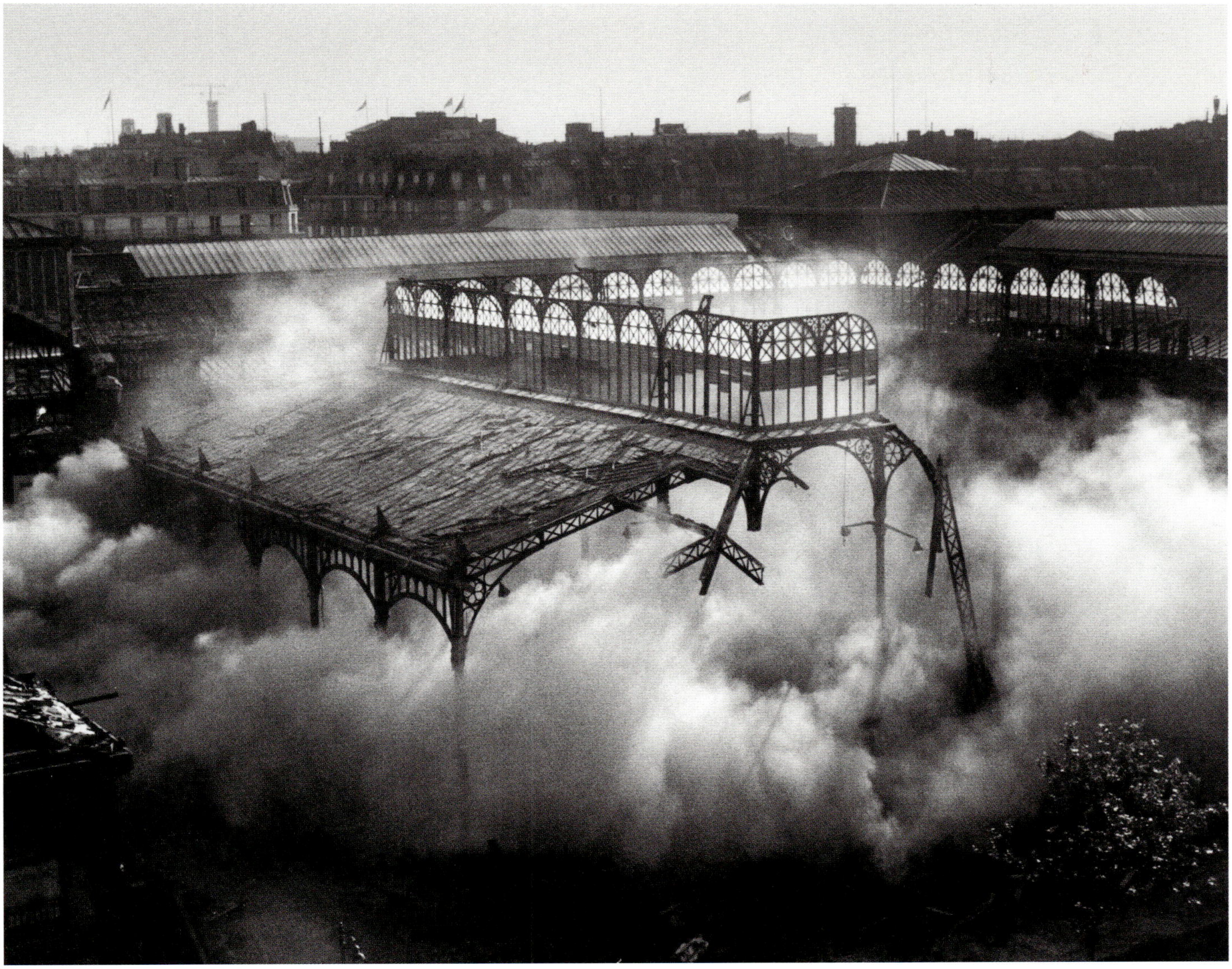

Villon, Nerval, Apollinaire and Desnos. In 1908, the novelist Huysmans gave the following picturesque description in his novel *Trois églises et trois primitifs* (Three Churches and Three Primitives): "The greater part is occupied by low quality wine merchants, bistros for pimps and especially by shoe repair shops, shops selling old boots; it's the market for used shoes! [...] The roadways reek of the swamp and wafting up from the gutters is an odour redolent of cauliflower water and marsh mud; a few of these narrow streets; whose names nor appearance have changed for centuries, nevertheless appear to have been disinfected; such as the Rue de Venise, where in bygone days the shops that opened onto the street were both hovels and storerooms."

"Insalubrious block no.1"

In the second half of the 19th century, during the period of Baron Haussmann's major urban works, the bad living conditions prevailing in the neighbourhood led him to declare it "unsanitary block no.1." However, it would only be demolished in the 1930s and nothing was proposed to replace it for over 30 years. It was this vast vacant lot, initially coveted by the National Library, which Georges Pompidou instructed the government to purchase for his cultural centre. Pompidou's vision converged with Le Corbusier's, who was entrusted with the project for a "museum of the 20th century" – interrupted by the architect's death in 1965 – and who declared: "A museum, to be really open to all, must be built in the heart of the city."

Les Halles Controversy

The simultaneous construction of the Centre Pompidou and the destruction of Les Halles, designed by Baltard, provoked quite a controversy. The public worried about these vast urban projects undertaken in the heart of Paris. But there was no link between the two projects. The decision to move Les Halles – which had remained in the same location since the 12th century – to Rungis had already been made in 1962 with the actual move occurring in 1969. Even the jury of the architecture competition organised for the Centre questioned the President about this project, arguing in favour of the preservation of the pavilions built by Baltard between 1852 and 1870, because "in the history of French architecture, they are a milestone and a success which would be difficult to equal, and they constitute, in relation to the future Centre Beaubourg, a vibrant meeting place whose disappearance risks compromising the building to which you are attaching your name."

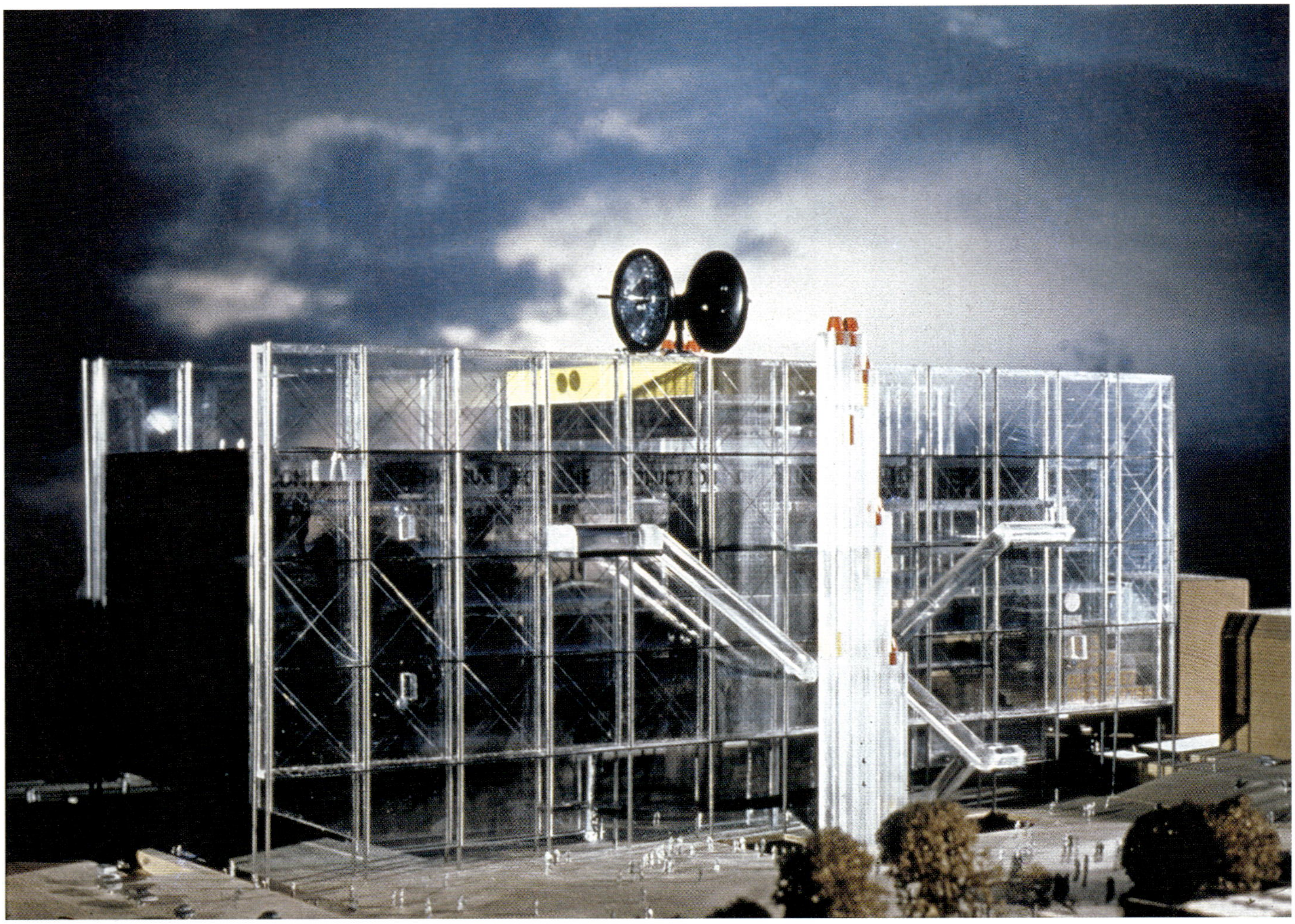

Winning model for the project entered by Renzo Piano, Richard Rogers and Gianfranco Franchini, 1970.

An international architecture competition

On 19 November 1970, a few months after the announcement of the creation of the future Centre Pompidou, followed the news that an international architecture competition would be held. This competition, called for by President Pompidou, was highly unusual in that it was to be anonymous and not reserved to "invitees" either, as was customary for this type of public project. Rather, it was open to all architects, regardless of their age, experience or nationality. Talent and creativity would be the most effective weapons. The candidates were given a "programme" which defined the main guidelines of the building but remained open to allow for dialogue between the winners and the future directors, who were already busy imagining how the Centre would operate.

An exemplary precedent

Another original aspect of the project was that to develop this programme, a team was built, one that included future users of the place, adding the strength of the knowledge they had in their respective domains and of their audiences.

This method of working – groundbreaking at the time – would later be implemented for all public museum buildings in France. Very quickly, the team drew up a detailed document, nurtured in part by the prior reflection done for the "Museum of the 20th Century," which already envisaged a "centre of artistic creation," with a "box of miracles" that would attract visitors through diverse events, and a forum-reception area for the public. After reviewing the historical data

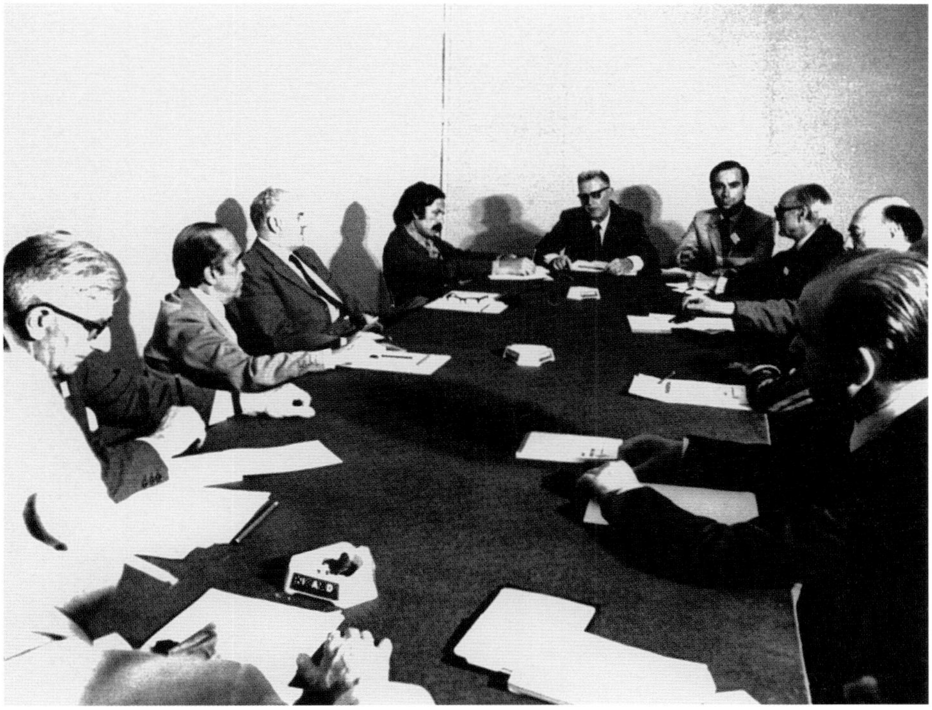

"The Republic of France has decided to build in the heart of Paris, not far from Les Halles, on the Beaubourg Plateau, a Centre dedicated to public reading, to art and to contemporary creation. The project's originality resides in the conjunction, in a single location, of books, the visual arts, architecture, music, cinema and industrial creation."

Excerpt from the competition programme, 1970

Jury meeting on the project presided over by Jean Prouvé (centre) at the Grand Palais from 5 to 15 July 1971 with (left to right) Oscar Niemeyer, Henri-Pierre Maillard, Sébastien Loste, Philip Johnson and Michel Laclotte.

of the operation and the features of the site, the programme described what the future institution had to be – the various activities, how they would function and their requirements in terms of surface area, technical services and personnel – but especially the requirements of the location, underscoring that "the project's originality lies in the conjunction of artistic and cultural activities in a single place [...] therefore, the extremely varied activities will have to be closely linked with each other."

Carefully written to be the least constraining as possible for the competing architects, the programme nevertheless imposed two objectives: interior flexibility, which had to be maximal, and the Centre's relation with its urban environment.

An exceptional jury

The success of the competition was extraordinary. By 28 June 1971, 681 briefs had been submitted, 500 of which came from foreign candidates. An exceptional jury would sort them out, presided over by the engineer Jean Prouvé and composed of internationally recognised architects and users: American Philip Johnson; Brazilian Oscar Niemeyer; Englishman Frank Francis, honorary director of the British Museum; Dutchman Willem Sandberg, former director of the Stedelijk Museum in Amsterdam; Belgian Herman Liebaers, director of the Royal Library of Belgium; and Frenchmen Émile Aillaud, Gaëtan Picon, former managing director of *Arts et Lettres*, and Michel Laclotte, chief curator of the department of Paintings at the Louvre Museum.

Deliberations took place in the Galeries Nationales du Grand Palais, where the competitors' models were on display. On 15 July 1971, the jury honoured 30 projects and agreed to designate as the winning project the one designed by a young, virtually unknown team of architects barely in their thirties: Renzo Piano, Richard Rogers and Gianfranco Franchini, assisted by Ove Arup & Partners, which counted Peter Rice on its team, an engineer who enjoyed a solid reputation.

Although the choice was made by the jury as a whole and particularly defended by Oscar Niemeyer and Philip Johnson, it bore the imprint of Jean Prouvé.

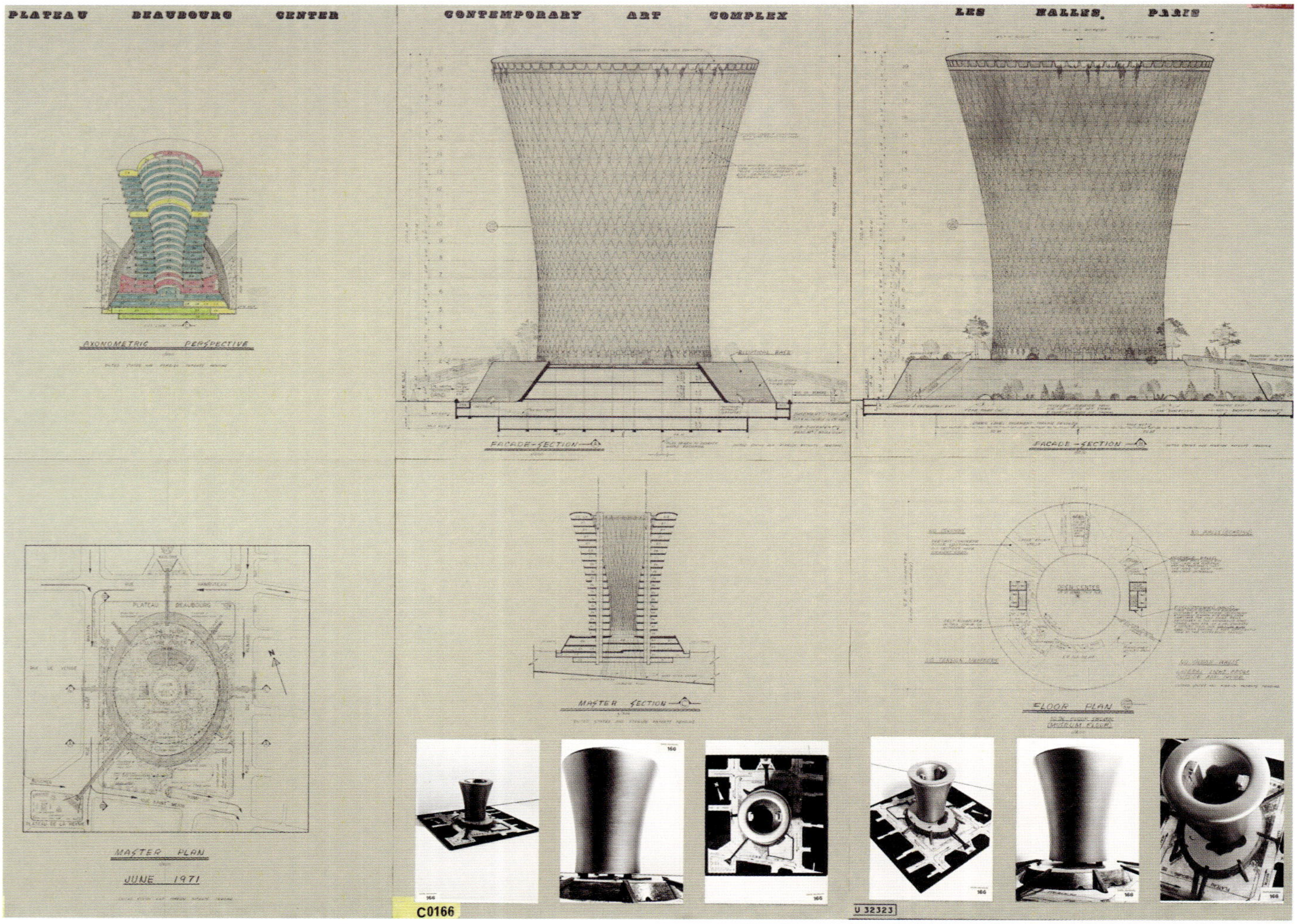

Projects presented in the 1971 international architecture competition for the design of the Centre Beaubourg: no.166, by Terrance J. Waters, United States (left page); no.272, by André Bruyère, France (right page, top); no.490, by Andres Perea Ortega, Ma Luisa Bujarrabal Fernandez, Juan Hernandez Ferrero and Javier Yeregui Aramendi, Spain, an award-winning project (right page, bottom).

In fact, Jean Prouvé advocated light prefabrication techniques against those traditionally employed in France of heavy prefabrication in reinforced concrete. President Pompidou did not participate in the deliberations of the jury and declared in *Le Monde* in January 1972: "We have accepted their choice, thinking that they [the jury] were better placed than anyone to give an opinion, in particular from the functional point of view."

Creative answers

In addition to designating the winner, the jury honoured the contestants, who presented a very broad range of proposals. "Whatever our judgement on this proliferation of forms, it is fair to acknowledge that one of the basic intentions of the programme, which was to allow the architects total freedom in their design, has been satisfied." The jury deemed that "in a period when the architects of the entire world are searching for new modes of expression, all interesting avenues had to be explored, even if they hadn't thus far led to perfectly satisfying results." The great majority of projects met the programme's requirements and time frames. So the decision came down to flexibility – essential, at least for the museum and the library (i.e. nearly half the surface area of the Centre) were vast open spaces without pillars – as well as the design of the articulations between activities and parts, light and the way with wich the urban context was dealt. Only two teams, including the winners, opted for partial occupation of the site. "Most of the other projects," the jury noted in its report, "filled the entire Beaubourg site like huge paving stones with heights from 30 to 50 metres, a few of them even up to 150 metres." However, this issue of the Centre's relationship to its environment wound up being the determining factor for the members of the jury, who returned to the site just before voting. "The idea that the whole environment – excluding the Rue du Renard which is without interest – might have been swept under the rug, appalled us. So we went back to the project that attracted us," Jean Prouvé recounted. "Let's have no regrets – the place is beautiful, and the contrast between the new building and the old houses is, in my view, thrilling in its reciprocity." (*L'Architecture d'aujourd'hui*, February 1977).

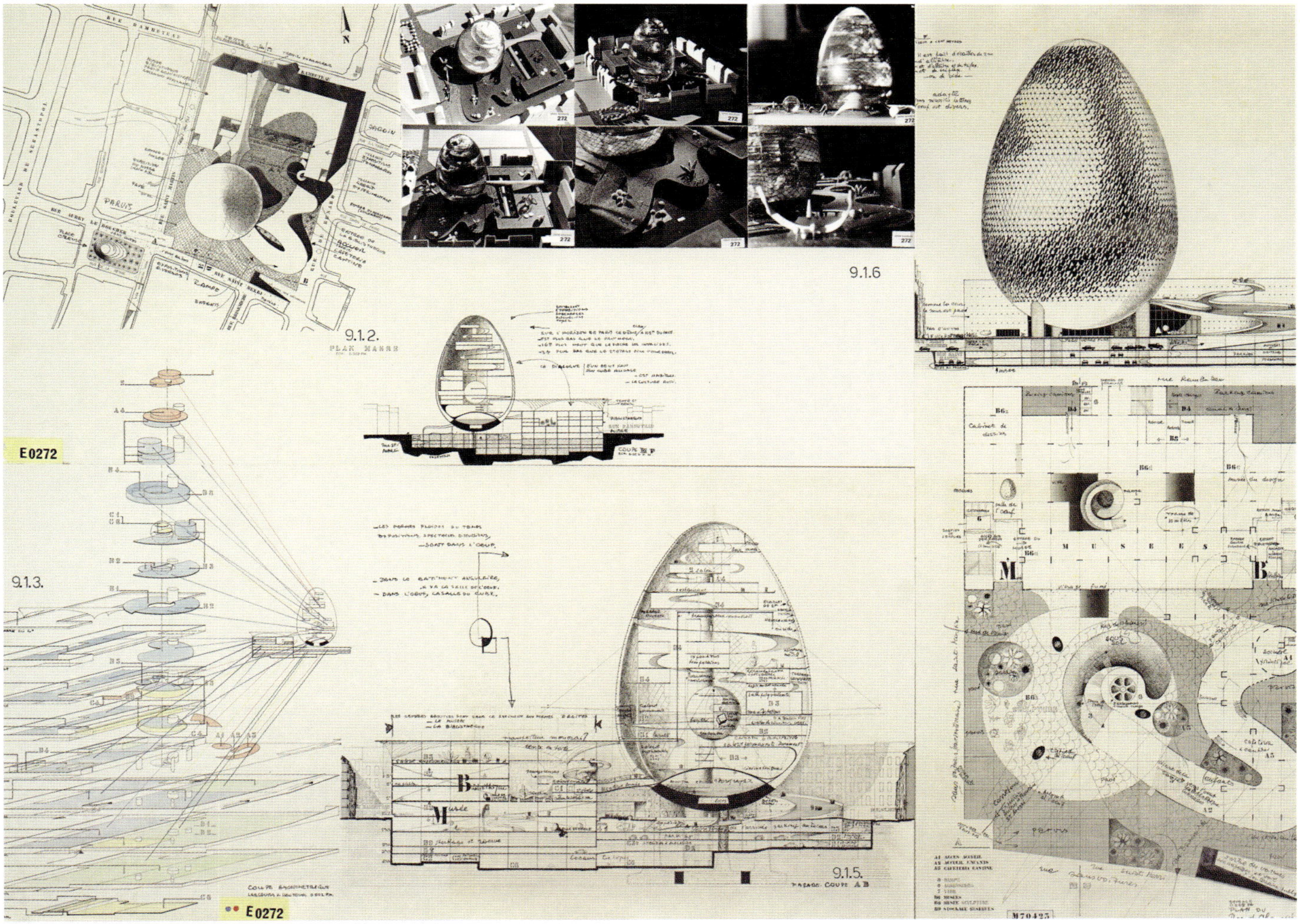

9.1.2.
PLAN MASSE
9.1.6
9.1.3.
9.1.5.
E0272
E0272

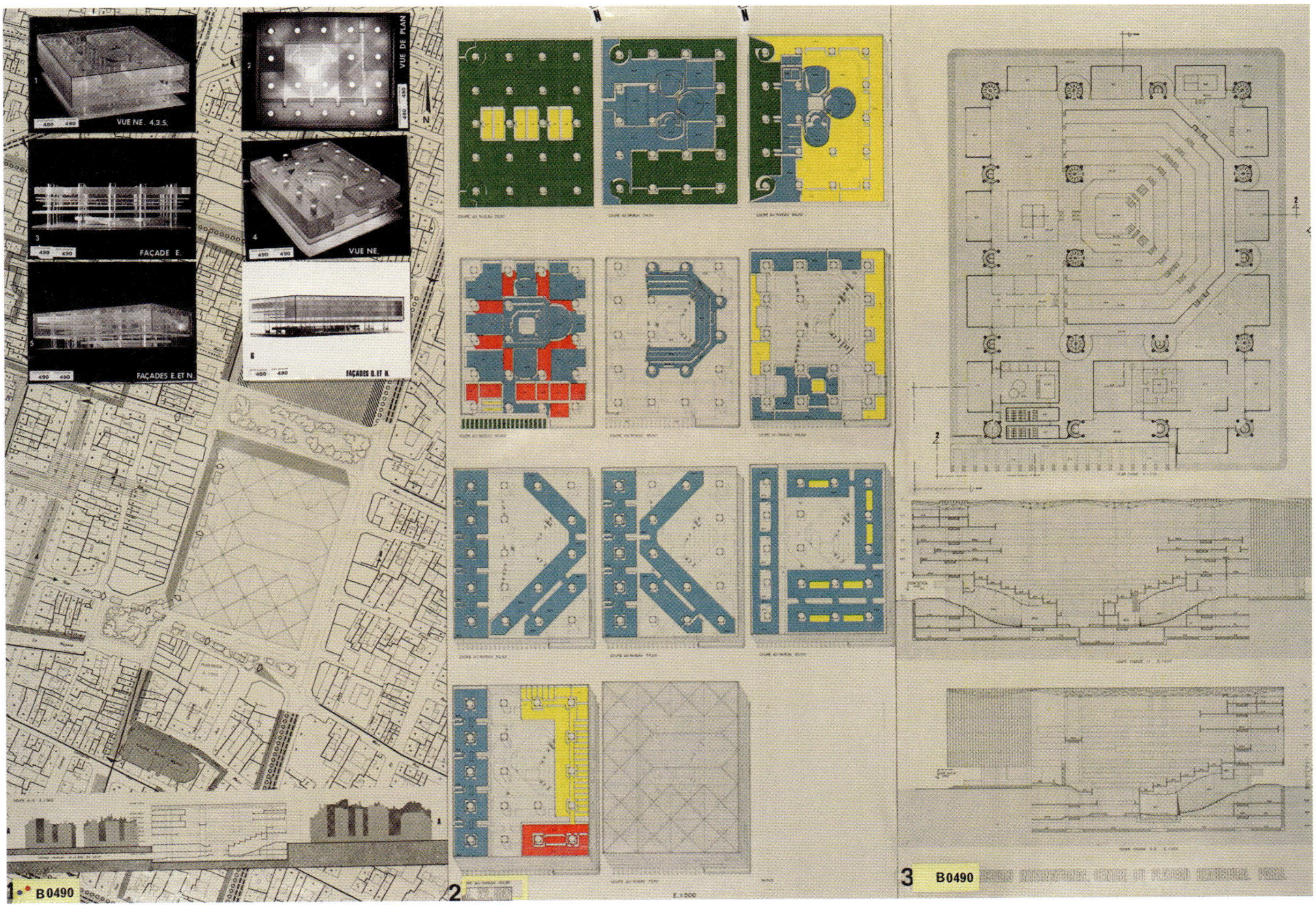

VUE NE. 4.3.5.
VUE DE PLAN
FAÇADE E.
VUE NE.
FAÇADES E ET N.
FAÇADES O. ET N.
1
B0490
2
3
B0490

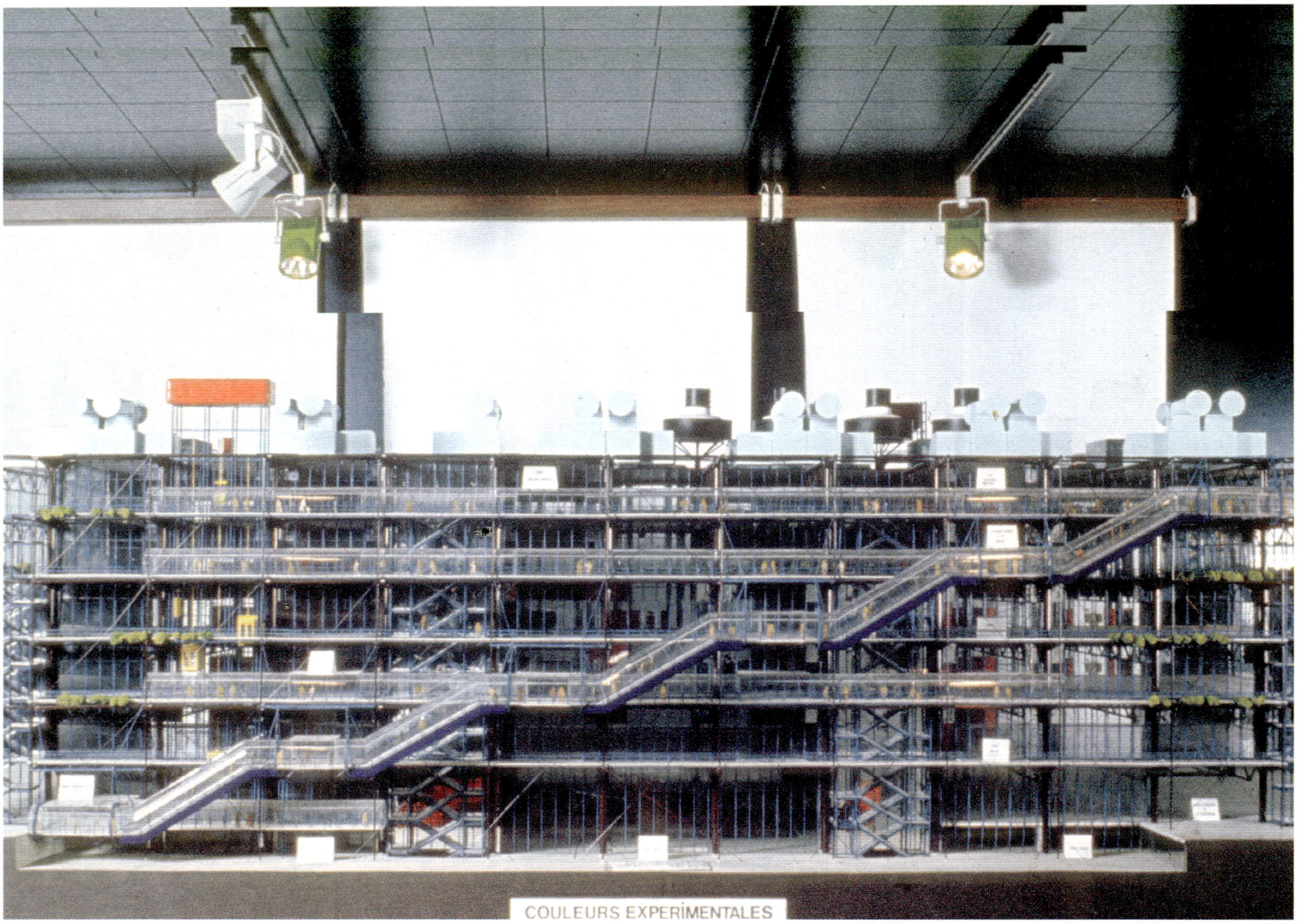

Model of the project's final draft (view of the west side of the Piazza), 1974.

The winning project

Project no. 493, by Piano and Rogers, won over the jury with its many original features and its perfect match with the project's philosophy.

An open place

The architects, attentive to the framework of the Parisian cityscape, aligned the building with the neighbourhood's north-south axis, parallel to the Rue Saint-Martin, whose dates trace back to Antiquity, and with the Boulevard Sébastopol. This positioning causes the Centre to stand out in the urban fabric, but without competing with the Cathedral of Notre-Dame de Paris and the Church of Saint-Eustache, two monuments with a comparable mass but both oriented east-west. The decision to only occupy half of the site in order to create a broad esplanade, made it possible to tie the building into the neighbourhood. To strengthen this link, the architects proposed turning the Rue Saint-Merri into a pedestrian street, bordering the esplanade on the west side. The building's elevation on pillars and the choice of glass façades completed this "liberation" from the ground, while also ensuring the continuity between the city and the Centre. Thus, the entire ground floor is permeable for the pedestrian who can see straight through to the Rue du Renard in the background.

Innovative solutions

The architectural design is radical in itself. The construction's simple plan and volume rests on a framework whose stress-bearing elements,

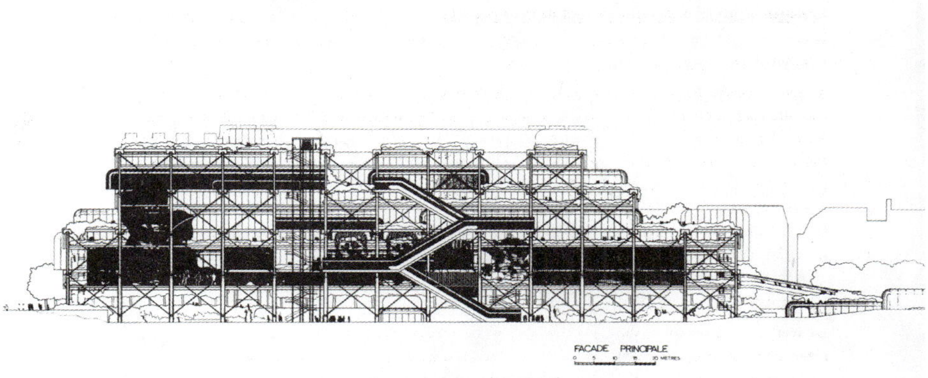

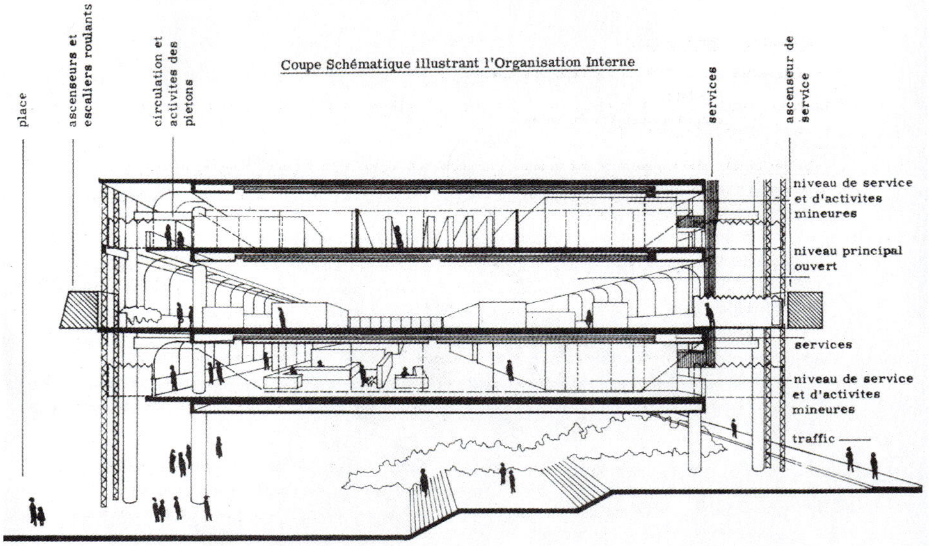

Draft of the main façade (top) and section of the building, still designed on piers (bottom), by Renzo Piano and Richard Rogers.

circulations and flows are pushed to the periphery, thereby opening up vast, superposed floors. These surfaces without partitions, of nearly 50 metres by 100 metres, were conceived not to receive specific functions, in compliance with the programme's flexibility requirement. Neutral and modular, they allow for multiple transformations. The entire structure can be read on the façade. Revealing its internal mechanisms to the gaze of passers-by, the transparent building seems to be turned inside out. The edifice is an evolving and functional structure, designed to host all its users' requirements. "Our building is a tool," Richard Rogers explains, "it must not be a conventional and rigid architectural monument, but fluid, flexible, easy to change, full of technical resources inside and outside, on top and underneath."

An anti-monument in movement

It is also a place designed to welcome the greatest number while doing away with the sacred aura of the solemn "museum monument." A playful project on the edge of architectural conventions, the Centre places the public at the centre of its systems and creates a new proximity between art and people. The Centre's permeability with the street, the flexibility of its spaces, their fluidity signal the erasure of frontiers, making all sorts of exchanges possible, notably between disciplines. Piano and Rogers' design transforms the Centre into a place of encounters and communication.

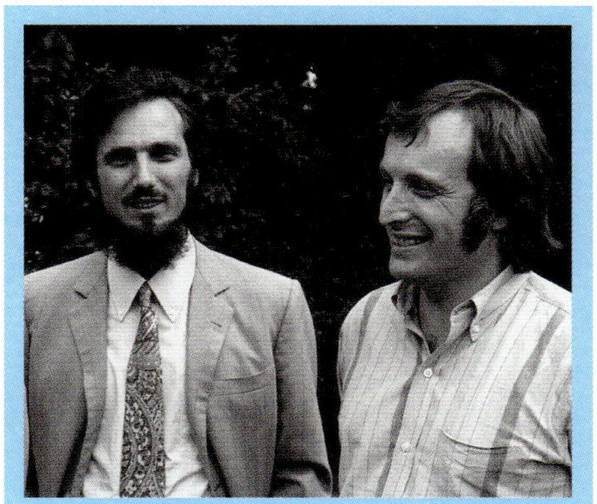

The architects

RENZO PIANO

(born in 1937 in Genoa)

A graduate of the Milan Polytechnic School in 1964, Renzo Piano completed his training in the 1970s in the United States, where he worked with Louis Kahn, and in England. It was during this period that he met Jean Prouvé, with whom he developed a friendship. He was interested in architecture that was rational, technological and considerate of its users' needs. In 1971, he became an associate of Richard Rogers before founding a new firm with the engineer Peter Rice in Genoa in 1977. After Rice's death in 1992, he founded the Renzo Piano Building Workshop. In 1998, he was awarded the Pritzker Prize.

Main buildings: the Kansai International Airport in Osaka (1988-1994); the Centre Culturel Jean-Marie Tjibaou in Nouméa (1991-1998); the Postdamer Platz in Berlin (1992-2000); the auditorium of the Music Park in Rome (1994-2002); the Paul Klee Centre in Berns (1998-2005); and the Cité Internationale in Lyon (1998-2006).

RICHARD ROGERS

(born in 1933 in Florence)

Briton Richard Rogers studied at the Architectural Association School in London, then at Yale University in the United States, where he graduated in 1962. It was there that he met Norman Foster, with whom he founded the Team 4 firm, which developed functionalist and high-tech industrial architecture. Following his association with Renzo Piano, in 1977, he created his own multi-disciplinary firm in London, Richard Rogers Partnership, and then Rogers Stirk Harbour & Partners. Awarded the Golden Lion at the 2006 Venice Biennale, he was also the recipient of the Pritzker Prize in 2007.

Main buildings: the Lloyd's Building in London (1979-1986); the Tribunal de Grande Instance of Bordeaux (1992-1998); the seat of the European Court of Human Rights in Strasbourg (1989-1995); the Millennium Dome in London (1999); Terminal 4 at Madrid-Barajas International Airport (1997-2005); the new building for the National Assembly of Wales (1998-2005).

In 1971, the two architects formed a partnership for the competition. Thereafter, they pursued their careers separately.

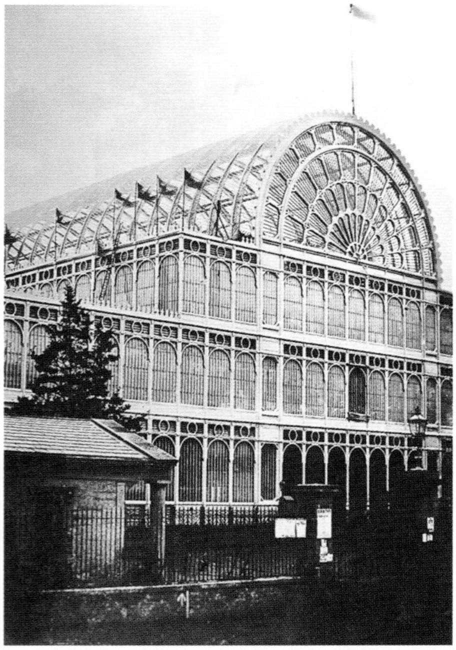

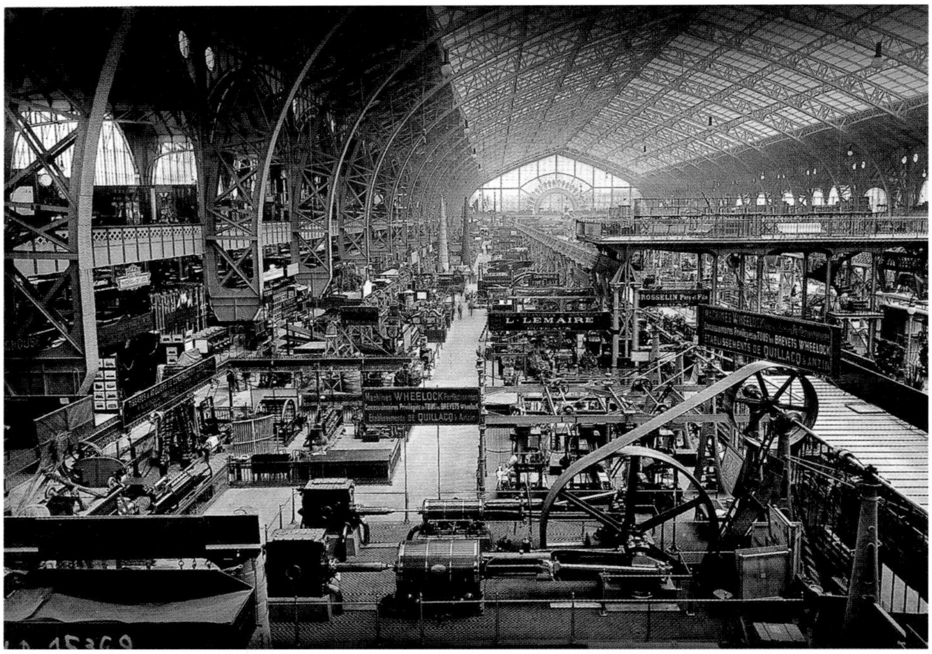

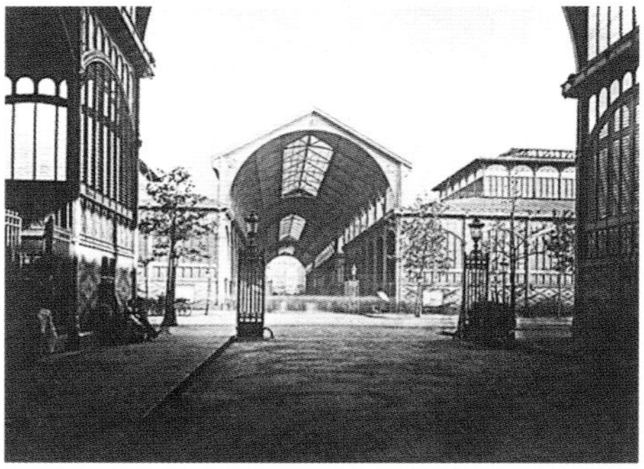

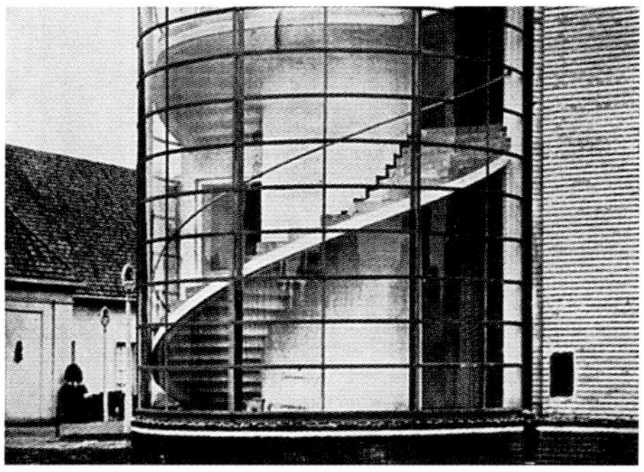

Buildings that inspired the Centre Pompidou (from top to bottom and left to right): the Crystal Palace by Joseph Paxton, London, 1851; the Gallery of Machines by Ferdinand Dutert and Victor Contamin, 1889; Les Halles Centrales de Paris by Victor Baltard, 1854-1870; the Model Factory by Walter Gropius, Cologne, 1914.

Inspiration, from the Crystal Palace to the Fun Palace

Though the radical and innovative architecture of the Centre Pompidou was perceived as revolutionary at the time of its construction, it is nevertheless heir to diverse historical currents.

Its metallic structure, based on a system of columns and beams, and prefabricated elements, echoes the architecture of cast iron and glass that triumphed in the 19th century by bringing luminosity, lightness and transparency to buildings.
The pavilions of the Expositions Universelles, the covered halls by Victor Baltard in Paris (1854-1870), the Crystal Palace built in London in 1851 by Joseph Paxton, and of course the Eiffel Tower, in 1889, as well as the geodesic domes of American engineer Richard Buckminster Fuller are some examples of experimentation, along with Charles Eames' 1949 house no.8, which blends prefabricated elements assembled in a light framework with glass curtain walls.
The choice of pushing circulations to the exterior of a structure so these spaces would not interfere with the spaces in the interior had already been made in 1914 by Walter Gropius, who placed the two stairwells of his model factory in glass cylinders at the ends of the building.
Even the "caterpillar" staircase that zigzags across the façade of the Centre has a forebear in the back façade of the MIT dormitory, designed by Alvar Aalto in 1948, and on the façade of the headquarters of the Neckermann Companies, conceived by German Egon Eiermann in 1960.

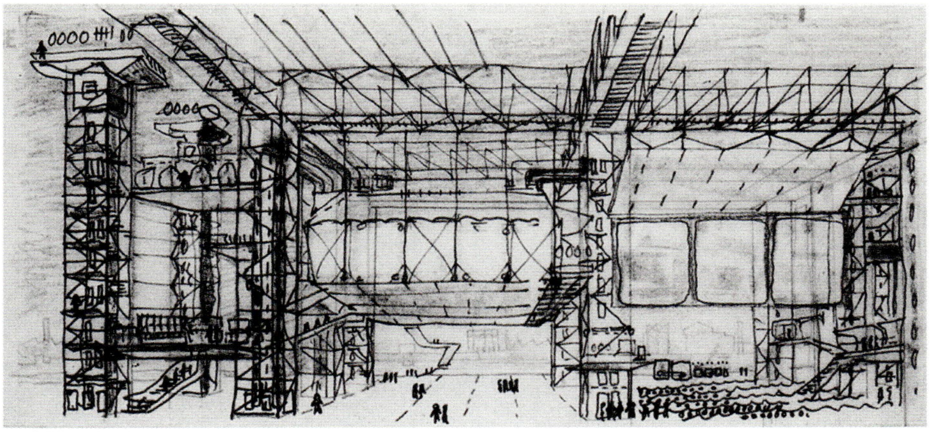

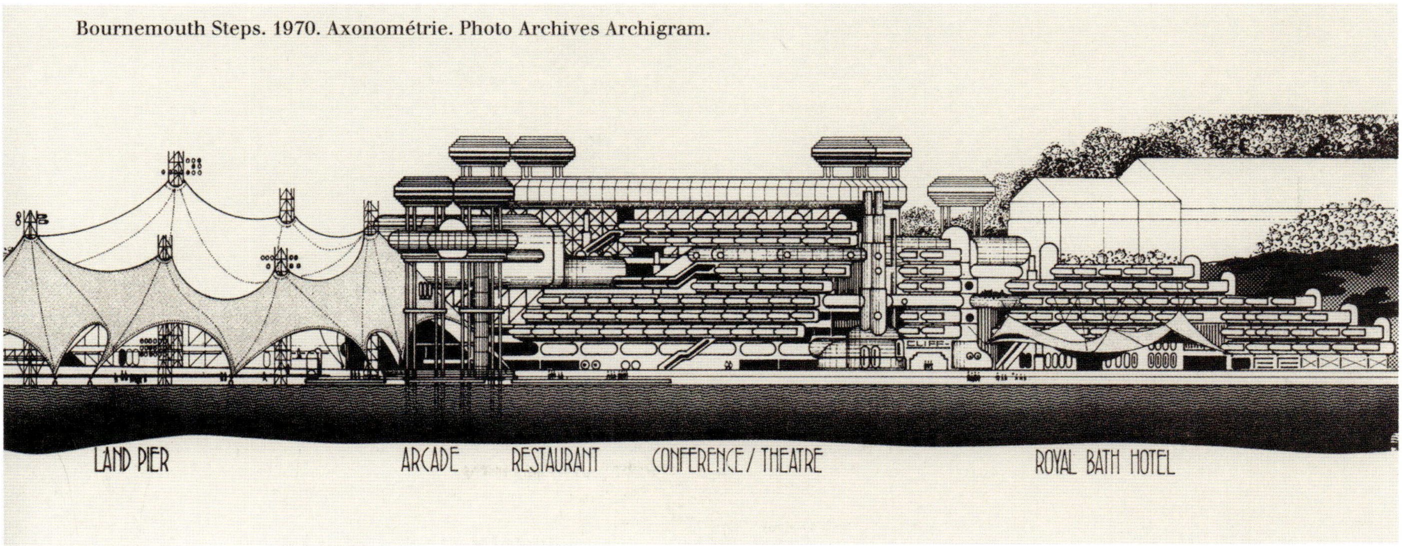

Other sources of inspiration for the architecture of the Centre Pompidou: the Fun Palace project by Cedric Price, 1960-1961 (top); the project for Bournemouth, known as the *Bournemouth Steps* by Archigram (collage by Ron Herron, Peter Cook and Dennis Crompton), 1968 (bottom).

The other major source of inspiration for the architects of the Centre Pompidou is, along with the utopian works designed by the British group Archigram in the 1960s, the Fun Palace designs of Britons Cedric Price and Joan Littlewood. Never actually built, theirs was a project for a "pleasure laboratory" for a new leisure society. "Its form and its structure, resembling a shipyard within whose walls are placed theatres, cinemas, restaurants, studios, gathering places, was designed to be assembled, moved about, reorganised and continuously fragmented." Entire sections are suspended on an exposed steel frame and these elements can be shifted about by means of mobile cranes attached to the exposed beams, according to the flow required by new projects. This modular concept of architecture, which poses basic questions about culture's place in society and the city and about how it should be defined, was a seminal work for a whole generation of practitioners, including Richard Rogers: "More than the form, it is Price's approach to his work – he was, after all, very political – which had an influence.
And naturally, we all admire Joan Littlewood, the stage director of the avant-garde. All these people are part of the roots of the Centre Pompidou".

The structure is designed to resemble a giant construction game. Metallic and painted in white, it is composed of repetitive elements that are assembled to form a regular framework.

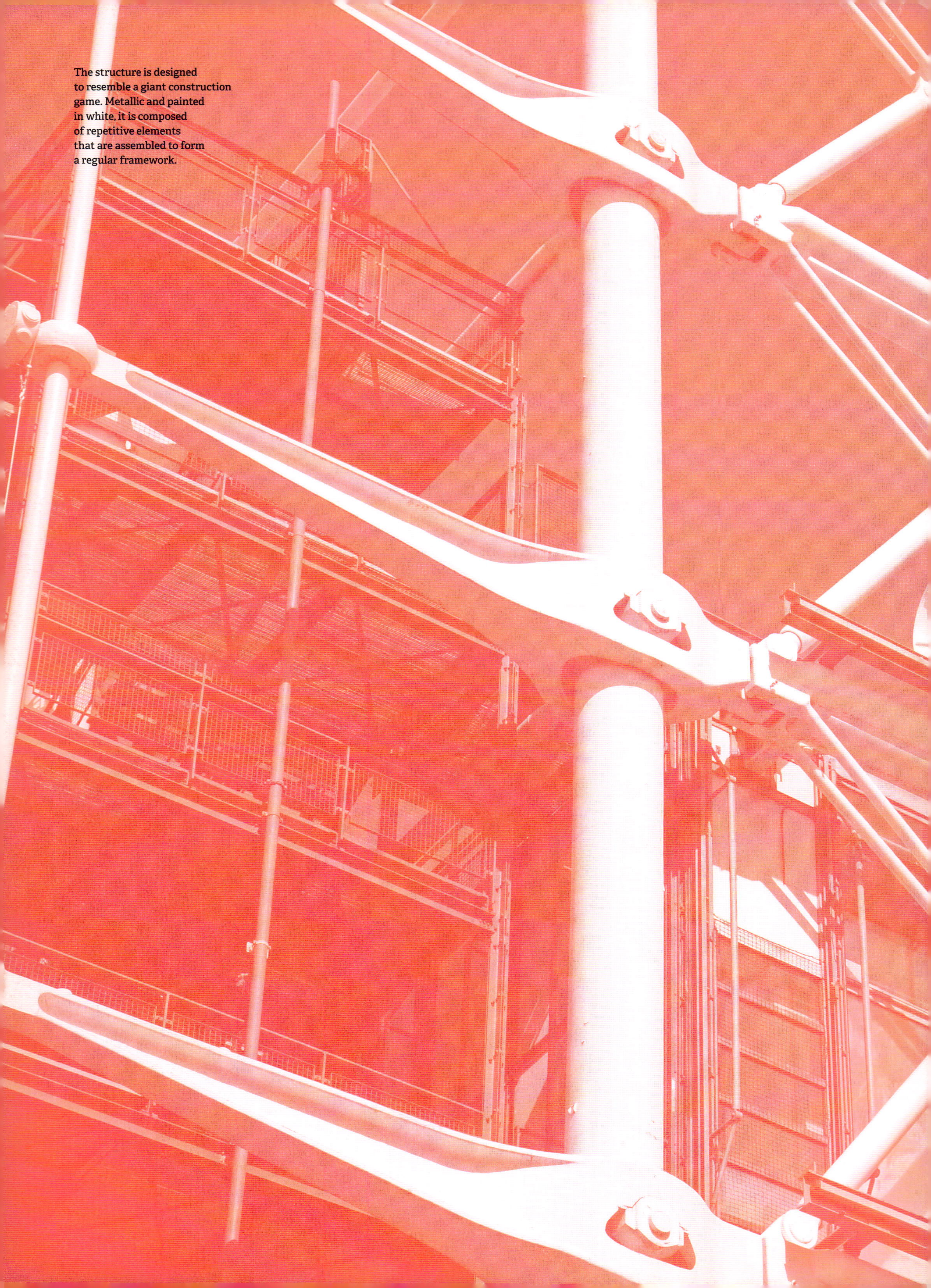

construction

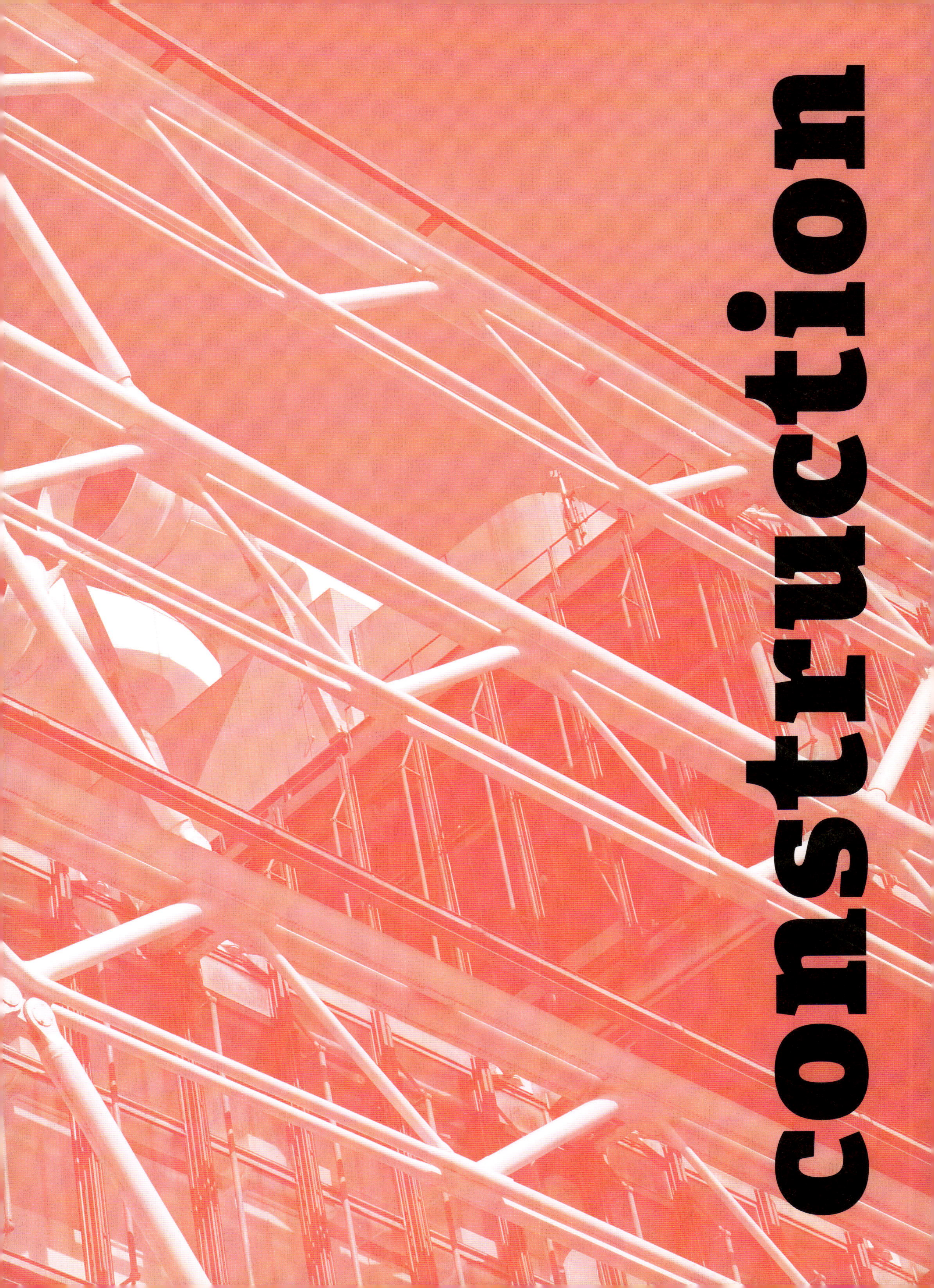

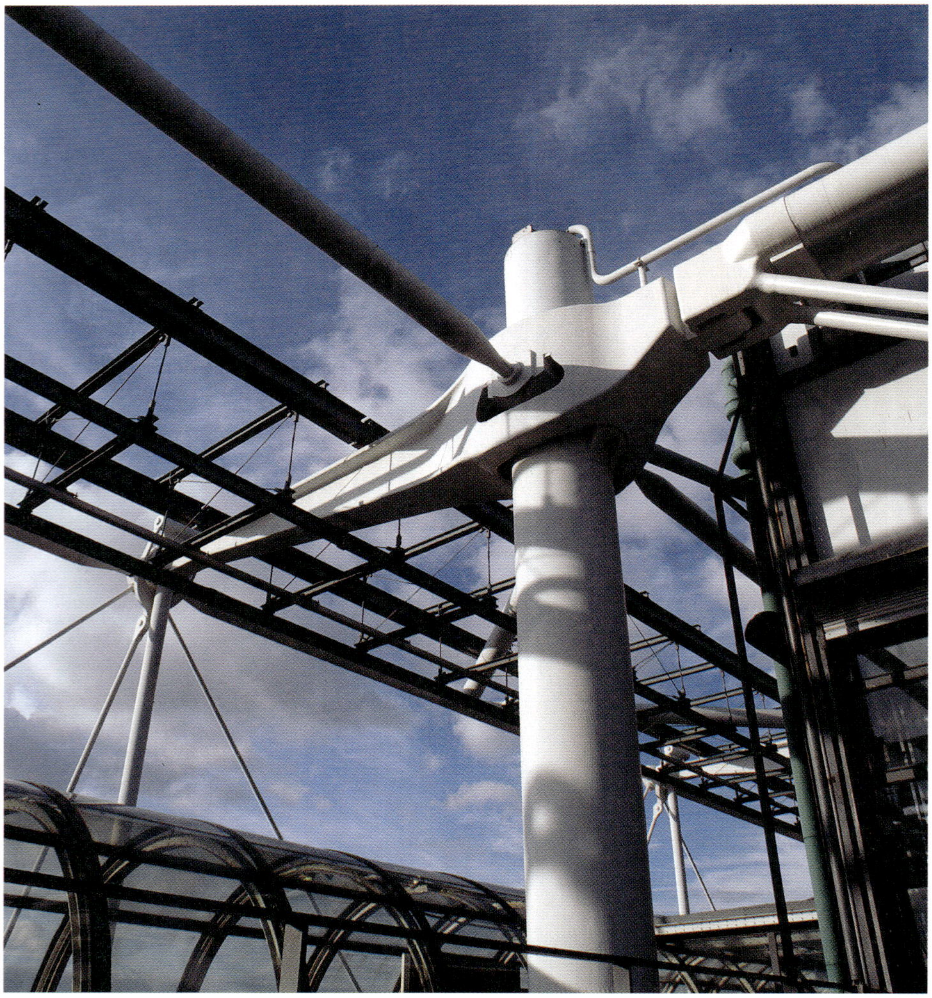
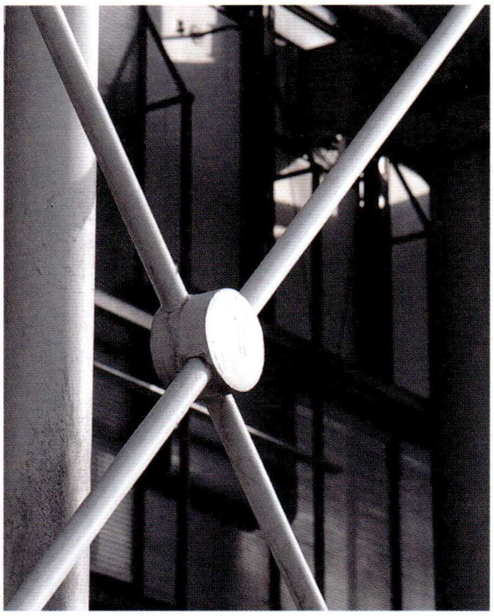
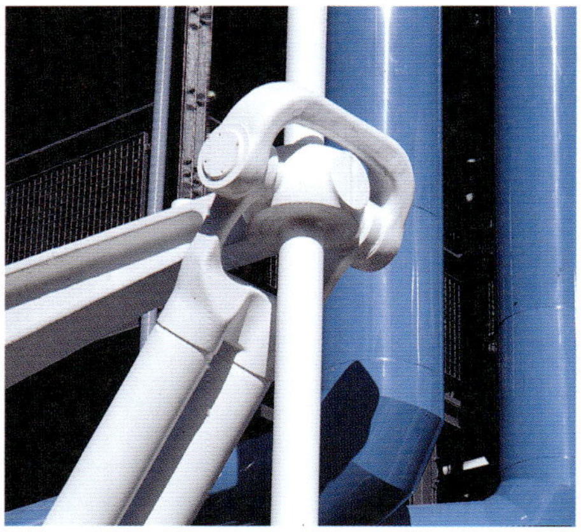

The core of the structure's assemblage comprises a pier, a beam, a beam hanger and a tie (left). If the weight of the beam is borne in part by the pier, the key to the structure lies in the end of the arm of the beam hanger, where an enormous vertically-stretched cable called a tie creates traction that acts as a counterweight (right, bottom).
The wind bracing system is composed of counter-braces, in the form of a Saint Andrew's cross with a height of two storeys (right, top).

A revolutionary design

Young, foreign born, with no understanding of the cogs of the French administration and with a mindset very far from the solemn air that can permeate an international architecture competition for a cultural institution, Renzo Piano and Richard Rogers thought they did not have a chance of winning. So, they allowed themselves free rein as they were designing a radical project, at a moment when, as Richard Rogers says, "the concept of culture seemed blurry enough to lend itself to this interpretation."

Function, first and foremost

They approached the exercise from the essential angle of functionality and technology. Their position was unwavering: it was not a question of "seducing" the client with a sophisticated formal aesthetic, but of "testing materials, of working with structural elements, in a precise and analytical frame of mind, in order to reach irrefutable conclusions."

No decorative elements, no flourishes and no variations of a classic architectural model either. Starting with only four basic modules – pillars, beams, beam hangers and ties – to which they added floors, the architects designed a regular and repetitive framework, a metallic structure like a giant construction set, simply painted white.

However, these elements were not mass-produced, but rather manufactured by craftsmen,

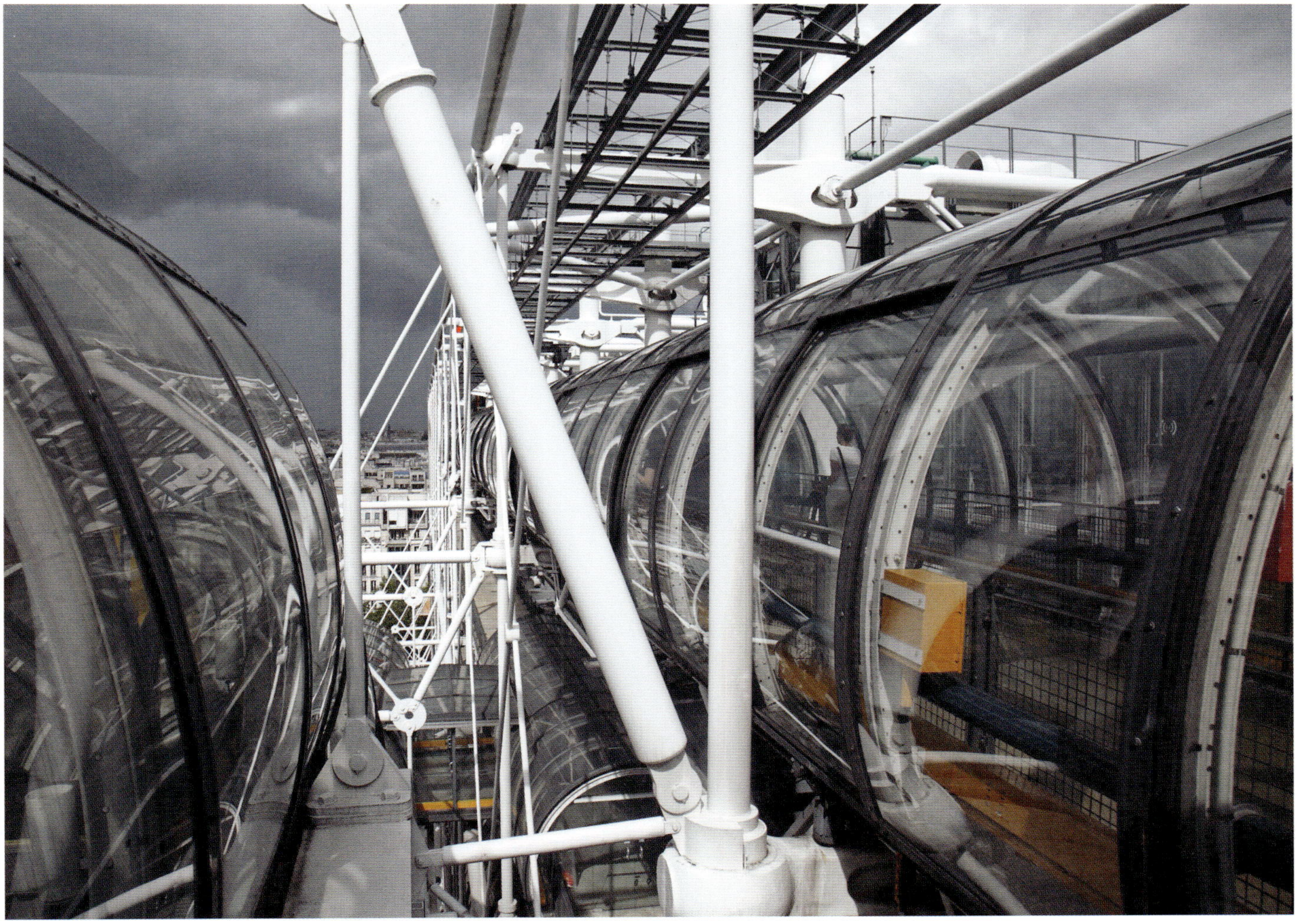

Entirely enclosed in glass, the escalator popularly referred to as the "caterpillar"
and the exterior metallic galleries running the length of the façade are attached to the metallic structure.

making the Centre a gigantic handmade prototype whose designers did not hesitate to qualify as a parody of the imagination of the times.
Tackling problems posed by the programme, Piano and Rogers proclaimed the sincerity of their approach and the care they took to effectively translate the needs of the users (department heads, curators, programmers, librarians, etc.) and the urban environment.
Their ingenious parallelepiped can be summarised as a stack of open-plan and flexible floors between two long façades, one dedicated to providing information to the public, on the Piazza side, the other technical, at the back. Function was given priority, a principle underscored on the exterior by exposed circulations that fulfilled a functional requirement, but which were also a sign of stylistic experimentation.
Inside, vast open, adaptable and modular areas were created, lighted and air-conditioned so that the freedom of installation and intervention would be as wide as possible.
"What we have built," wrote Renzo Piano, "is a big cube open to everyone, a neutral interior space, one bordering on indifference with regard to function. Despite that, Beaubourg is not a neutral container, in the way a state can be, for example."

"A big urban toy"

If certain aspects of the building do recall a factory or a machine – a fact which earned it numerous criticisms and nicknames – its utopian and playful dimension even further removed it from the classical canons of palaces of culture. This was one of the strongest guidelines in the architects' thinking, who, thumbing their noses at the establishment, strove to design a "building that wouldn't be a monument, but a party, a big urban toy." To receive the public and change its relationship to art, they inverted the codes, created conditions fostering exchange and relied on the human scale. Convivial and joyful, the building makes fun of conventions and currents.
If specialists have often assimilated the architecture of the Centre with the high-tech style that incorporates industrial

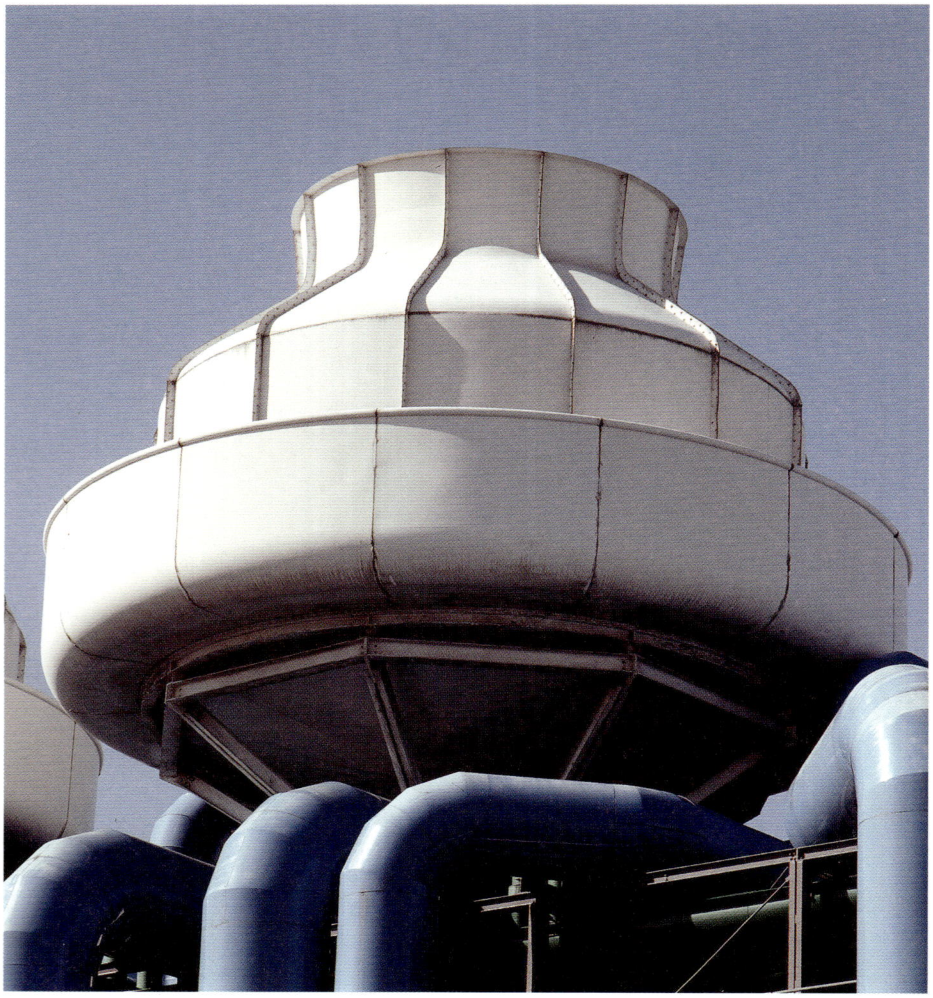

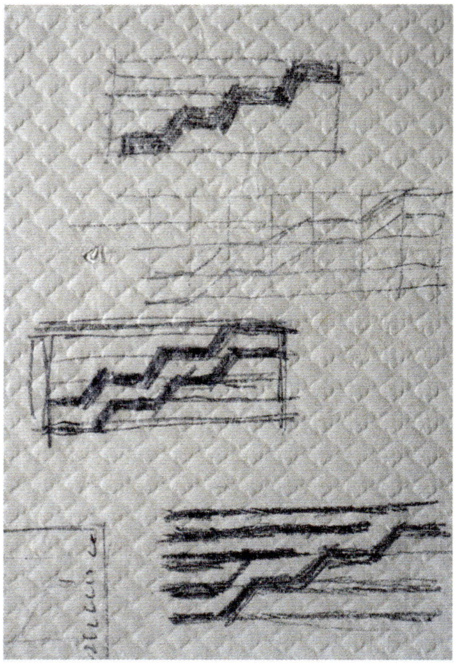

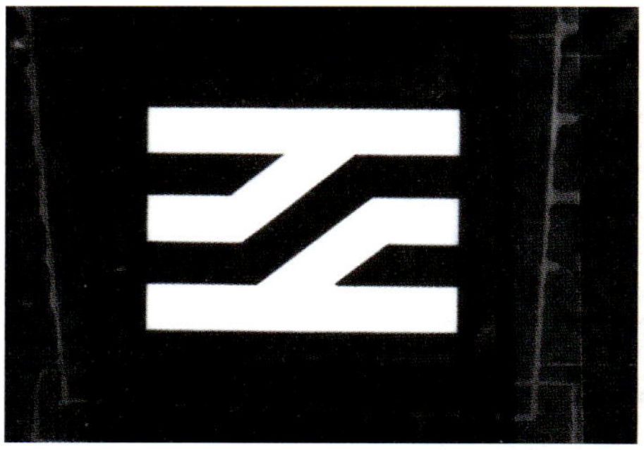

One of the four air-cooling towers placed on the roof of the Centre Pompidou (left page, on the left).
Jean Widmer, *Study of the logo* (detail), 1976-1977, and *Logo*, 1977 (left page, from top to bottom, on the right).
View of the first of fourteen gantries comprising the structure of the Centre Pompidou and upon which the building's six levels are stacked (right page).

high-technology into architecture, Piano prefers to speak about playing with technology, necessary to be able to design an escalator that zigzags across the façade in a dynamic movement, or utilise beams 50 metres long and weighing 120 tonnes, which made it possible to lighten the structure – but not insufficient to express the soul of the project. The building's lightness is as physical as it is philosophical. The times were not indifferent to the blossoming of such a project. The spirit of 1968 was still coursing through the Centre's architectural competition and its programme, which advocated the abolition of frontiers between disciplines and the confrontation of experiences.

The logo: history of a scratched rectangle

The Centre Pompidou's logo, six black, superimposed horizontal bars – the six floors of the building – forming a rectangle struck with a broken diagonal bar, the escalator running across the entire façade – has become a graphic design icon. Jean Widmer created it just before the inauguration, compelled by the Centre's management, which was adamant about the Centre having a sign of this type. In fact, the Swiss designer, who along with Ernest Hiestand won the international competition to design the Centre's graphic identity in 1974, initially refused to include a logo, which he deemed useless and even harmful. The three elements of the "brand image" that the two graphic designers imagined would have to suffice: typography breaking with tradition and inspired by typing, the symbol of communication that was not solemn yet democratic; a colour code (yellow for administration, green for the BPI, blue for the CCI, red for the MNAM and violet for the IRCAM); and vertically hanging signage. But the management insisted: a logo is eminently practical for "signing" a book as well as a ticket or a piece of furniture. Hiestand withdrew. Widmer, inspired by Piano and Rogers' façade, designed this minimalist, immediately recognisable abstraction of the building, which now seems so obvious. The logo is the last remaining element of the original graphic identity.

When under threat during the major renovations in the 2000s and the accompanying design of a new graphic identity, the whole international graphic design community rose to defend this now historical sign.

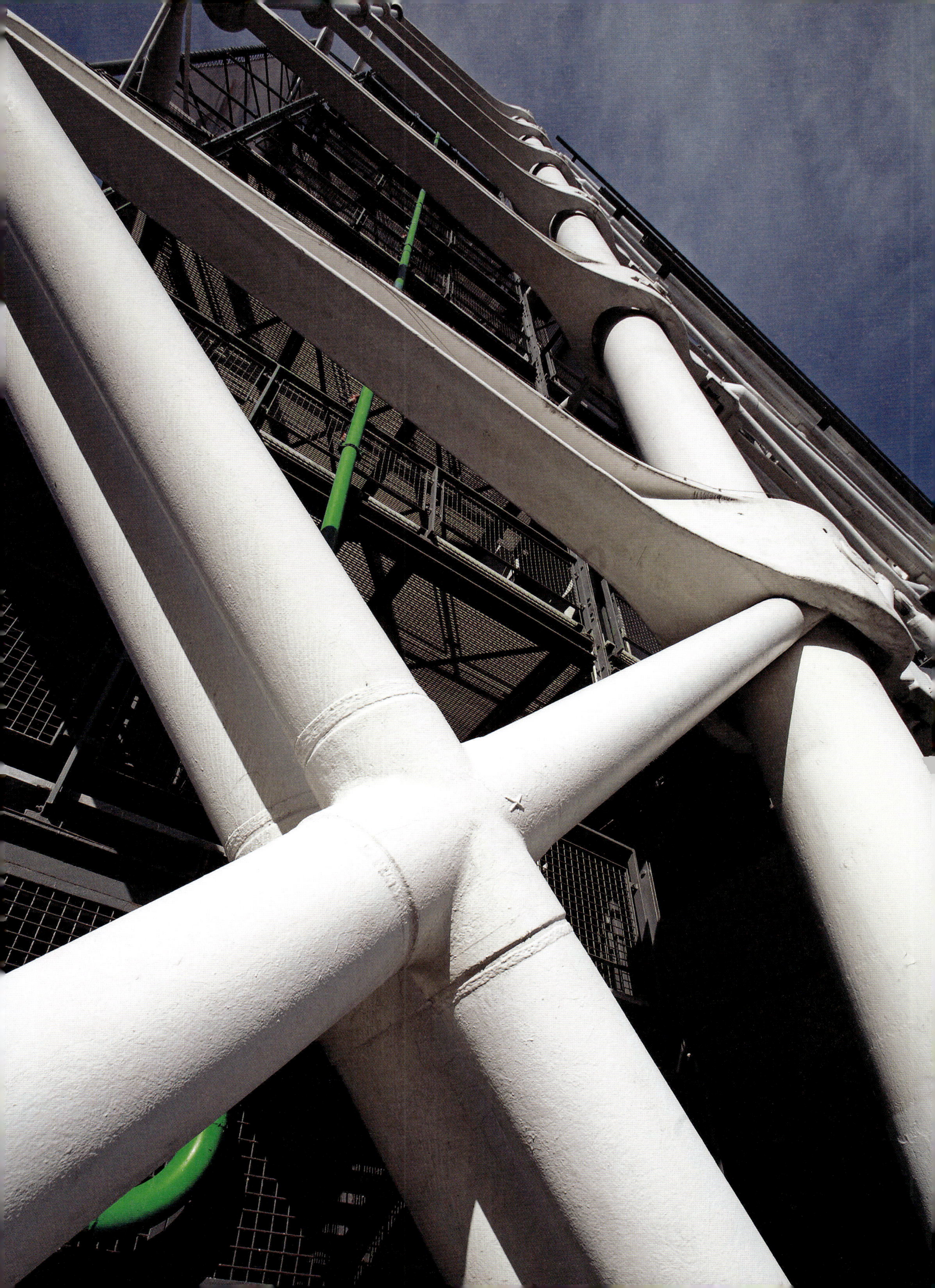

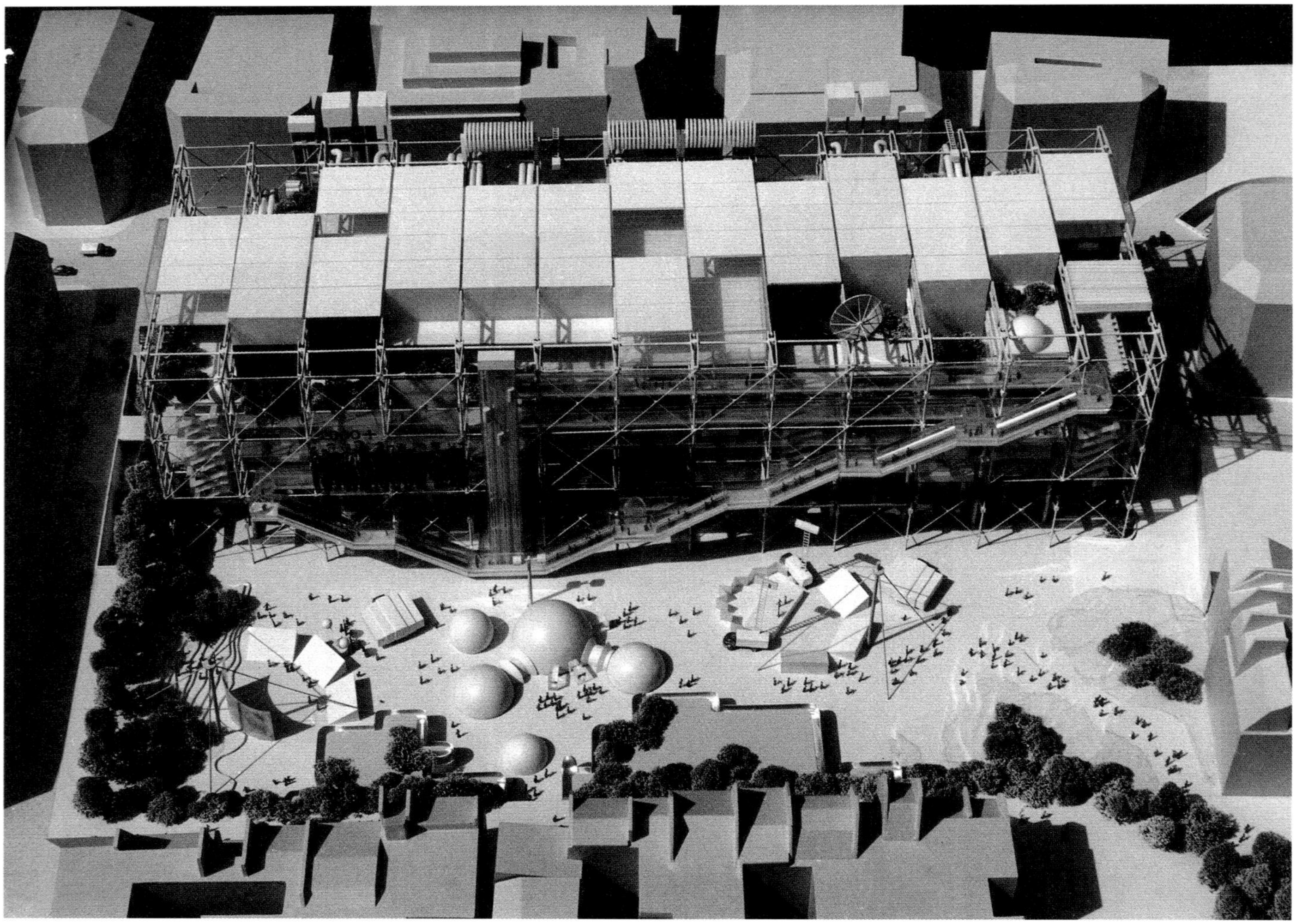

Second model, construction permit and Piazza development, May 1972.

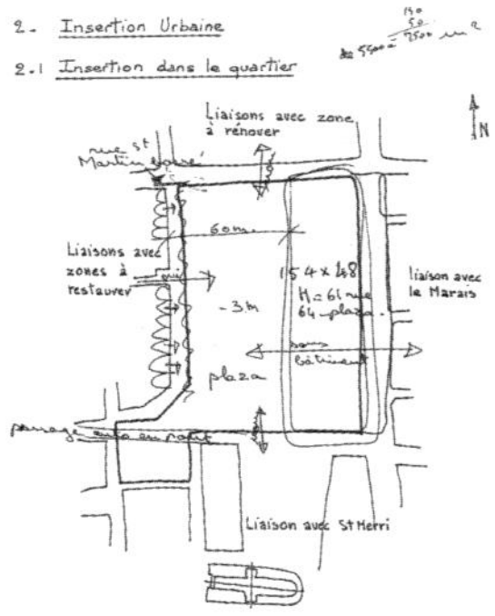

From project to completion

Between the model presented in the competition and the building that was actually constructed, two notable changes occurred – at the level of the Piazza and the Centre's ground floor – during the so-called "project-programme" adequacy phase, intended to enable the architects and users to dialogue in order to adapt the project to fit everyone's wishes and to deal with real constraints.

A gently sloping piazza rather than an inner courtyard

The original project envisaged a horizontal, hollowed-out plaza three metres below street level, even with the buildings. The façades of houses bordering the plaza were extended downward, all the way to cellar level. To access this enclosed plaza, subterranean passageways were planned, notably from Les Halles – where the first phase of the main hub of the regional trains and the metro was to open in 1977 – by passing under the Boulevard Sébastopol. To the north and the south, Rue Rambuteau and Rue Saint-Merri remained open to traffic. The plaza in this design was a sort of inner courtyard in continuity with the totally open ground of the Centre resting on pillars. For various technical and practical reasons, it was finally decided to build a plaza gently sloping downward from the Rue Saint-Martin, turned into a pedestrian street like its neighbouring streets, all the way to the foot of the building. This created a more natural

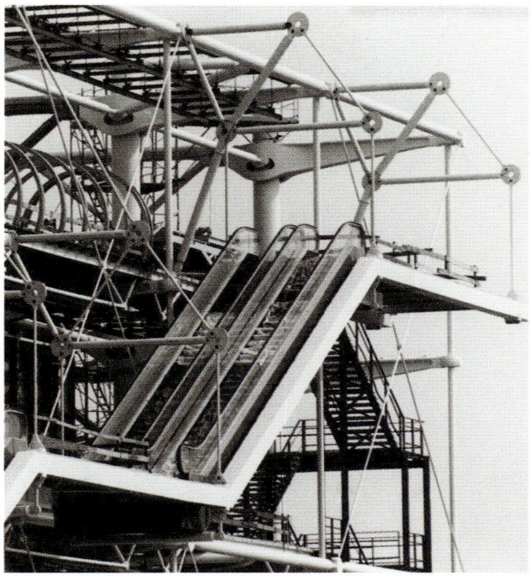

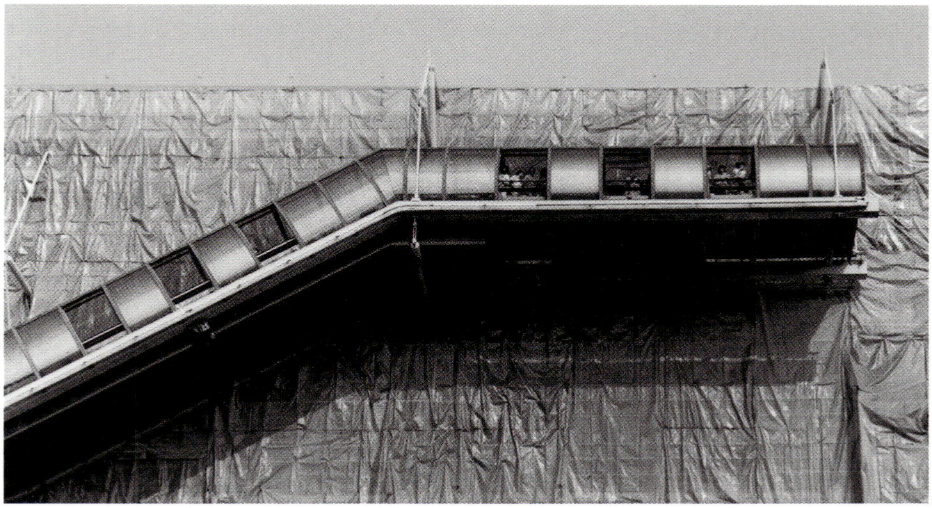

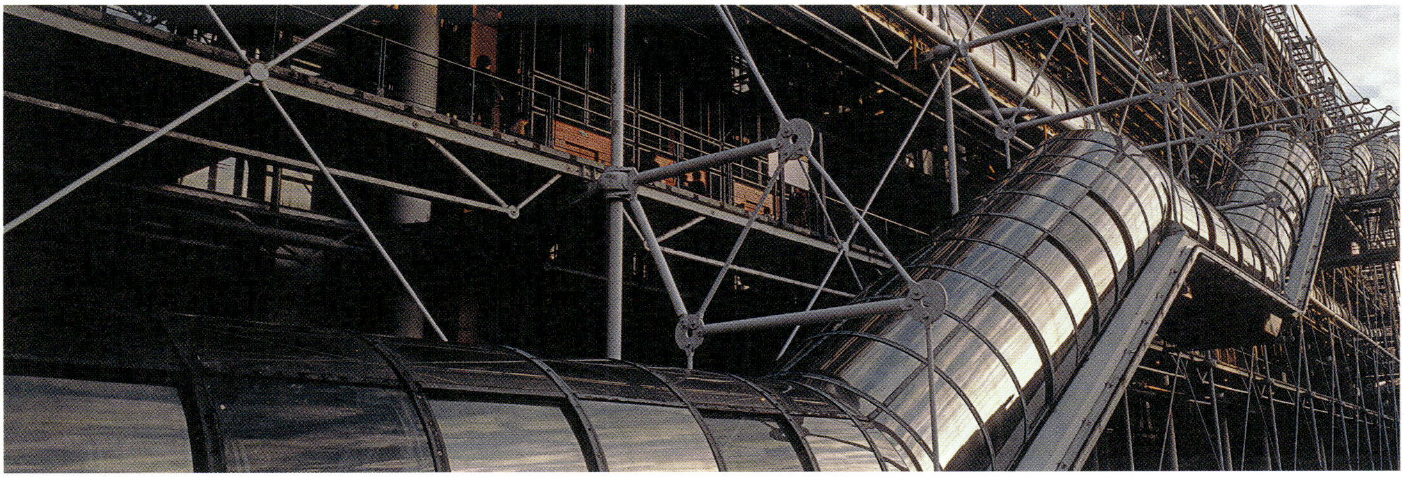

The "caterpillar": view of the escalator suspended from the façade, before installation of the glass-enclosed arcade (top, left); renovation for the 10th anniversary of the Centre Pompidou, June 1986 (top, right); current view (bottom).

link with the neighbourhood.
The ground floor had to be closed with glass curtain walls, like the rest of the building.
Yet it retained an aspect of an inner courtyard, a welcoming place for encounters and shows.

The "caterpillar": a vertical street

With the ground floor now to be closed, the idea of a vertical plaza on the façade remained; one that would enable free access to every floor.
To achieve this, the architects first imagined a bank of lifts and escalators distributing the circulations, then a cascade of escalators on the building's axis, before proposing a system composed of lifts and two escalators, one very short on the north end, the other stretching southward. Finally, they came up with what would become the signature of the Centre: a hanging escalator diagonally zigzagging across the entire building, marking a landing at each level.
This "caterpillar" encased in glass, which makes the flow of users visible, is a veritable vertical street where visitors extend their stroll, discovering the panoramic views of Paris as they ascend.

Key dates of the construction of the Centre

May 1972:
start of earthwork

1973:
fabrication and assembly of beams at the Krupp factory in Germany

1 July 1973:
definitive architectural programme

December 1973:
construction of the infrastructure begins

September 1974:
arrival of the first beam

October 1974-June 1975:
construction of the metallic framework

1976:
mounting of the escalator, installation of the air-conditioning towers on the roof, completion of construction

31 January 1977:
opening of the Centre National d'Art et de Culture Georges-Pompidou

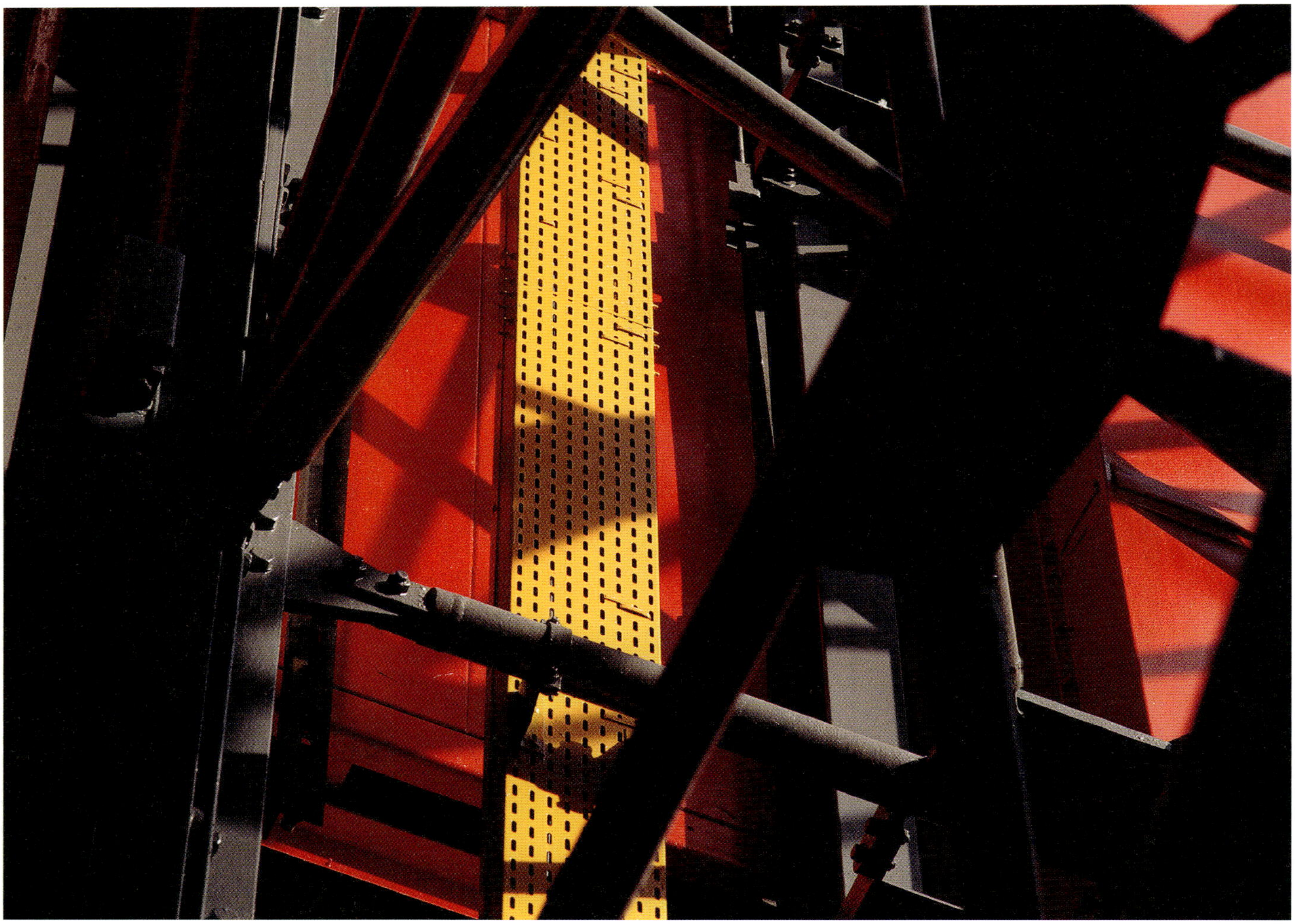

Painted in red, one of the lifts installed on the façade by Rue du Renard is notably utilised for transporting works inside the Centre Pompidou.

Colour code

One of the Centre Pompidou's specific features is its utilisation of bright colours, unusual for architecture. Though joyful and playful, these colours have precise functions because each one symbolises one of the flows feeding into the Centre from its periphery – blue for air, yellow for electricity, green for water and red for circulations.

Blue for the air

For the conservation of artworks and books and for the public's comfort, the Centre is equipped with a heating and cooling system, whose distinguishing feature is that it is entirely exposed. At the foot of the building, big white air intake vents in the shape of the curved smoke stacks of cruise ships mark a sort of frontier at the top of the Piazza. They are also placed at the back of the Centre, in the Rue du Renard. On the roof, four enormous cooling towers supply the air-conditioning. Between the two façades, a multitude of exposed pipes in the galleries and reading rooms and outside, all painted blue, ensure the distribution of air.

Yellow for electricity

Everything involving the distribution of electricity, whether transformers, cable ducts, shafts, etc., is equally exposed and signalled in yellow. Thus, the visitor can follow the pathway of electricity to any facility in the Centre, whether it is a lift, an escalator, a computer or a simple lamp. The fact that the entire system is "exposed" in this way greatly facilitates maintenance.

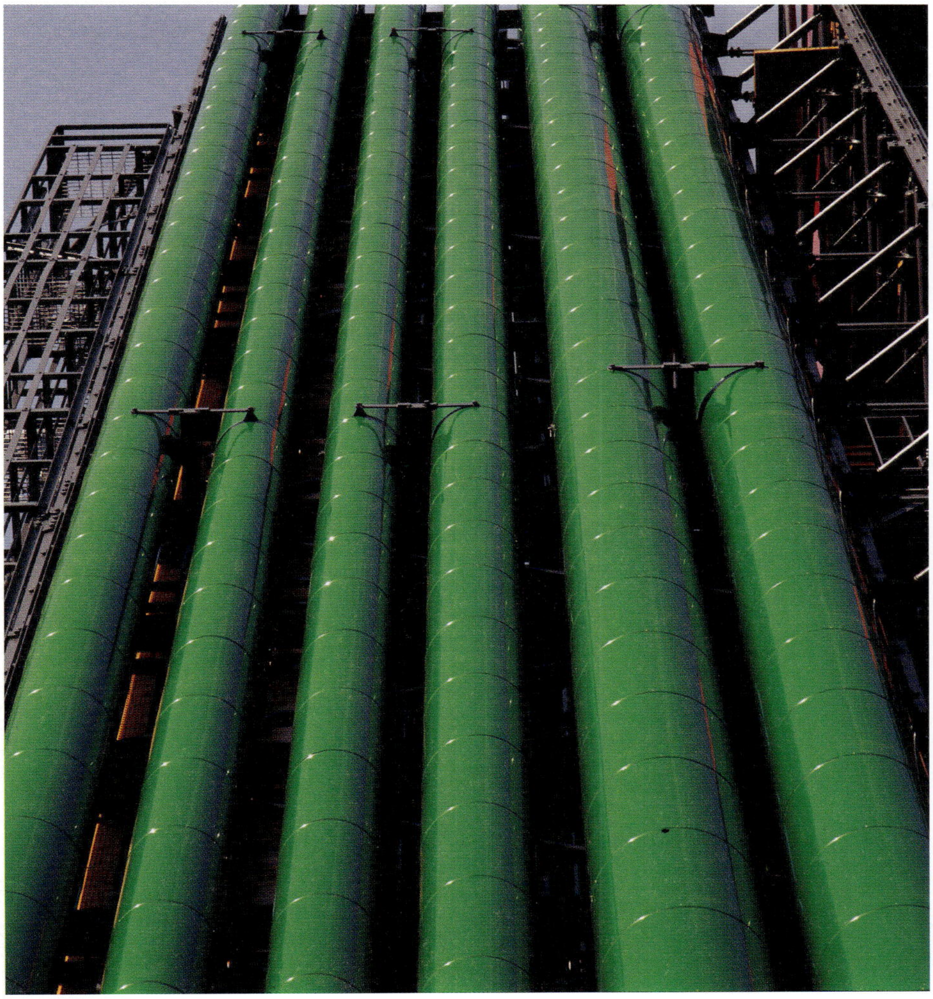

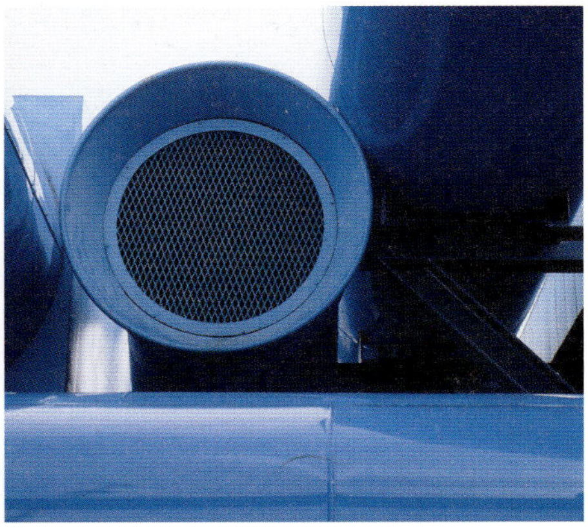

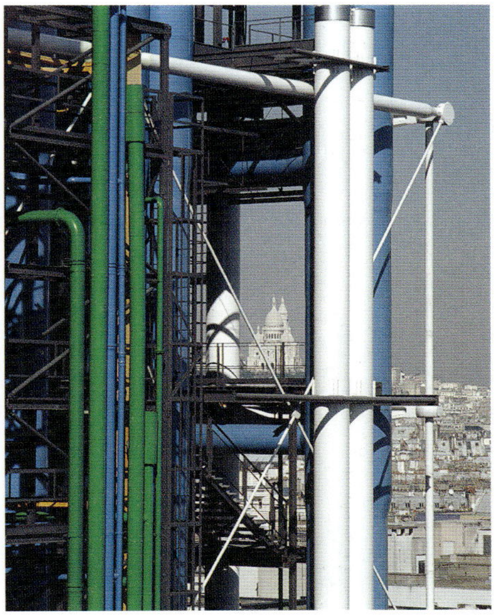

Like organ pipes, the water conduits run the entire height of the façade (left).
One of the blue vents on the roof of the Centre Pompidou (right, top).
The basilica of Sacré-Cœur, seen through the forest of pipes (right, bottom).

Green for water

Next to blue ducts and yellow tubes, green hoses carry the water required to ensure building functions and safety. They too are openly attached to façades or suspended from ceilings.
The distribution of all flows – water, air, electricity – is organised on the back façade, a solution whose cleverness was highlighted by the president of the jury, Jean Prouvé: "This is a qualified, very well-designed technical façade. Moreover, the Rue du Renard, where traffic will increase, offers no real architectural interest. However, the great organs of the Centre, whose utility cannot be denied, offer a big, entertaining show. The architects have turned all these pipes and lifts into a magnificent decor, whose polychromic programme they have sentimentally and scientifically developed." (*L'Architecture d'aujourd'hui*, February 1977).

Red for circulations

The Centre's arteries, its circulations, are for the most part in red: on the front façade, the public lifts; on the back façade, the service and freight lifts for artworks. Only the "caterpillar" is transparent, but its underside is painted red. The circulations are also pushed to the building's exterior to leave the floors wide open.

The artist consultations

The first model presented by Piano and Rogers was all in white. However, a though President Pompidou approved the overall project, he wished to see colour added to mark the "whole with a part of his character." He requested the consultation of "a talented colourist," and suggested Vasarely, Agam and Cruz Diez. Agam proposed a system for varying the building's exterior colour scheme according to the time of day. Then the team thought about focusing on two colours that obtained a consensus, blue and brown. Georges Pompidou intervened once again: "garish colours must be avoided as they quickly become annoying. Therefore, if we want to go with the pair brown and blue, I suggest brown and light blue or a pale blue-grey, a model for which can be found in Braque's lithographs." The painter Jean Dewasne, reacting negatively to this 'grey," proposed enlivening the exterior forms with bright primary colours.

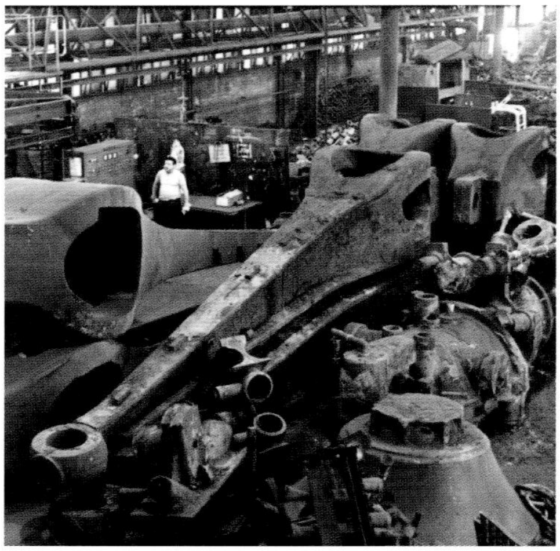
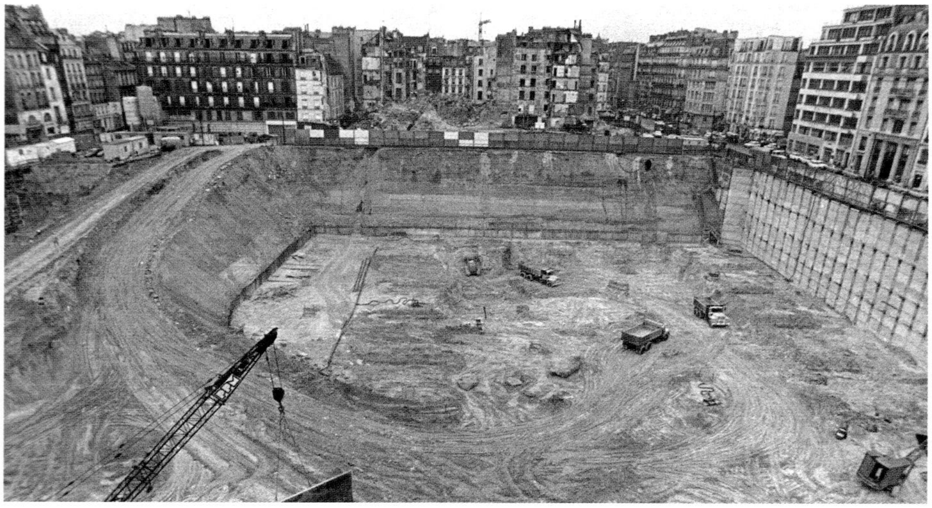
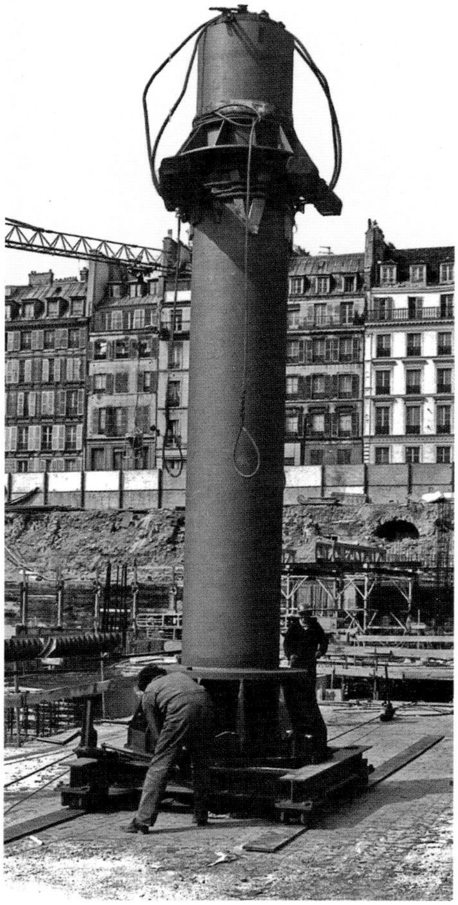

Preparation of the Centre Pompidou construction site: fabrication of the beam hangers at the Krupp factory, in Germany (top, left); the start of the earthworks, April 1972 (bottom, left); the start of construction of the infrastructure with the installation of the first pillar column, December 1973 (right).

The construction site

In May 1972, the monumental construction site of the Centre Beaubourg was launched. It would be completed on schedule, less than five years later, and despite several interruptions due to no less than six lawsuits filed against it by the numerous opponents of the project.

Titanic foundations

First, the site had to be prepared by excavating an enormous hole to a depth of 20 metres over an area of 16,000 square metres, whose sides had to be reinforced by retaining walls capable of supporting the very heavy load of the future structure. This hole would receive the only elements of the building that would remain invisible: the foundations, to which the pillars would be anchored, and the reinforced concrete infrastructure that would house the four-level car park, technical areas, storage space, reserves and rooms for the public. Meanwhile, in Germany, at the Krupp factory, the steel pieces of the metallic structure were cast in special moulds (French steel manufacturers had declined the order). The pieces arrived in Paris by train and were transported to the site by special convoys which crossed the capital during the night.

A spectacular assembly

By October 1974, and after only nine months, the entire metallic structure was assembled by very tall cranes that lifted and adjusted various elements under the watchful eye of many onlookers, attracted by the spectacular dimensions of this ballet.

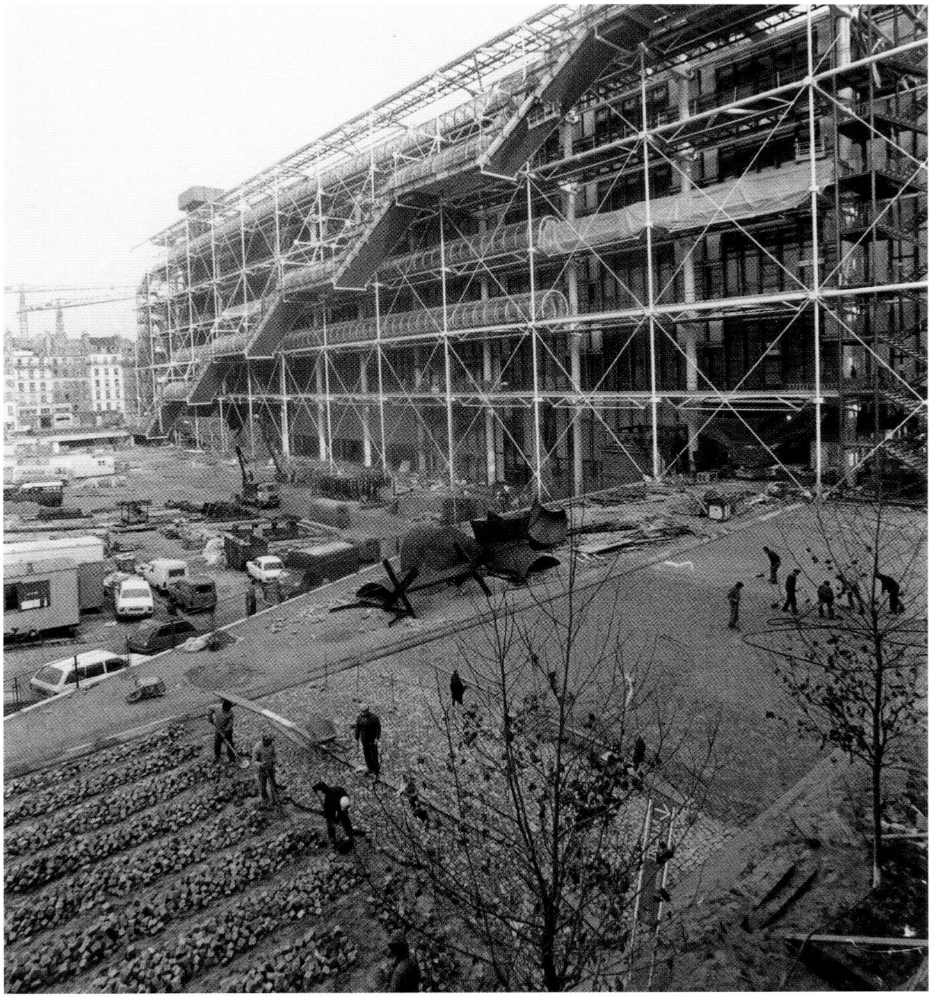

"I really loved, for years before the construction of the Centre Georges Pompidou, to venture onto the Beaubourg Plateau, smooth, cleared of its rubble and fenced off in the distance by the obscure mass of the buildings that had been saved, stitched up tears in their walls of phantom staircases, and marked off at the base by a feeble, thinly stretched cord of light: it was the only spot in Paris where you could see the moonlight in the open sky, like a glade in the forest."

Julien Gracq, *La Forme d'une ville*, ed. José Corti, Paris, 1985

During the installation of the glass curtain walls of the Centre Pompidou, a field of paving stones was prepared on the Rue Aubry-le-Boucher, awaiting the moment they would cover the Piazza.

The choreography was planned to the millimetre: first, the bottom piece of the pillars – the part that remains underground – was anchored to the foundations, to which the two other segments were then soldered. Then, onto these gigantic 49-metre pillars, the cranes slipped the beam hangers, resembling brackets (also referred to as "gerberettes" after the name of their inventor, Gerber), which were placed one by one in their designated positions. These pieces, which look like keys, are the nodal points of the structure because they constitute the interlocking system of the full set of elements.
After which, beams were put in place, each one weighing the equivalent of 70 cars, which were then raised and hooked to the beam hangers spaced at 12.8 metres from each other, and which create thirteen bays running the length of the building.
The "ties" – cables of 22 centimetres in diameter – are also affixed to the ends of the arms of the beam hangers facing outwards and vertically stretched and anchored to the ground to serve as a counterweight to the pillars.
Finally, between the two pillars, the floors in reinforced concrete were laid and bolted. Floor by floor, bay by bay, like an immense Meccano, the framework rose.
To ensure their stability and avoid any deformation, braces two storeys in height – also called "Saint Andrew's cross" – were affixed to the tips of the beam hangers.
The third phase consisted of "trimming" the structure painted in white. The fire escapes were installed, the exterior galleries attached and the "caterpillar" hung.
The elements required for the circulation of the various flows were laid: pipes and ducts along the façades and cooling towers installed on the roof, like big hats. The big panels 7 metres in height, in glass for the most part, were finally installed inside the structure, to protect what it would eventually contain.

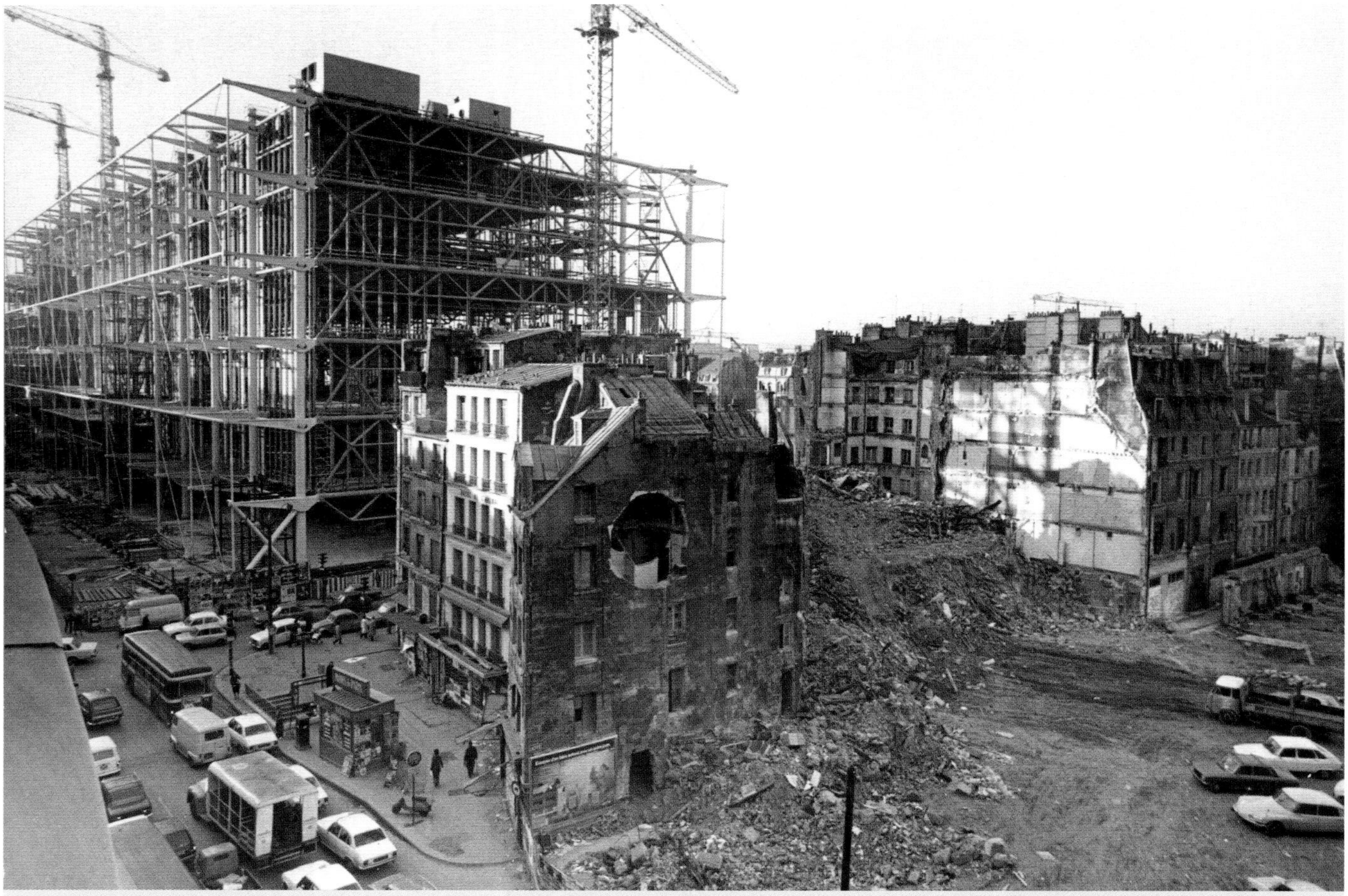

Robert Doisneau, photography of the construction site and the piece by Gordon Matta-Clark, *Conical Intersect* (1975), at 27-29 Rue Beaubourg (top).
One of the beams, a gigantic piece of steel 45 metres long, weighing the equivalent of 70 cars, is transported by night through Paris to the construction site (bottom).
View of the construction site during the placement of the second beam (right page).

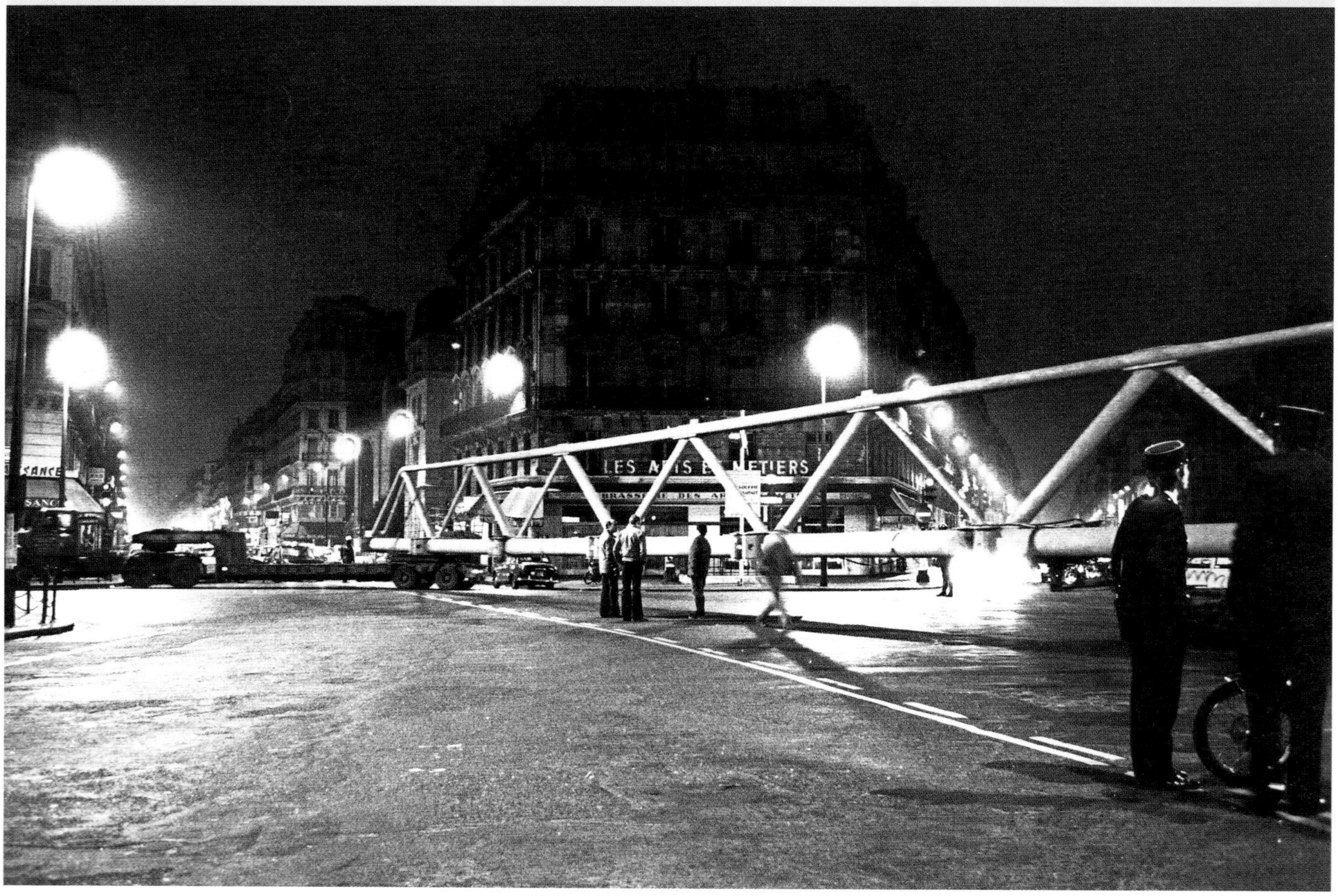

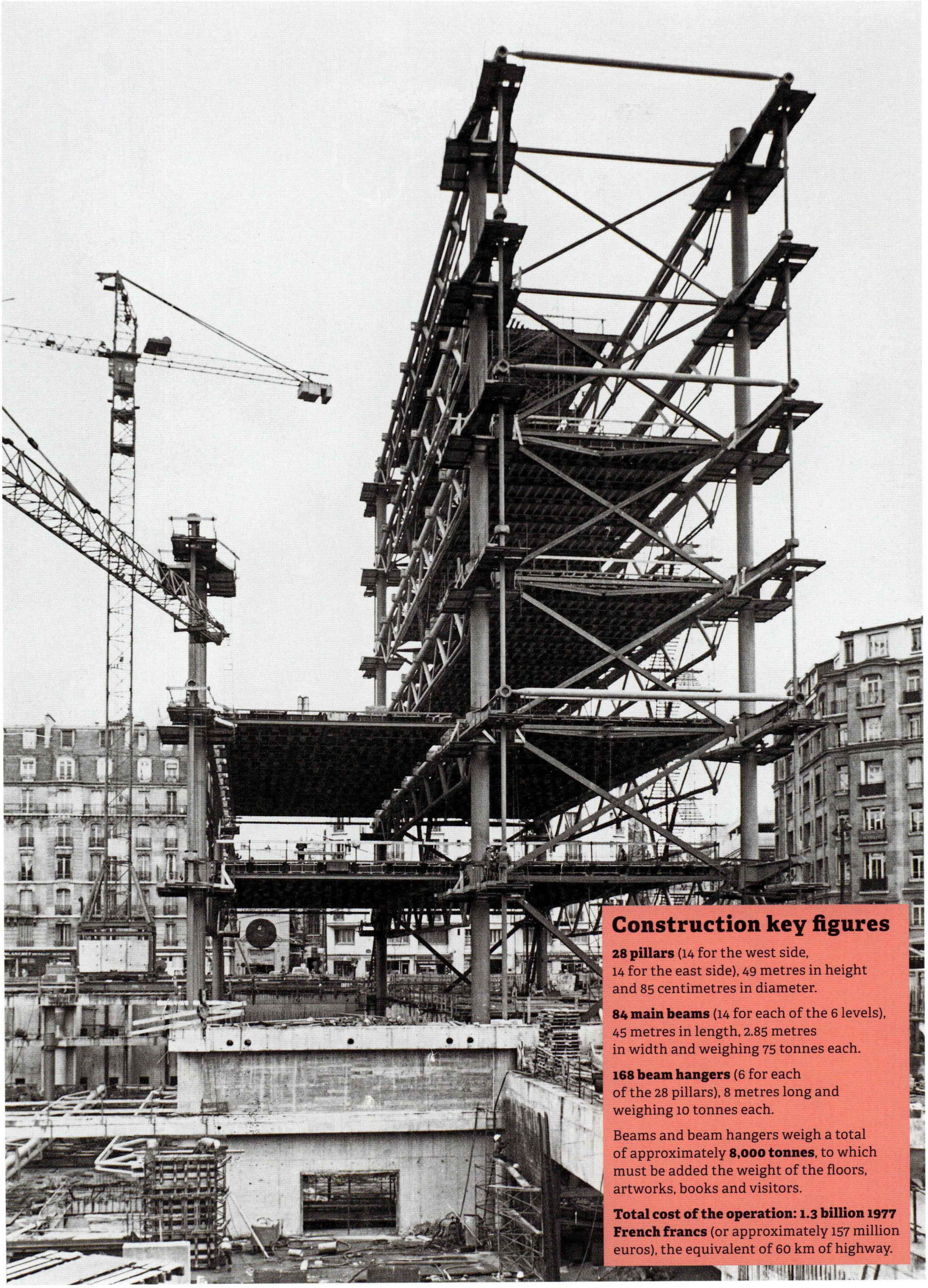

Construction key figures

28 pillars (14 for the west side, 14 for the east side), 49 metres in height and 85 centimetres in diameter.

84 main beams (14 for each of the 6 levels), 45 metres in length, 2.85 metres in width and weighing 75 tonnes each.

168 beam hangers (6 for each of the 28 pillars), 8 metres long and weighing 10 tonnes each.

Beams and beam hangers weigh a total of approximately **8,000 tonnes**, to which must be added the weight of the floors, artworks, books and visitors.

Total cost of the operation: 1.3 billion 1977 French francs (or approximately 157 million euros), the equivalent of 60 km of highway.

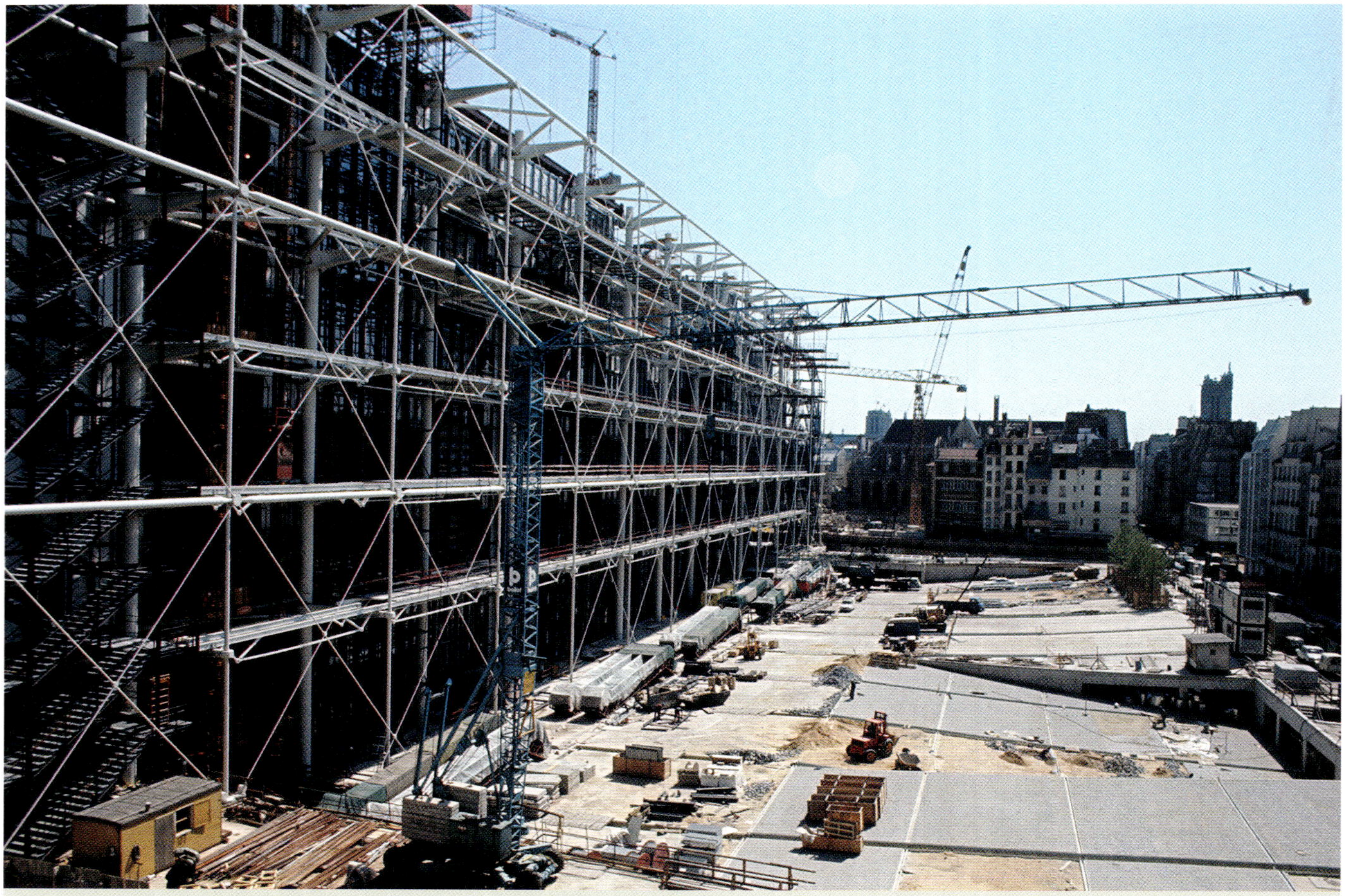

View of the building nearing completion: the infrastructure under the Piazza is covered over (top). The exterior galleries on the Piazza side are placed on the arms of the beam hangers (bottom). View of the construction site from the top level of the Centre Pompidou, which has a series of terraces. The metallic framework has not yet been painted white (right page).

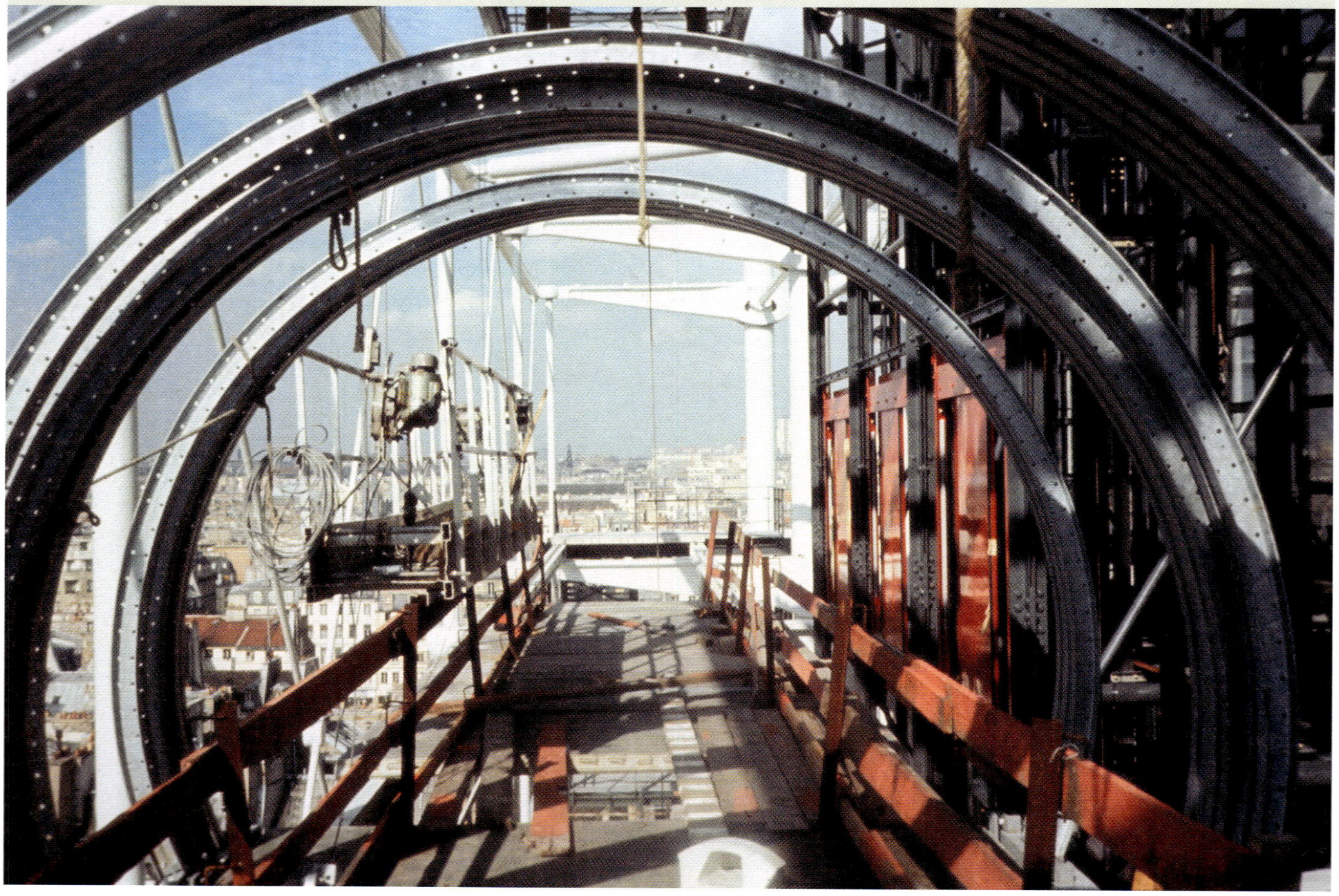

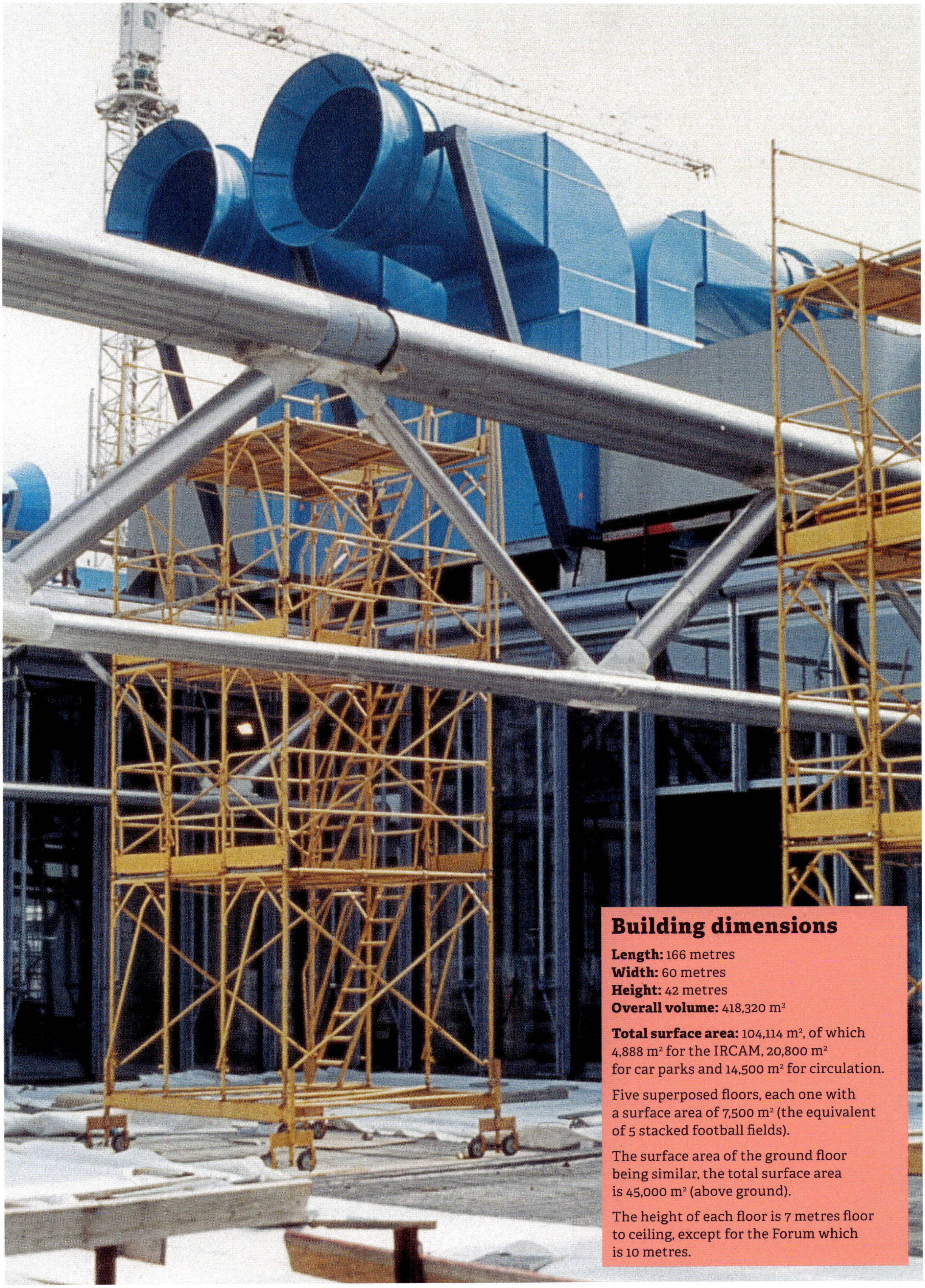

Building dimensions

Length: 166 metres
Width: 60 metres
Height: 42 metres
Overall volume: 418,320 m^3

Total surface area: 104,114 m^2, of which 4,888 m^2 for the IRCAM, 20,800 m^2 for car parks and 14,500 m^2 for circulation.

Five superposed floors, each one with a surface area of 7,500 m^2 (the equivalent of 5 stacked football fields).

The surface area of the ground floor being similar, the total surface area is 45,000 m^2 (above ground).

The height of each floor is 7 metres floor to ceiling, except for the Forum which is 10 metres.

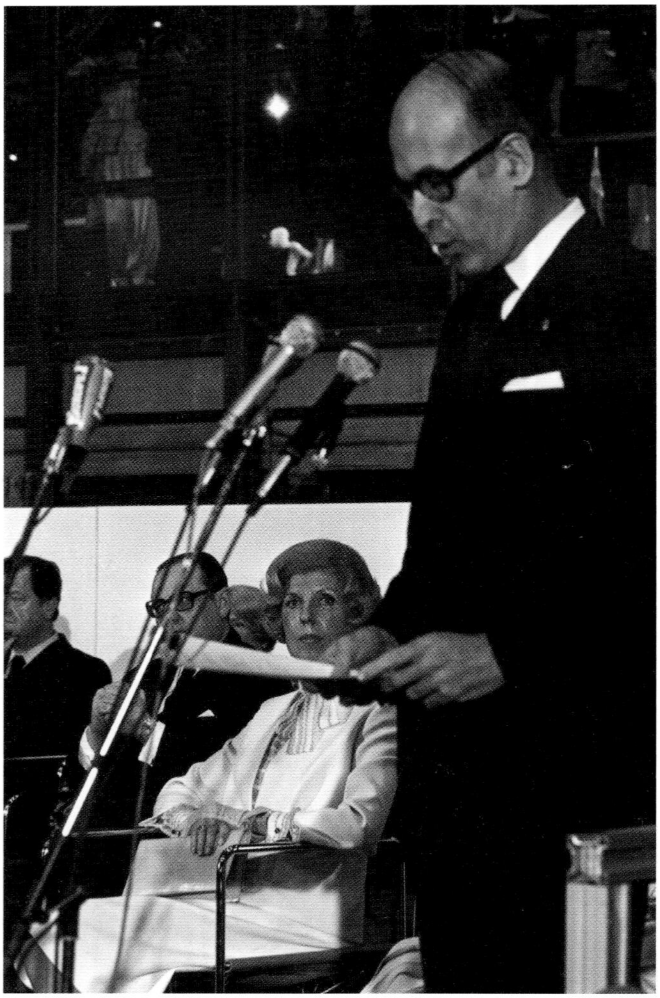

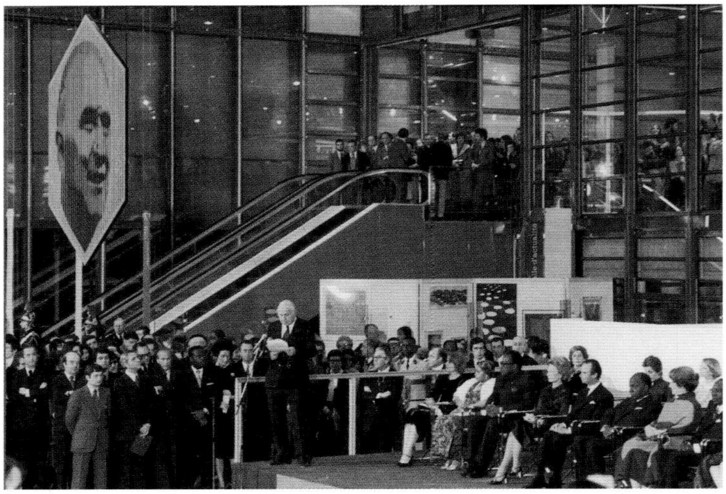

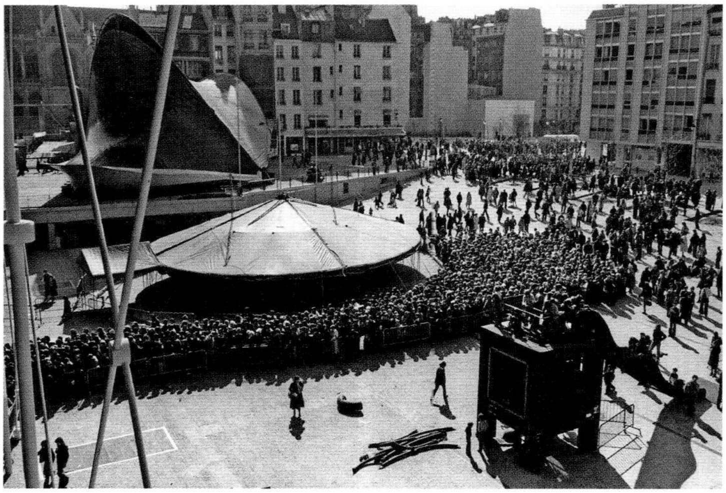

Opening in 1977: Monday, 31 January, the Centre National d'Art et de Culture Georges-Pompidou is inaugurated by President of the Republic Valéry Giscard d'Estaing (left), in the presence of Prime Minister Raymond Barre, Mrs. Georges Pompidou and numerous other personages. Robert Bordaz, President of the Centre, giving a speech (top, right). The *Diatope* by Iannis Xenakis and the *Toboggan* by Bernhard Luginbühl on the Piazza, March 1977 (bottom, left).

The "Beaubourg model"

If a few institutions in the world created a stir in the museum world prior to 1977, nowadays the model for museum, the Centre Pompidou for its part launched a genuine revolution in museum architecture, design and audience.

Demystifying culture

All the codes are inverted. On the outside, passers-by are no longer blocked by a closed monument. They can now cross through it or continue their stroll vertically; on the façade, large glass curtain walls have replaced colonnades; an immense escalator diagonally rises to the top of the building, replacing the big escalator at the entrance; the traditional citation inscribed on the building's fronton has become a wall of information (in the initial plans, this idea was eventually dropped).
Exchange and communication become the watch words, between the disciplines and between the Centre and the street – the transparency of the walls reinforces this – the frontiers are now permeable. Inside, the succession of closed galleries where visitors "content themselves" with contemplating the artworks gives way to open spaces with evolving dimensions where all sorts of dynamic relations can be created between the users and the Centre.

A tool in the service of the public

Consideration of the public is at the centre of this new conception, which is what makes the museum a place open to all. "Culture is static

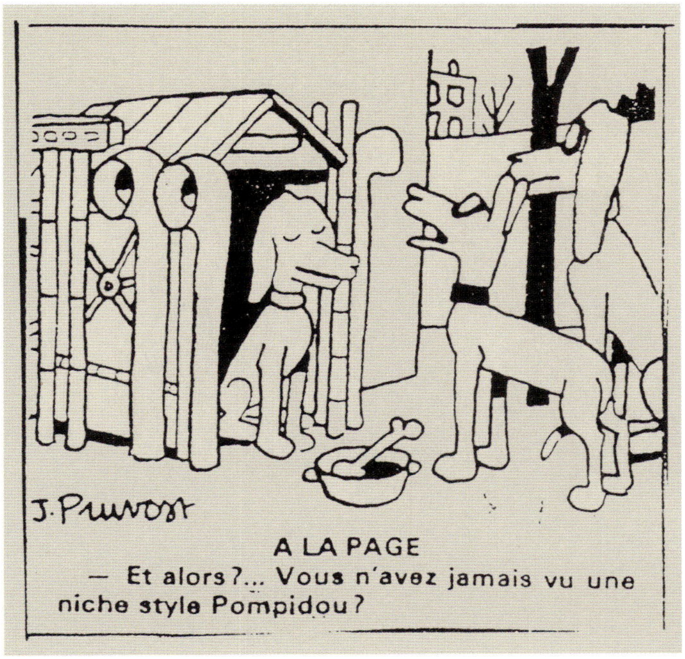

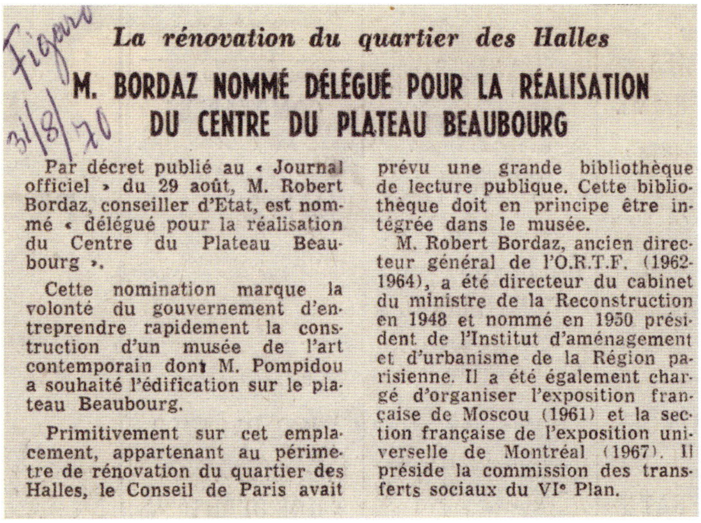

Figaro 31/8/70

La rénovation du quartier des Halles

M. BORDAZ NOMMÉ DÉLÉGUÉ POUR LA RÉALISATION DU CENTRE DU PLATEAU BEAUBOURG

Par décret publié au « Journal officiel » du 29 août, M. Robert Bordaz, conseiller d'Etat, est nommé « délégué pour la réalisation du Centre du Plateau Beaubourg ».

Cette nomination marque la volonté du gouvernement d'entreprendre rapidement la construction d'un musée de l'art contemporain dont M. Pompidou a souhaité l'édification sur le plateau Beaubourg.

Primitivement sur cet emplacement, appartenant au périmètre de rénovation du quartier des Halles, le Conseil de Paris avait prévu une grande bibliothèque de lecture publique. Cette bibliothèque doit en principe être intégrée dans le musée.

M. Robert Bordaz, ancien directeur général de l'O.R.T.F. (1962-1964), a été directeur du cabinet du ministre de la Reconstruction en 1948 et nommé en 1950 président de l'Institut d'aménagement et d'urbanisme de la Région parisienne. Il a été également chargé d'organiser l'exposition française de Moscou (1961) et la section française de l'exposition universelle de Montréal (1967). Il préside la commission des transferts sociaux du VIe Plan.

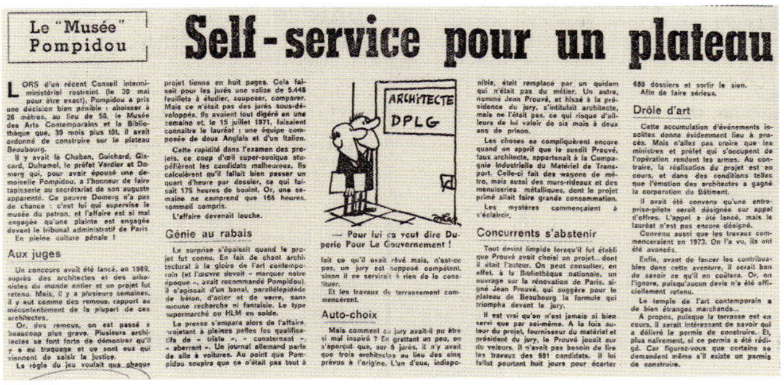

Le "Musée" Pompidou

Self-service pour un plateau

Aux juges

Génie au rabais

Auto-choix

Concurrents s'abstenir

Drôle d'art

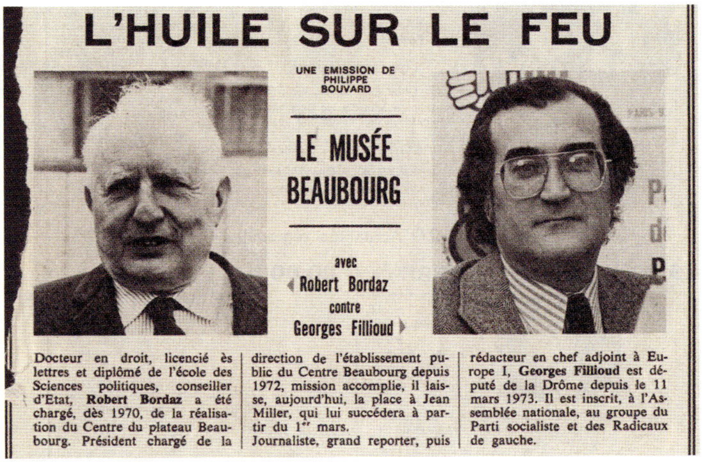

L'HUILE SUR LE FEU

UNE ÉMISSION DE PHILIPPE BOUVARD

LE MUSÉE BEAUBOURG

avec Robert Bordaz contre Georges Fillioud

Docteur en droit, licencié ès lettres et diplômé de l'école des Sciences politiques, conseiller d'Etat, **Robert Bordaz** a été chargé, dès 1970, de la réalisation du Centre du plateau Beaubourg. Président chargé de la direction de l'établissement public du Centre Beaubourg depuis 1972, mission accomplie, il laisse, aujourd'hui, la place à Jean Miller, qui lui succèdera à partir du 1er mars. Journaliste, grand reporter, puis rédacteur en chef adjoint à Europe I, **Georges Fillioud** est député de la Drôme depuis le 11 mars 1973. Il est inscrit, à l'Assemblée nationale, au groupe du Parti socialiste et des Radicaux de gauche.

Press clippings testifying to the violence of the controversy surrounding the Centre Pompidou.

and remains the privilege of the elite," in the analysis of Renzo Piano. "Our challenge is to give it life. It has to be able to entertain as well as inform not only tourists or specialists, but also those who live nearby, in an environment in crisis." For the first time, the users' well-being is placed at the heart of the concerns of the architect and the programmer, who create clear, calm and comfortable spaces, while increasing the means of access to knowledge (library, lectures, films, documentary resources, etc.). The Centre is above all a cultural tool aimed at welcoming the greatest number, by offering services, activities for children and families as well as colloquia disseminating the current state of research, which today seems indispensable.

The art critic Pierre Restany was already emphasising the necessity of this renewal of missions in the April 1974 issue of *Combat* magazine: "It was necessary to shift to another rhythm, to radically restate the problem in another way, to gain a firm grasp of the concept of dynamic museography and to make information and engaging mediation on the art of today a permanent public service. This has been achieved with Beaubourg." From its opening 31 January 1977, despite the amount and violence of the criticism leading up to its inauguration, the popular success has been immense and the public has voted in favour of the formula. Over 25,000 people cross the threshold of the Centre each day, whereas the most optimistic estimates forecast a mere 5,000.

The fire of controversy

Right from the announcement of its creation to its opening, the Centre was the target of virulent attacks, widely distributed via the press. These were opened on multiple fronts. For one, the very idea of a multi-disciplinary centre was contested and its opponents asked the public if the Centre Beaubourg would become the "meeting point for snobs, or a supermarket of culture?" The architectural project also provoked a great deal of ridicule and the nicknames would only increase in number: "refinery," "Notre-Dame of the pipes," "elephant of the Beaubourg Plateau"... To the point that the death of President Pompidou in April 1974 and the scepticism of his successor, Valéry Giscard d'Estaing, cast doubt on the future of the Centre. However, the project eventually went forward, thanks to the determination of then Prime Minister Jacques Chirac. On 3 December 1974, the bill on the creation of the "Centre National d'Art et de Culture Georges-Pompidou" was adopted, with its original status as a "public institution with a cultural purpose".

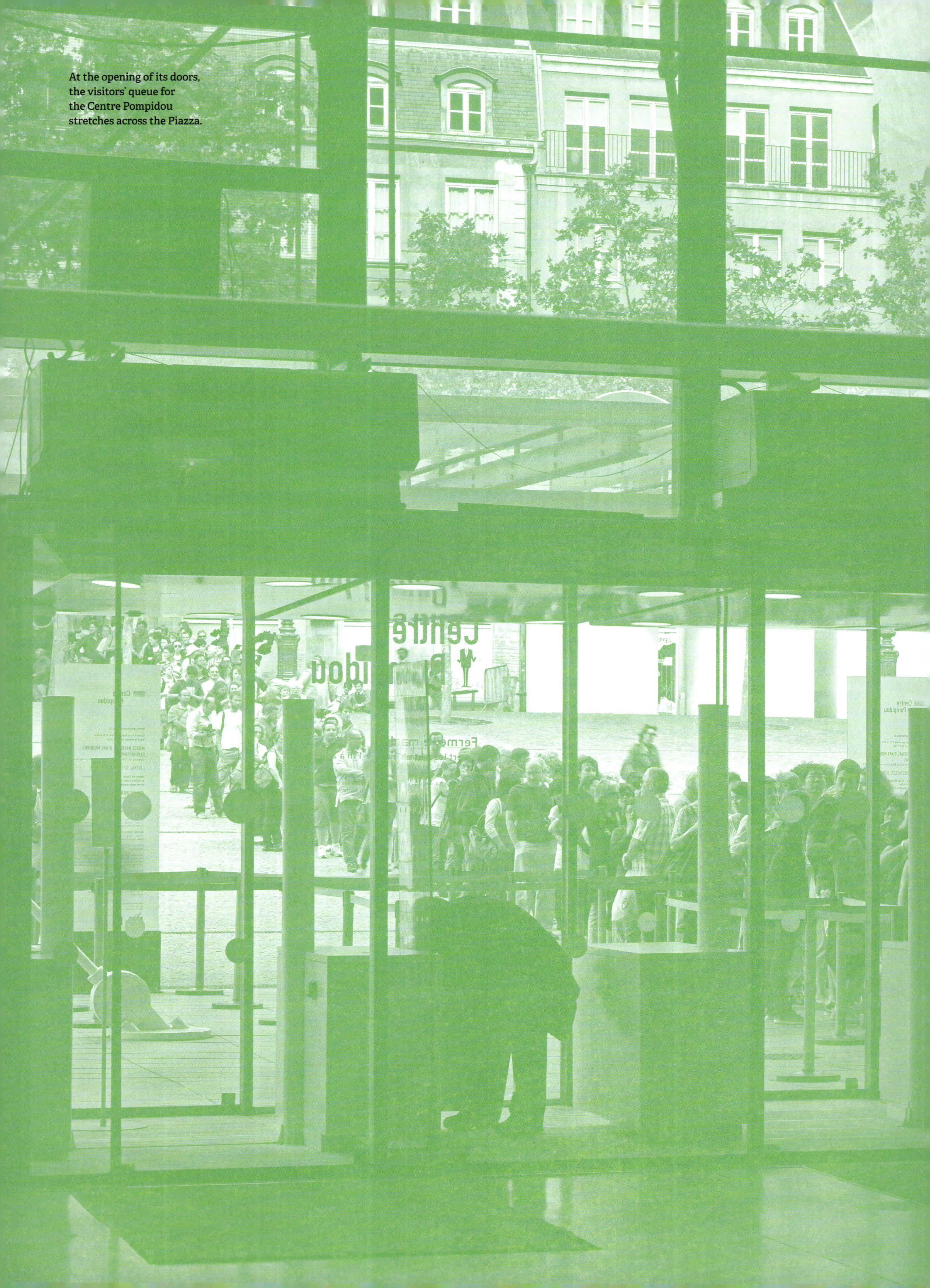

At the opening of its doors, the visitors' queue for the Centre Pompidou stretches across the Piazza.

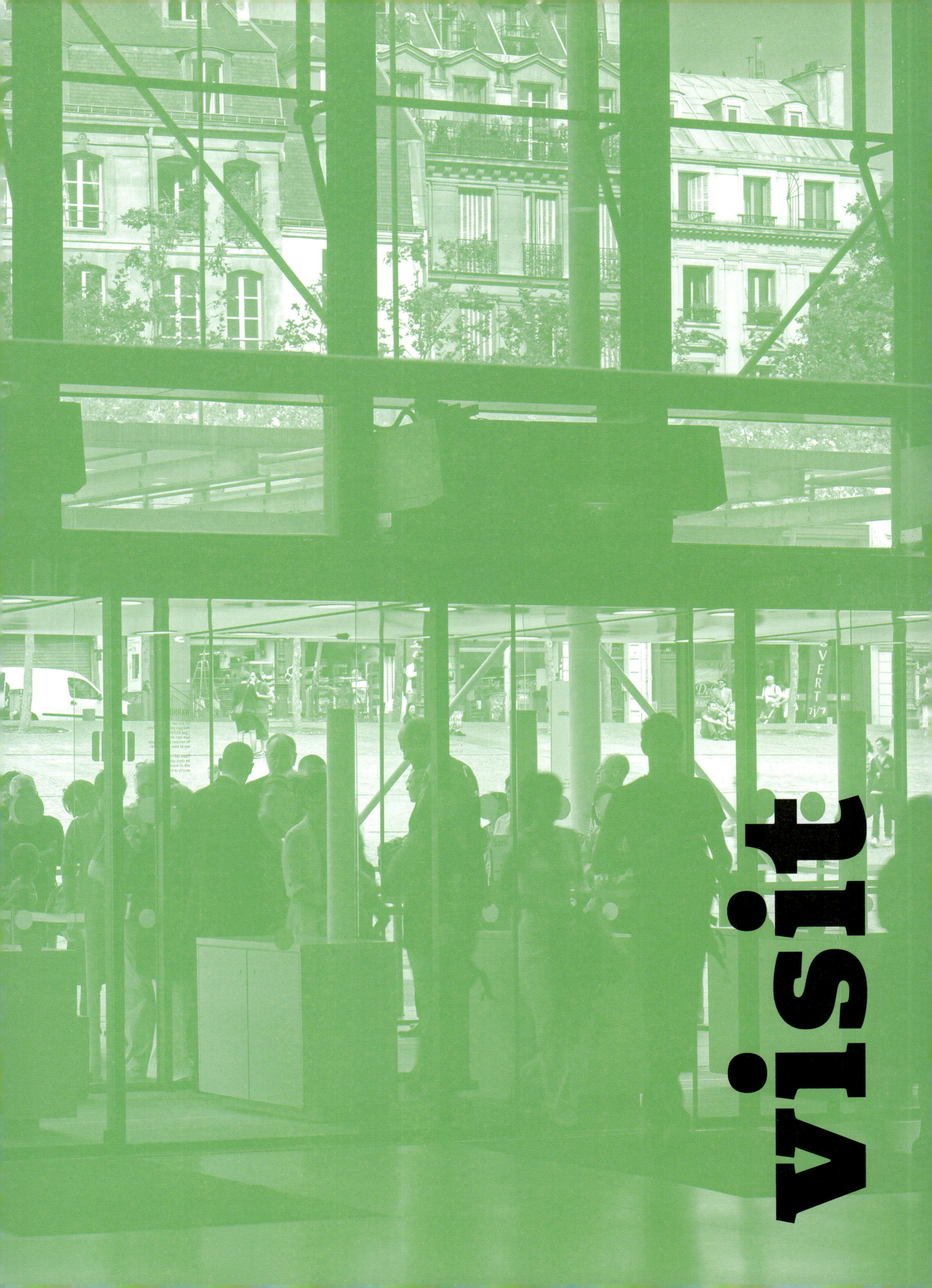
visit

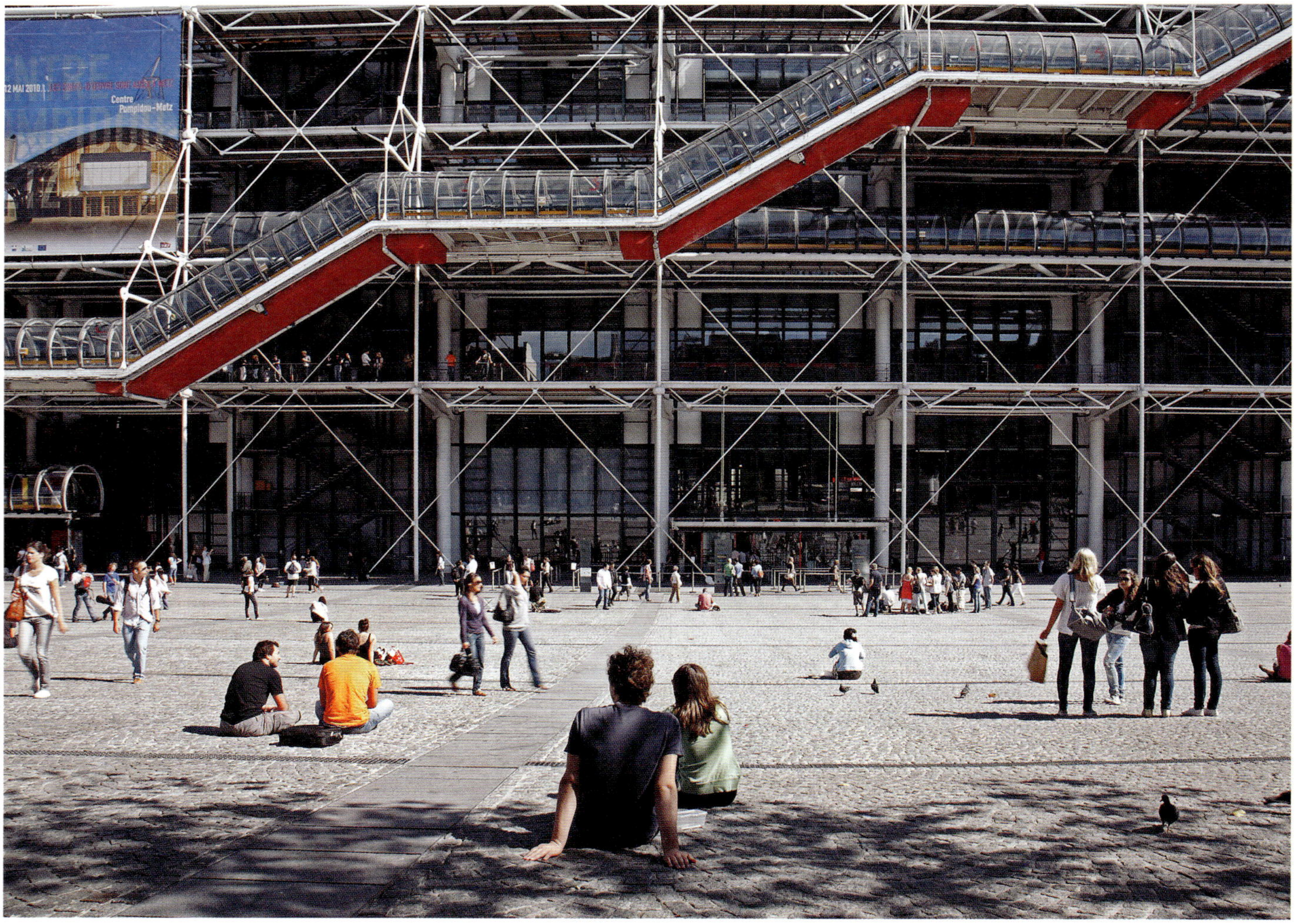

The Piazza today, a place for strolling and relaxation. Passers-by do not hesitate to sit down directly on the paving stones.

The Piazza

The big, gently sloping plaza that leads visitors towards the Centre Pompidou has the same surface area as the building. The architects designed it to be an integral and essential part of their project, a space reserved for pedestrians that is both an extension of the Centre – which can occasionally organise events there – and its link with the city.

First look

The plaza opens up a view of the entire building, setting off the singular architecture of the Centre Pompidou, which, with its transparent façades and hanging exterior circulations, reveals everything about how it functions and its structure.
From the plaza, passers-by grasp the movement coursing through the edifice, and notably the rolling flow of visitors taking the escalator hung on its façade, a veritable vertical extension of the city's circulations.
The descent, situated below street level, orients and focuses the stroller's gaze on the Centre, in response to the ascent on the mechanical "caterpillar," which gradually offers the discovery of a unique panoramic view of Paris.
This dynamic relation is enhanced by mirror effects as the surrounding buildings are reflected on the Centre's glass façades while "observers" on the plaza are in turn observed by visitors walking along the exterior galleries and on the huge diagonal escalator.

A convivial place

If the plaza officially bears the same name as the Centre, Georges-Pompidou,

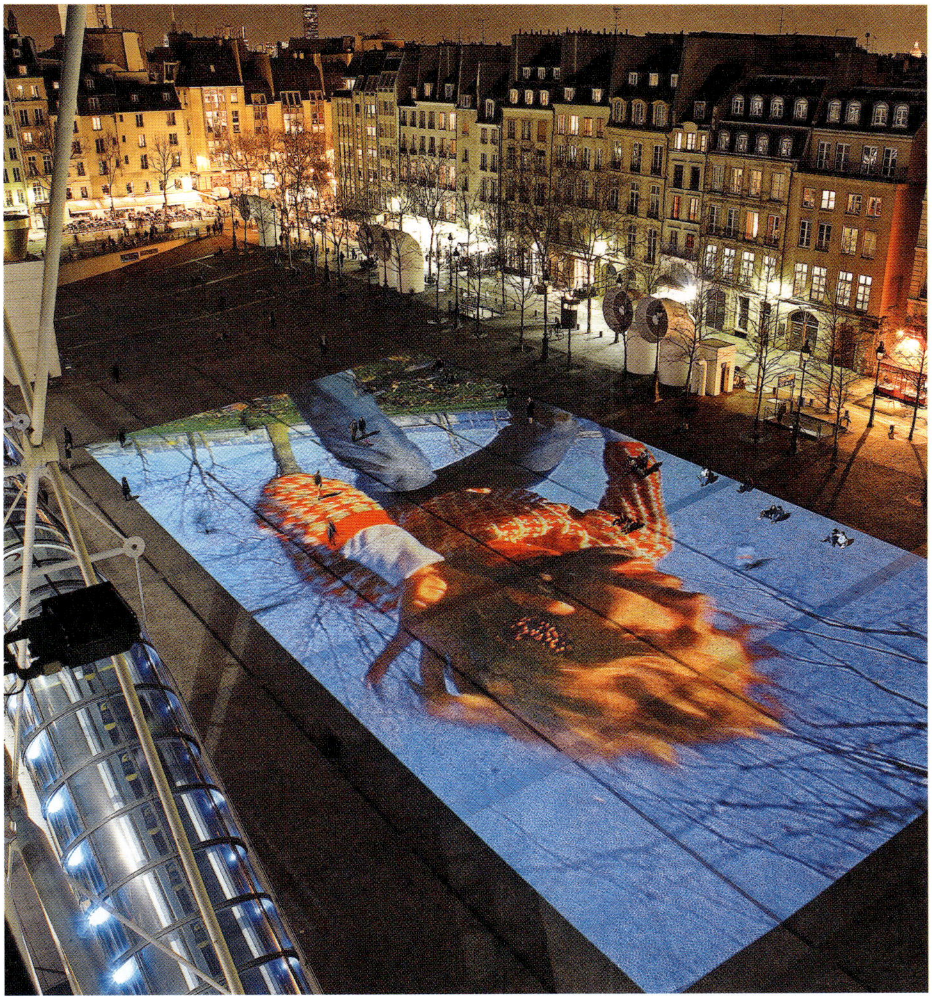

"In a city of heavy traffic like Paris, the pedestrian zone was essential because it is obvious that the Centre Pompidou landed in this neighbourhood like a sort of giant catalysing magnet and it needed a physical space around that was free of vehicular traffic, the noise, the danger... but clearly available for leisure activities."

Renzo Piano, excerpt from an interview published in *Domus*, January 1977

Pipilotti Rist, *À la belle Etoile (Under the Stars)*, installation commissioned for the occasion of the 30th anniversary of the Centre Pompidou, on the Piazza, 2007.

it is commonly referred to as the Piazza and has been from the moment of its conception by the architects, in homage to the Piazza del Campo in Sienna, also sloping. Inspired by the urban model of Italian Renaissance cities, it perpetuates the tradition of conviviality of a public place where all pathways intersect: visitors from the museum, readers from the BPI (whose exit is also onto the plaza), tourists, tramps, street artists, local inhabitants, strollers, etc. It is also indissociable from the Centre the way a forecourt is from a cathedral, a place filled with life and exchanges between the city and the building, which one does not necessarily enter. It has even been compared to a duty-free zone like the ones that encircled religious buildings during the Middle Ages. And with good reason, because even though it opens onto the public street, it falls under the authority of the President of the Centre, and an administrative decree authorises forms of entertainment and other activities there that are prohibited almost everywhere else in Paris. Caricaturists, musicians, acrobats, mimes, clowns and jugglers perform there, children run, youngsters gather to chat, visitors queue, passers-by relax or stop to admire the building...
The absence of urban furniture encourages people to sit down on the ground and to make it their space. Thanks to its diversity, relaxed atmosphere and the festive ambiance, the Piazza is one of the things that make the Centre so inviting.

The Piazza as seen by the jury of the architecture competition

"The building only occupies half the Beaubourg Plateau; the other half being covered by a long plaza on a slightly lower level [...], the space it creates makes it possible to have enough perspective to clearly view the Centre [...]. In its exterior forms, the winning project was of course designed with great simplicity and purity of line, further strengthened by the inevitable dryness of its minimalism, but everything there is made to attract, stimulate and retain life: placement at the forefront of the most creative and the most lively activities, current events room, permanent design gallery; constant exchanges with the neighbourhood, partially restricted to pedestrian traffic and linked to the Centre by an open space, which must not be a dreary esplanade, but a meeting place, a place of assembly, entertainment, a constant focus of life and movement."

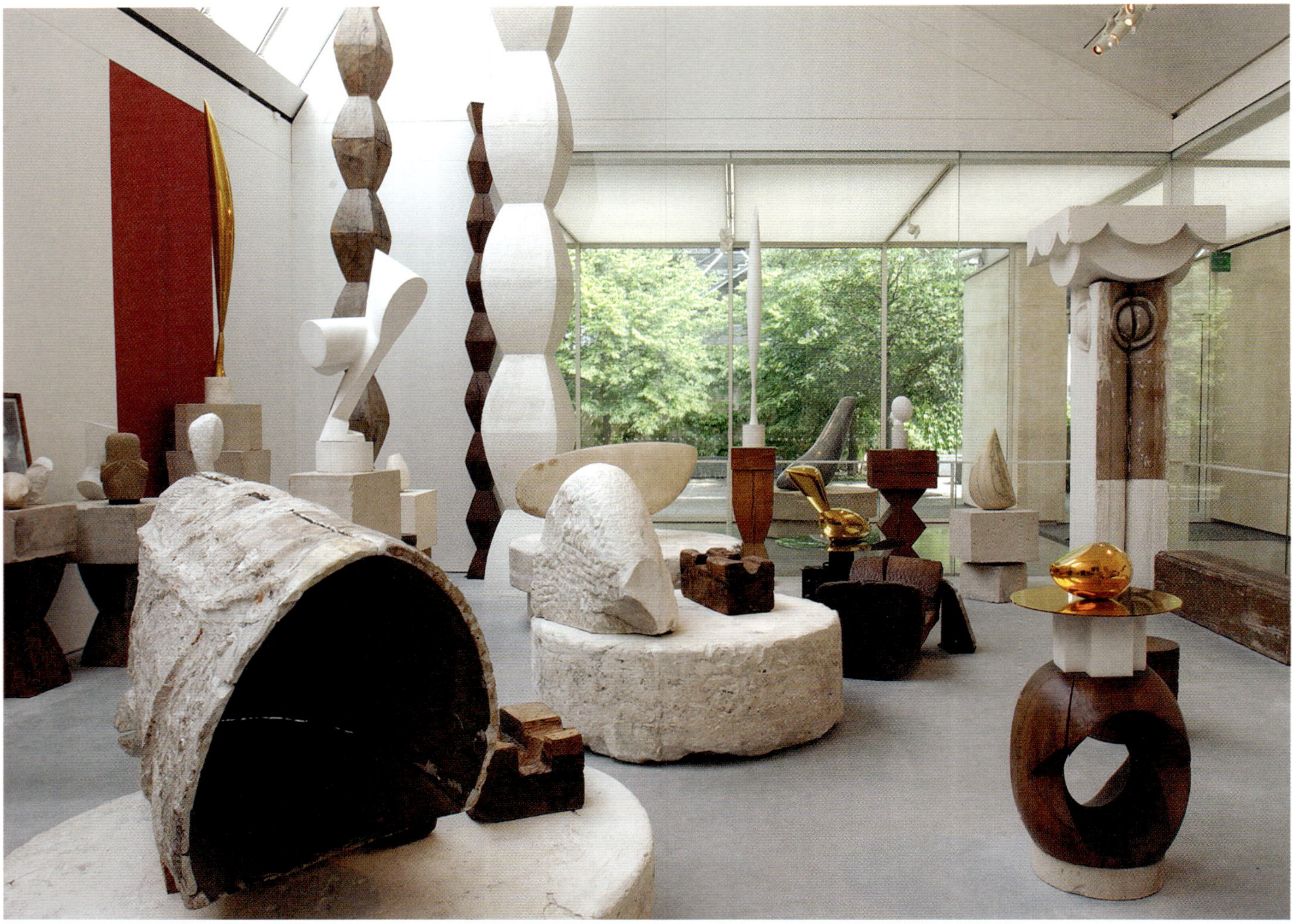

View of one of the four spaces in the Brancusi Studio, north side, with, in the foreground, the mould for the *Coq IV (The Rooster IV)* and various plinths.

The Brancusi Studio

In 1956, just a year before his death, the Romanian sculptor Constantin Brancusi, who had settled in Paris in 1904, bequeathed his entire studio in the Impasse Ronsin, near Montparnasse, to the French state – works, sketches, workbenches, tools, furniture, photographs, library, record collection, etc. – on the condition the state would undertake to reconstitute it as it would be found on the day the artist died. Thus, it is this studio, essential key to understanding Brancusi's work that today stands on the northern edge of the Piazza, at the foot of the Centre Pompidou.

For Brancusi, the relation between his works and the space containing them was of the utmost importance. Therefore, his studio was not only the place where he conceived his sculptures, but also the privileged space in which to perceive them.
He was constantly moving them round it, beginning in the 1910s, to form "mobile groups," as if to continuously transform them into new works.
He took hundreds of photographs of these evolving installations, sometimes waiting hours for the light of day to dissolve a contour or underscore a ridge.
Displayed in a row and isolated from each other, as they were during the Contemporary French Art Exhibition of 1922 in New York, which Brancusi was unable to attend, his sculptures seemed "inert." After this exhibition he refused to show again, even going to the lengths of having the plaster casts made of the works he sold to avoid compromising the unity of the ensembles he so painstakingly

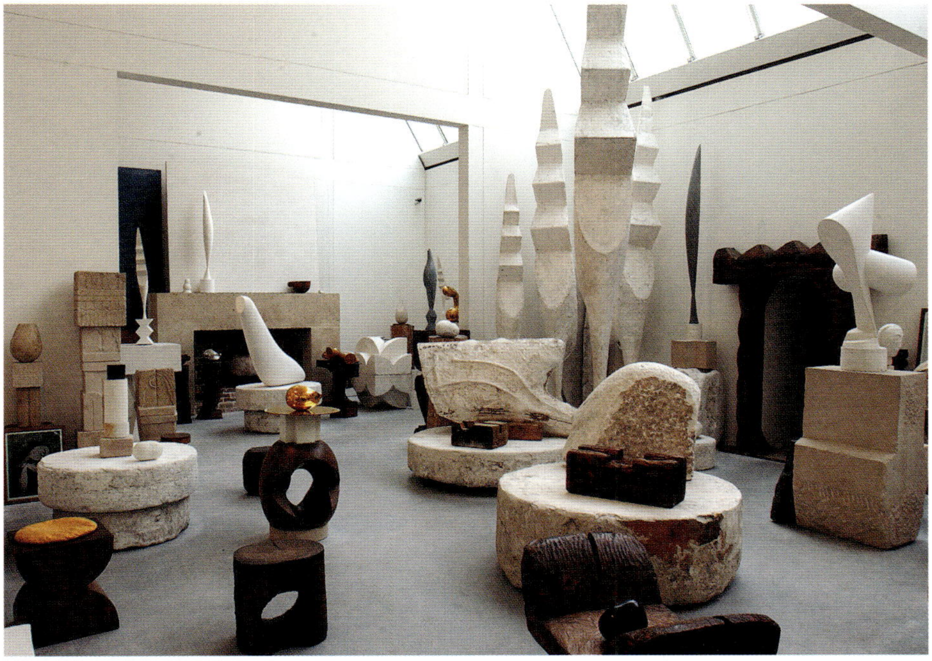

“Brancusi worked alone and his only contact with people outside was with those who loved his sculpture. In his case, the war between the artist and the collector does not exist, for no one can see this sculptor’s works anywhere else but his studio.”

Marcel Duchamp,
***De retour en Amérique* *(Back to America)*, 1933**

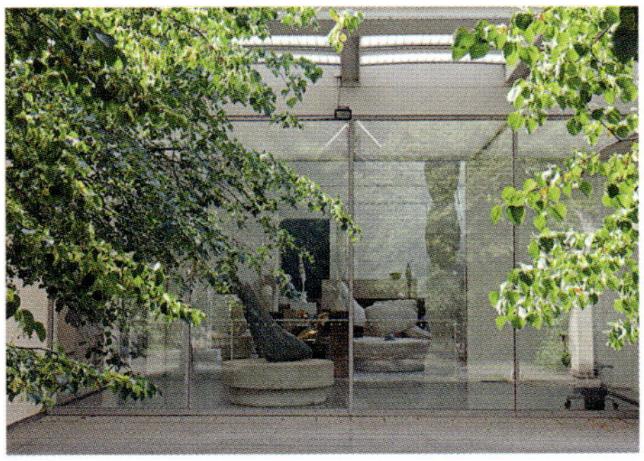

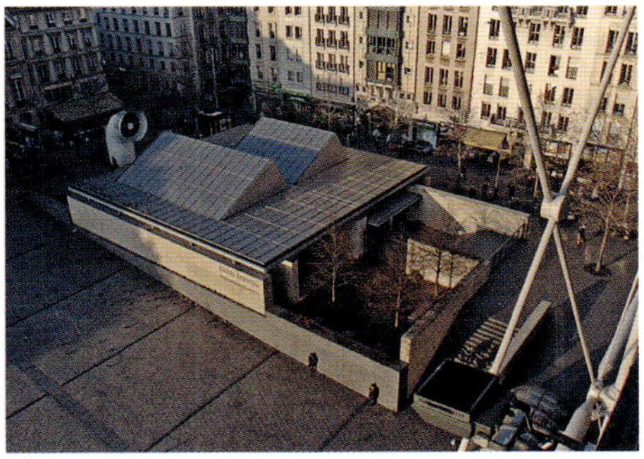

View of one of the four spaces in the Brancusi Studio, south side (top); an enclosed garden was laid out in the courtyard of the Brancusi Studio, which isolates it from the Piazza and recalls the Impasse Ronsin of the original studio (bottom, left); the new Brancusi Studio, whose architecture was designed by Renzo Piano, was inaugurated on 28 January 1997. It replaced the one dating from 1977 (bottom, right).

composed. Towards the end of his life, Brancusi dedicated himself entirely to the study of the relations between his works, focusing on his groupings, such as the *Endless Columns* or the *Big Roosters*. The studio became a work of art in its own right, and the ultimate achievement of the artist’s approach.
In addition to the 137 sculptures, 87 plinths, 41 drawings, 2 paintings and nearly 1,700 negatives and prints, the studio also houses the artist’s library and record collection.
This comprises some 160 literary works and books on art as well as on geometry and mechanics, and over 200 records, ranging from classical music to the repertory of his contemporaries, including those by his friend Erik Satie. The first replica was built inside the Musée National d’Art Moderne – Palais de Tokyo in 1962. In 1977, when the MNAM moved to the Centre Pompidou, Brancusi’s bequests were arranged in an exact replica of the studio, on the Piazza. This replica of Brancusi Studio was replaced in 1997, following closure of the previous one due to flooding in 1990. Renzo Piano designed and built it to ensure it was protected from the surrounding intensely urban agitation, his attempt to restore something of the more intimate atmosphere of the Impasse Ronsin, located in the heart of a neighbourhood of narrow streets. Isolated by a small garden and a covered passageway, the studio has regained its original light thanks to big picture windows. Here Brancusi’s works are displayed just as he wished.

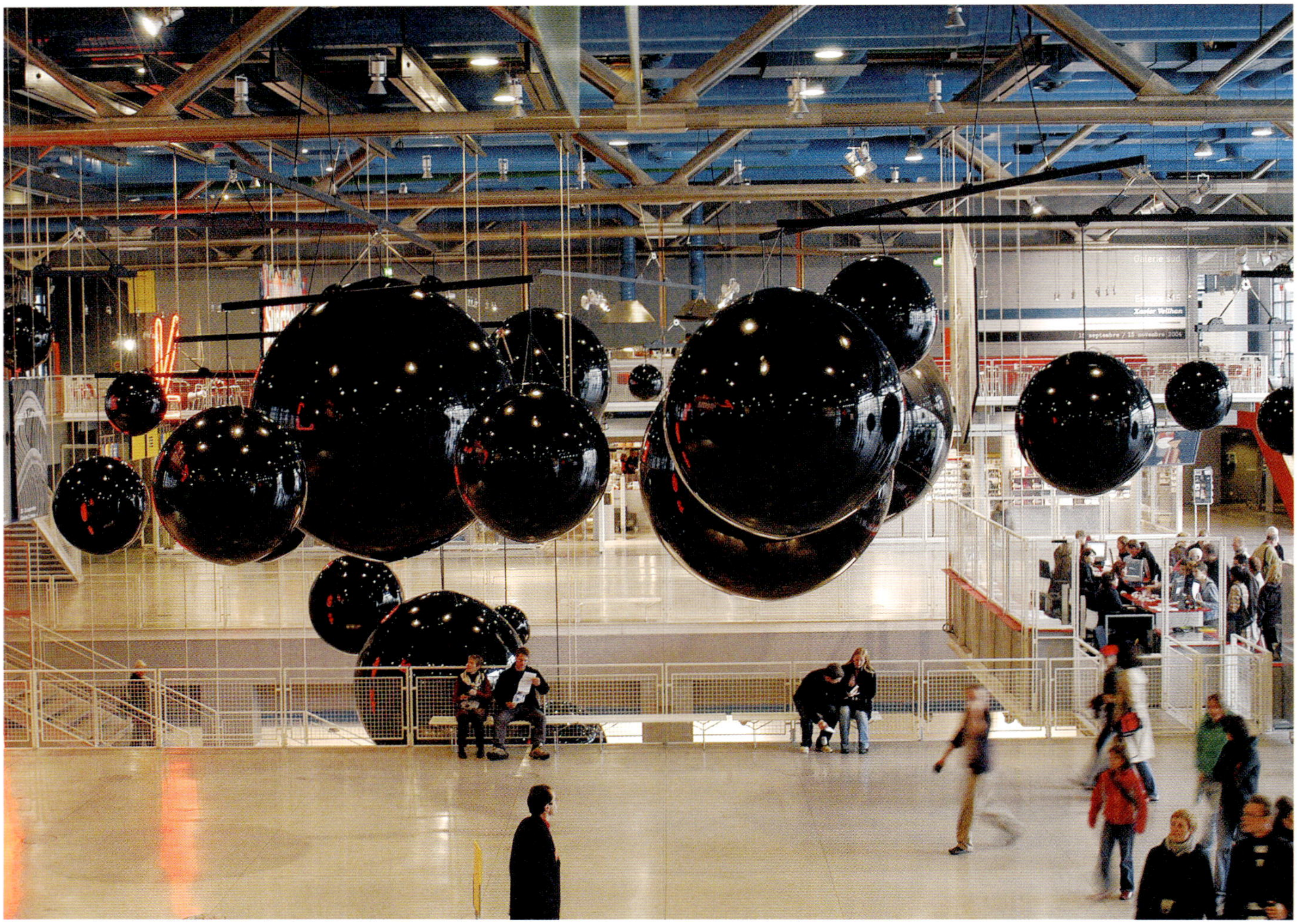

Xavier Veilhan, *Le Grand Mobile*, shown in the Forum in parallel with the exhibition dedicated to the artist in the Espace 315 (20 October 2004-3 January 2005). Metallic structure, 25 spheres of 75 to 350 cm in diameter in PVC; approximately 440 m².

The Forum

The Forum is the natural and fluid extension of the Piazza. No threshold, or porch, or steps mark the break between inside and outside, separated only by a simple glass wall. Located at the centre of the west façade, the main entrance to the Centre Pompidou (the BPI has its own entrance located on the opposite façade, in the Rue du Renard) is not underscored by any architectural sign or visual landmark that would interrupt one's gaze. This continuity was even stronger in the architects' original project, which foresaw a Forum entirely open to the Piazza, which in the end could not be built, mainly due to reasons involving the climate. But once it was enclosed, the space retained some of the feel of a covered urban plaza with its café, bookstore, shop and cinemas. Inside, the transparency of the façades enables one to sense the surrounding city and to perceive pedestrians on the Piazza as well as the cars in the Rue du Renard.

The crossroads of "Beaubourg city"

With its three levels – basement, ground floor and mezzanines – it extends virtually the entire length of the building. It is the heart of the Centre, the point of contact with 25,000 daily visitors and the common area for all the departments, which organise there, either separately or in groups, events which are most frequently multi-disciplinary. A reception area, a space for temporary exhibitions and performances,

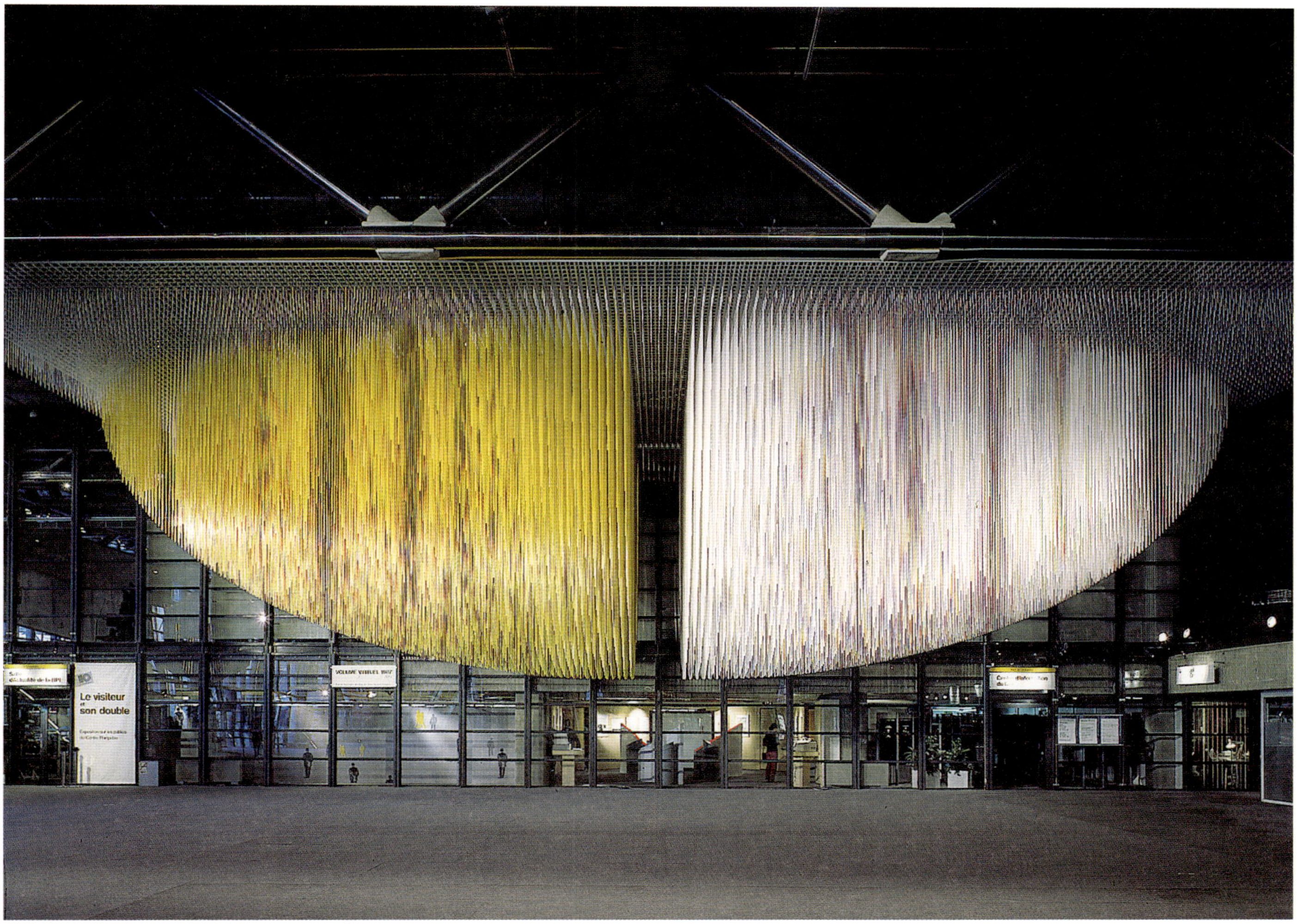

Jesús Rafael Soto, *Volume virtuel (Virtual Volume)*, commission of the Society of Friends of the Musée National d'Art Moderne, installed in the Forum on the occasion of the 10th anniversary of the Centre Pompidou, 1987.

its arrangement and functions have evolved over time. In its initial form, it was hollowed out by an immense trough of 900 square metres, which enabled the organisation of all sorts of events that were visible from the ground floor. Tinguely's *Crocodrome*, a gigantic and playful piece of collective machinery reminiscent of carnivals, initiated in 1977 a series of spectacular events where the public was in direct contact with contemporary creation. Then it was Dalí's turn two years later, who transplanted his universe there, during his Heroic Kermis, with the very significant reinforcements of a giant spoon and of forward suspended traction, the prelude to a more traditional exhibition of his work on the fifth floor. During the "Vienna. Joyful Apocalypse" show, stupefied visitors stepped into the Austrian capital, notably with a replica of an authentic Viennese café in the Forum and a bookstore, public readings and concerts. *Parade*, the stage curtain by Picasso was also restored right under the public's eyes, and rehearsals of artists, such as the dancer Merce Cunningham or the musician John Cage, were held in plain sight throughout the day, for performances held before a paying public the same evening. A space of initiation for the visitor and a proving ground for artists and their work, this version of the Forum was in sync with early spirit of the place. Then the trench was largely covered over to create spaces for new requirements of the times, but still retaining an opening overlooking the basement. Numerous contemporary events, programmed by all the departments, continue to attract and amaze the public.

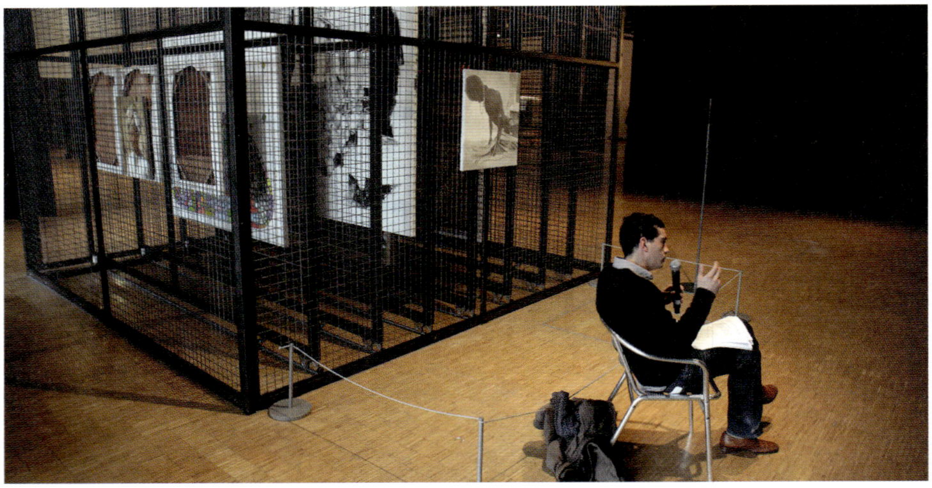

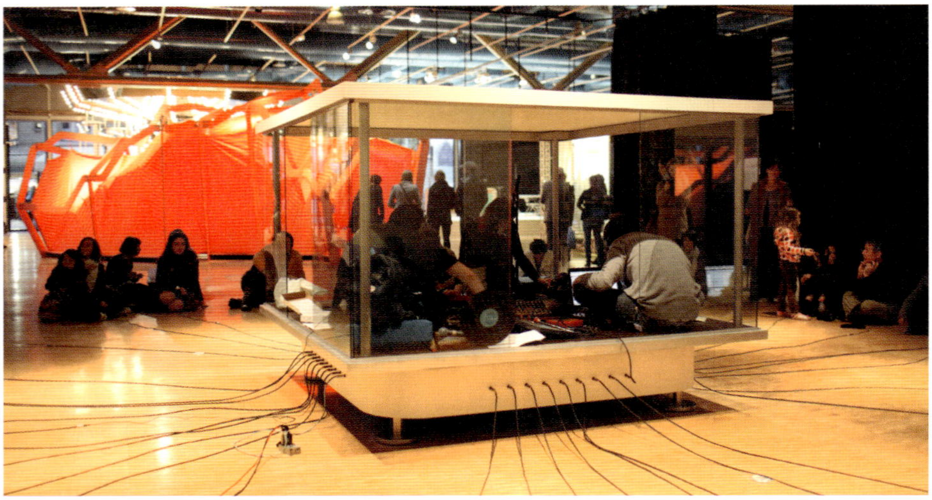

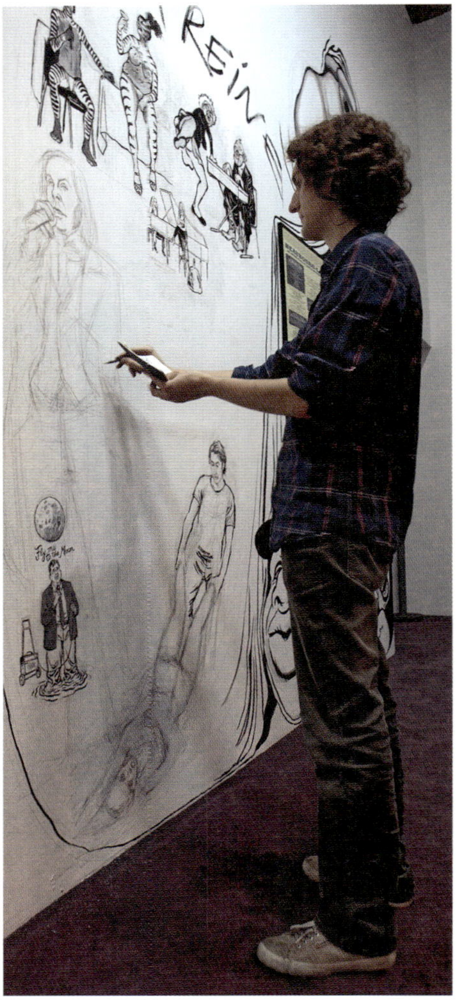

Nouveau Festival, 2009 edition, held in the South Gallery and the Espace 315: art critic Judicaël Lavrador shows and comments on the works of Luc Tuymans in the context of the "Spoken Painting" cycle (left, top); the band Hypo and EDH Friends occupies the "kiosk" (left, bottom); *Les Vestiges de Beaubourg-la-Reine (The Vestiges of Beaubourg-la-Reine)*, intervention of the artist Erwann Terrier (right).

The South Gallery (Galerie Sud) and Espace 315

Observation and support for contemporary creation, both French and international, are part of the basic missions of the Centre Pompidou. On level 1 of the Forum, two places are dedicated to it: the South Gallery and Espace 315. These places convey the Centre's mission to be at the forefront of creation, in all disciplines of the visual arts and their interdisciplinary extensions, and to ensure its dissemination to the widest possible public. Here, the visitor encounters the latest trends in the art of today, younger generations of artists, the most innovative forms.

The South Gallery

Spread across the entire width of the Centre, on the same level as the Rue Saint-Merri, the big South Gallery is entirely transparent. Passers-by do not even have to enter the Centre to discover the artworks, installations and arrangements on display there as if in a giant showcase. Some stop, taken aback or fascinated, and come closer, once to discover the slow moving carrousel of mirrors by the German Carsten Höller, or on another occasion, the amateur film factory by Frenchman Michel Gondry, which transformed the space into a genuine film studio. At the rhythm of two exhibitions per year, without forgetting the Nouveau Festival that has also occupied the space every year since 2009, the place alternates, architecture or contemporary design and one-person shows, with overtly cross-disciplinary ambitions. Creators, such as Renzo Piano, as well as David Hockney,

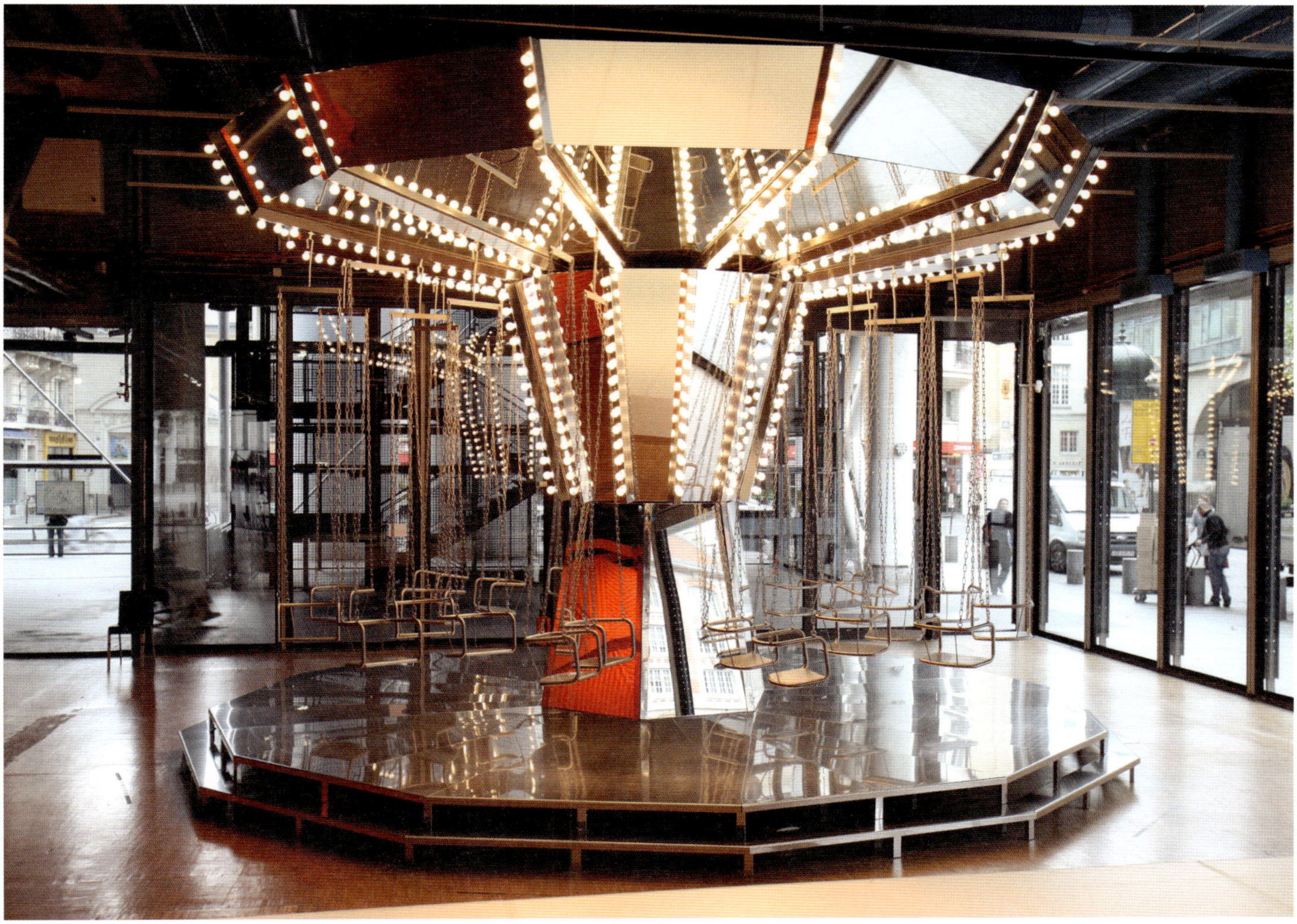

The scenography of the South Gallery, during the first edition of the Nouveau Festival in 2009, hosted several enormous sculptural creations, of which a carrousel of mirrors by Carsten Höller.

Giuseppe Penone, Nan Goldin, Annette Messager or Gabriel Orozco, come to show their work and their latest experimentations. And the visitor, from the inside, sees the kinetic sculptures of the Stravinsky Fountain, created by Jean Tinguely and Niki de Saint Phalle in 1983 in the context of the 1% for culture of the Centre construction budget.

Espace 315

A long space, extending between the South Gallery and the Forum, Espace 315 owes its name to its surface area of 315 square metres. It presents the most contemporary scene at the Centre, proposing two to three exhibitions per year – both group and monographic shows of up-and-coming artists, but also linked to the Nouveau Festival.

If it is difficult to quantify the added value of this space, for an artist, the value of a show here is incontestable, notably on the international scene. Since its creation in 2003, Espace 315 has hosted the winner of the Marcel-Duchamp Prize, awarded by the ADIAF, the most important association of private collectors of contemporary art in France. This prize is intended to contribute to the influence of the French art scene by confirming the notoriety of an artist residing in France and working in the domain of the visual and plastic arts. Among its winners are Claude Closky, Tatiana Trouvé, Saâdane Afif and Cyprien Gaillard. The prize-winning artist benefits from a monographic exhibition in Espace 315.

The Nouveau Festival

Since 2009, an event is held over several weeks that simultaneously involves both Espace 315 and the South Gallery (Galerie Sud): the Nouveau Festival, which extends its programming even further into the Forum, the Mezzanine, the Grande Salle and even outside the walls. This event is in keeping with the founding principles of the Centre Pompidou, i.e., to be multi-disciplinary, free and festive. It aims to serve as an interface between society and contemporary creation. It is an experience led in close collaboration with the artists on the areas of art, an ephemeral laboratory very diverse proposals and practices can intersect.

The programming changes every day and blends all fields: visual arts, cinema, literature, dance, theatre, music... Traditional formats of representation and exhibition are questioned, challenged, overturned. It is a maelstrom placing creation at the heart of the Centre Pompidou.

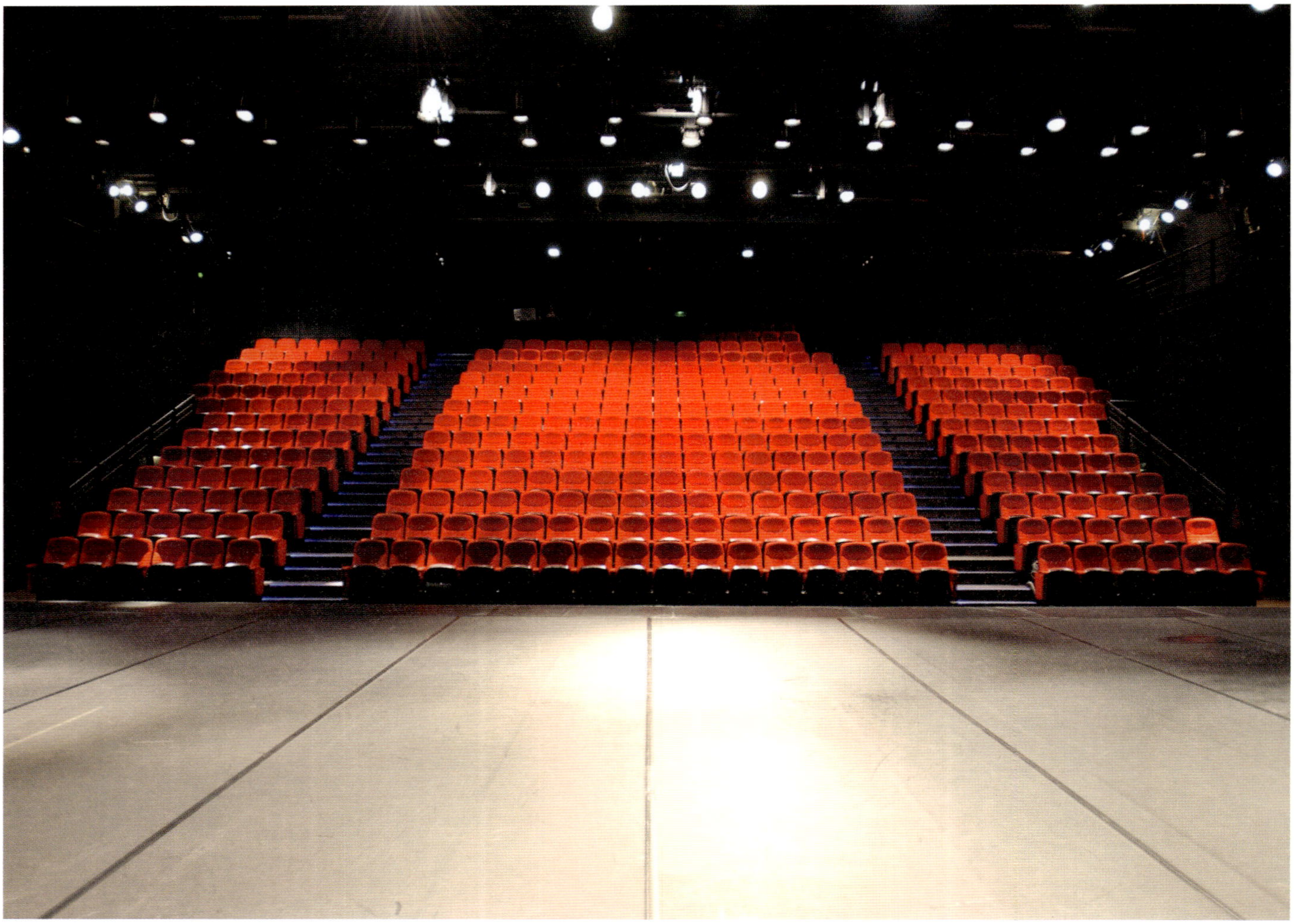

The four theatres for films, shows and lectures on level -1 host a multitude of cycles, retrospectives, encounters and festivals, linked or not with the programming of the other spaces of the Centre Pompidou.

The cinemas at the Centre

While the cinema in most major cultural institutions is confined to a complementary documentary role, often situated at the end of the course, it is everywhere at the Centre Pompidou, where it is considered as an art on the same level as painting or photography. At the Museum, which collects experimental films of the avant-garde and by artists since it moved into the Centre; at the BPI, which focuses on documentary films and more specifically on the disciplines of ethnography and sociology through its "Cinema of the Real" festival; at the Kandinsky Library, which produces its own films on artist studios... even the Cinémathèque Française came close to moving under its roof. The Centre Pompidou treats cinema as both an object of exhibition – through monographic exhibitions, such as "Hitchcock and art. Fatal Coincidences" or "Voyage(s) in Utopia. Jean-Luc Godard" – and of programming. For the purposes of programming, it possesses two movie theatres totalling over 450 screenings and 50,000 spectators per year. Its programming is flourishing: retrospectives dedicated to a cineaste in which many actors and professionals of the cinema participate, a multitude of cycles, including "Video and After," a monthly program dedicated to videos made by French and foreign visual artists in the Museum's collections, the multi-disciplinary festival "Hors-Pistes," which focuses on new trends in the contemporary image. Exhibitions and programming nurture each other and the screen becomes a picture rail.

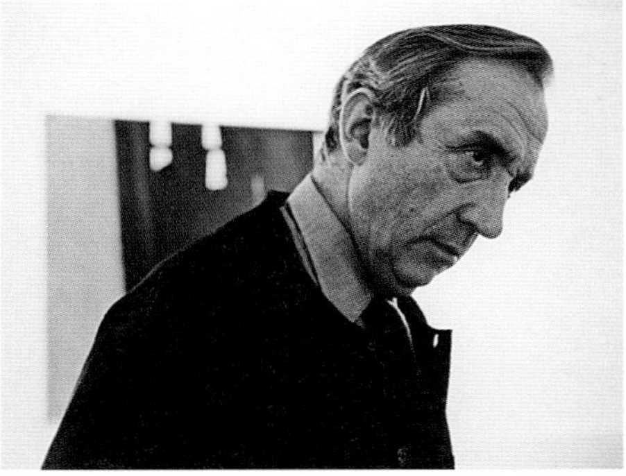

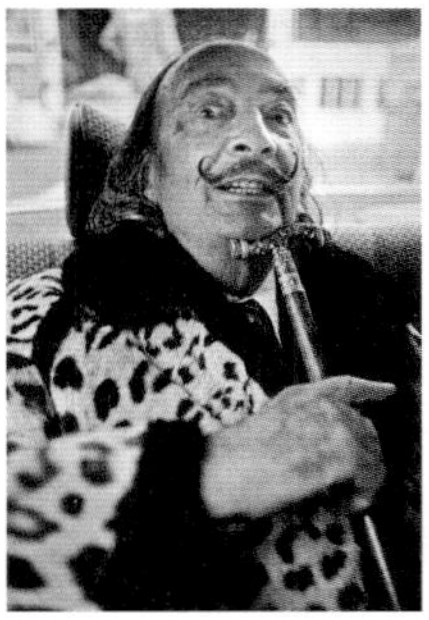

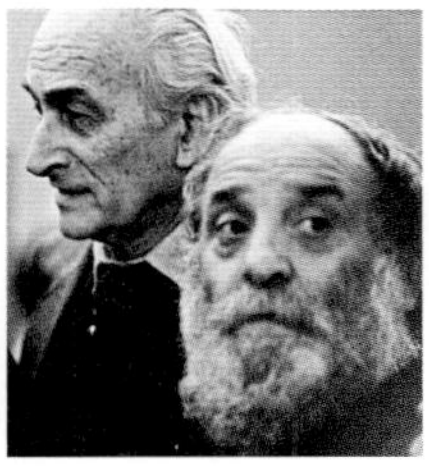

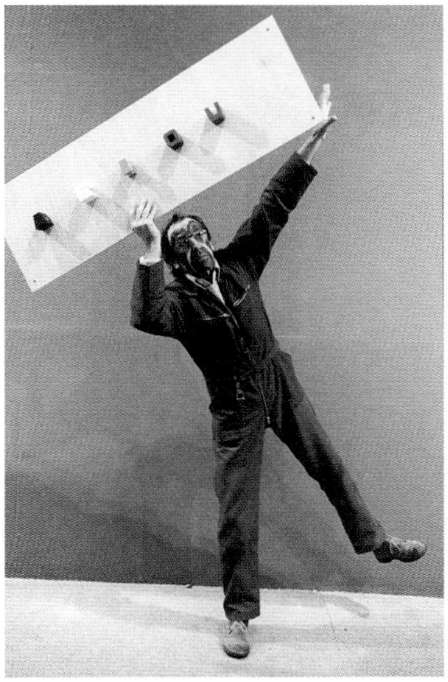

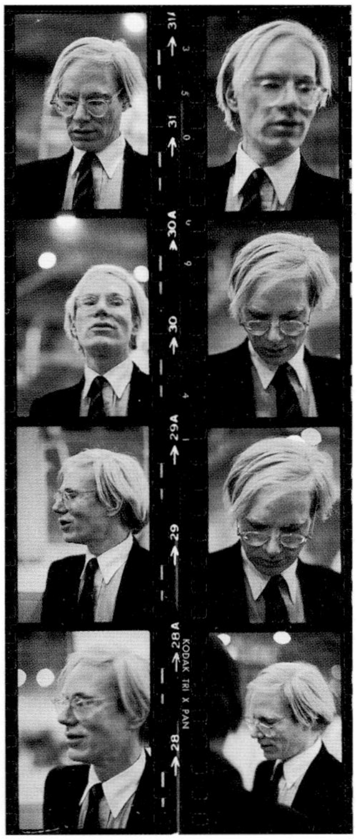

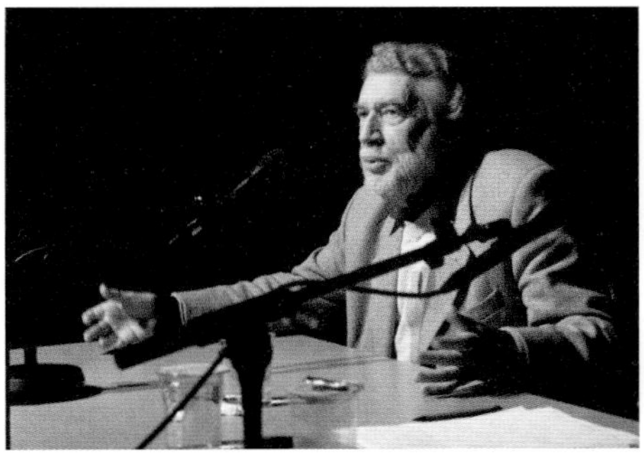

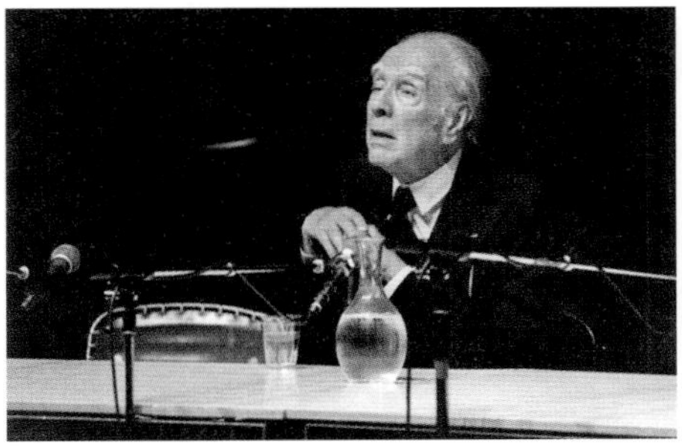

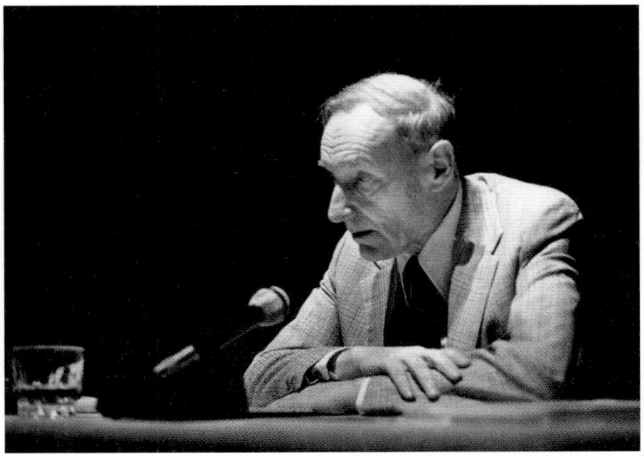

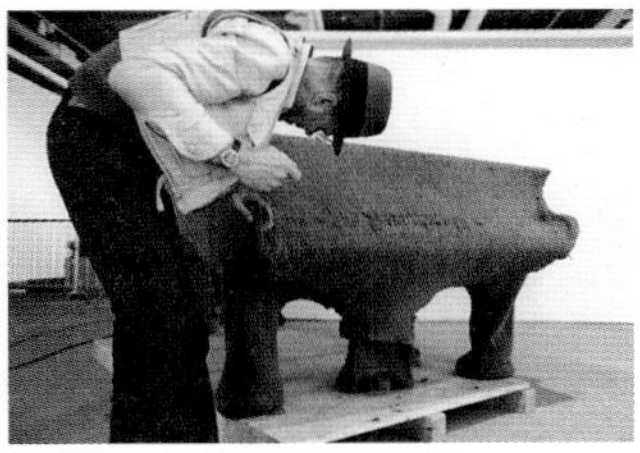

Numerous cultural personages appearing at the Centre Pompidou (from top to bottom and left to right): Pierre Soulages, 1979; Alain Robbe-Grillet; Jorge Luis Borges, 1986; Salvador Dalí, 1979; Balthus and César, 1983; Robert Filliou and his *Poïpoïdrome*, 1978; William S. Burroughs; Andy Warhol, 1977; Joseph Beuys, 1977.
Drawing of the *System Layout* (exterior system for television projection) by Billy Klüver for the façade of the Centre Pompidou (below).

The project for an audiovisual façade

In the initial proposal, the façade overlooking the plaza was equipped with audiovisual systems continuously broadcasting cultural events from around the globe, presentations of artworks or even electronic games. Another project involved implementing a system that enabled the public to create forms on the façade via screens made available on the Piazza, and to install buttons on the pavement of the Piazza to activate luminous signs on the same façade. These projects were abandoned because of their costs and technical complexity and in favour of the "caterpillar." However, the Centre Pompidou did commission an audiovisual installation by Billy Klüver for its inauguration, which could be viewed on a giant twelve-metre screen protected from the sun by an awning.

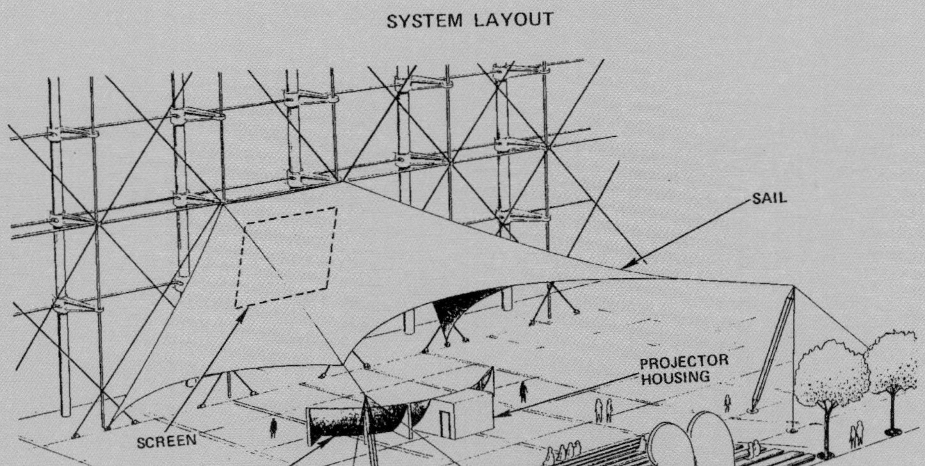

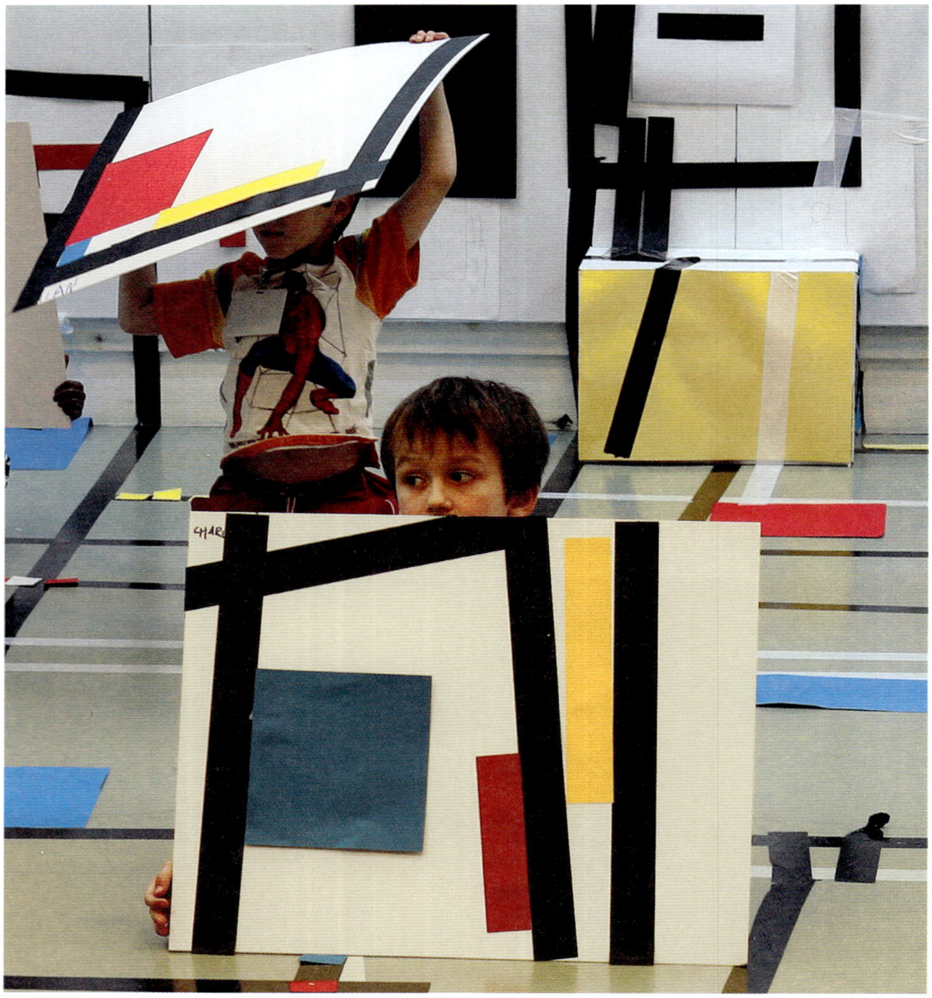

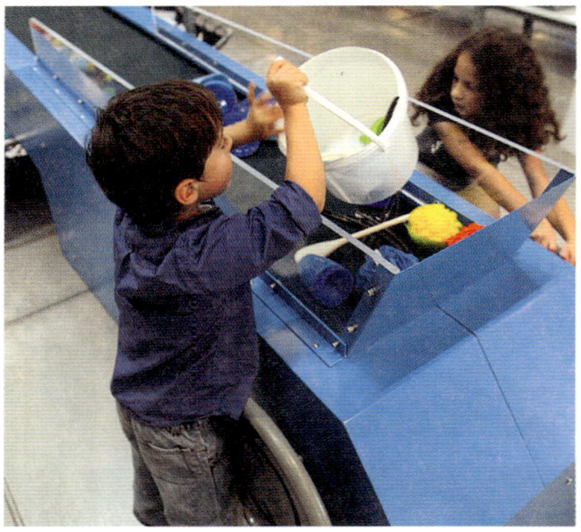

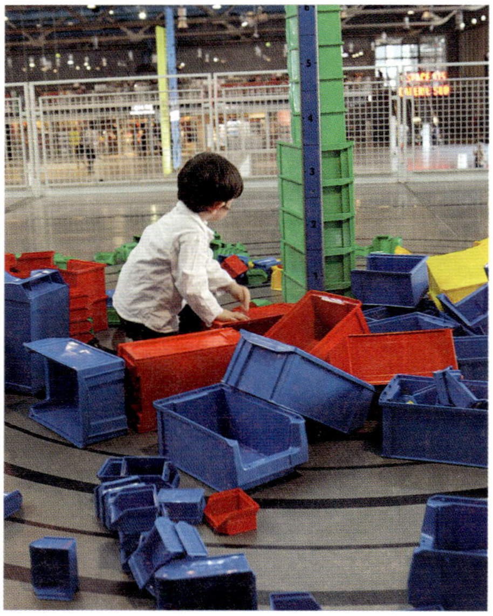

A children's workshop built around the work of Mondrian (left).
In the Children's Gallery, "The Adventure of Objects," exhibition-workshop built around *Arman* (22 September 2010-10 January 2011) (right).

Workshop (Atelier), Children's Gallery (Galerie des Enfants), Studio 13/16

Playing with concepts of balance and movement to understand Calder's sculptures, imagining the home of the future with the designer Matali Crasset, selecting and accumulating objects by following Arman's gestures, participating in a workshop with a street artist or discovering how to make an art video are a few of the activities offered by the Centre Pompidou to the younger public. From 2 to 16 years of age, children and adolescents are welcomed here like nowhere else, in areas designed just for them and with specific programming, usually linked with the featured exhibitions. In addition to traditional school and family related visits, it is about challenging the imagination and creativity of the youngest generation and providing them with a privileged contact with the art they make.

From 2 to 12 years of age: doing to understand

On the ground floor of the Forum, the Children's Studio – already present at the creation of the Centre Pompidou, at a time when no other structure dedicated to them existed in museums – is a place where young visitors exchange the passive attitude of the spectator to become actors. They observe, experiment and familiarise themselves with world of artists, developing their imaginations utilising contemporary creation as a medium.
The children engage with the artworks they study, which helps to foster their encounter with all artists' work.

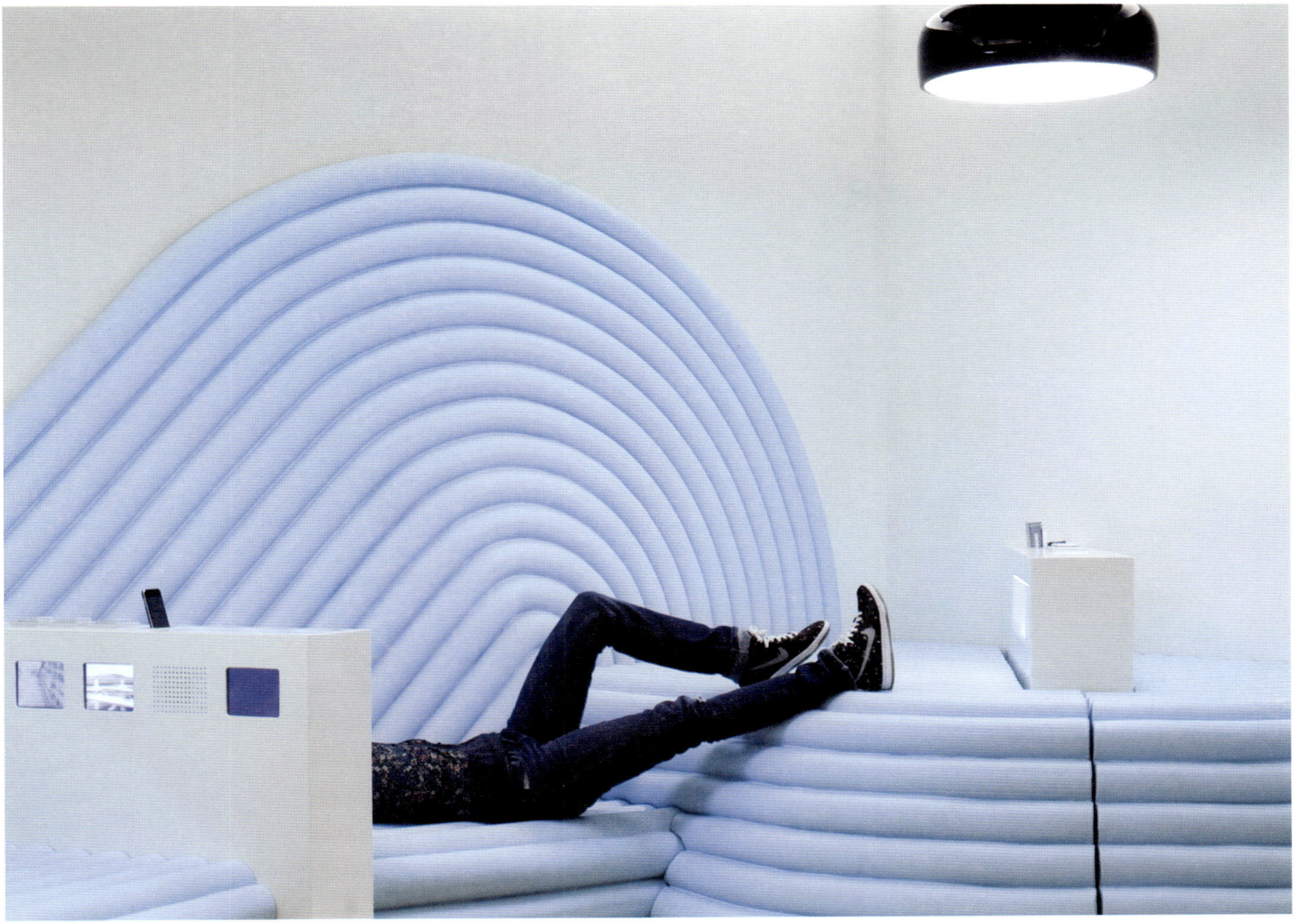

The Studio 13/16, an open-access space dedicated to adolescents, conceived by designer Mathieu Lehanneur.

In 2000, as an addition to the Studio (Atelier), a unique temporary exhibition space was set up: the Children's Gallery (Galerie des enfants), now located on the mezzanine of the Forum, which is perhaps the most visible space of the entire Centre Pompidou. Two exhibitions aimed at children are programmed every year, either linked to the major exhibitions at the Centre – Jean-Michel Othoniel showed his glass sculptures here, rich in symbols and therefore stories – or on an autumnal theme, as the case for example with Tadashi Kawamata and his cardboard huts. Here, there are no works hanging from the picture railings but workshops for "doing" and learning to see while having fun.

From 13 to 16 years of age: open access

Since September 2010, the Centre Pompidou has been equipped with a hitherto unheard of space in a museum, the Studio 13/16, specifically targeting adolescents, who are treated as autonomous visitors. This free and open space requiring no reservation was imagined by taking account of the expectations, tastes and behaviours of 13 to 16-year-olds: at an age when they are building their personality and their rapport with the world crystallises, art can prove to be a structuring element. A place filled with life, a factory and an open stage, the Studio 13/16 allows adolescents the freedom to participate in the creative process in the domains that interest them, and more specifically – graphic arts, fashion, dance, design… – or just to come for the pleasure of getting together with their friends or to listen to music. Their mere presence in a place dedicated to culture is a first step that may lead to a video in a workshop, to a discussion about a particular work of art, to an idea for an artist, or to an artist in the museum.

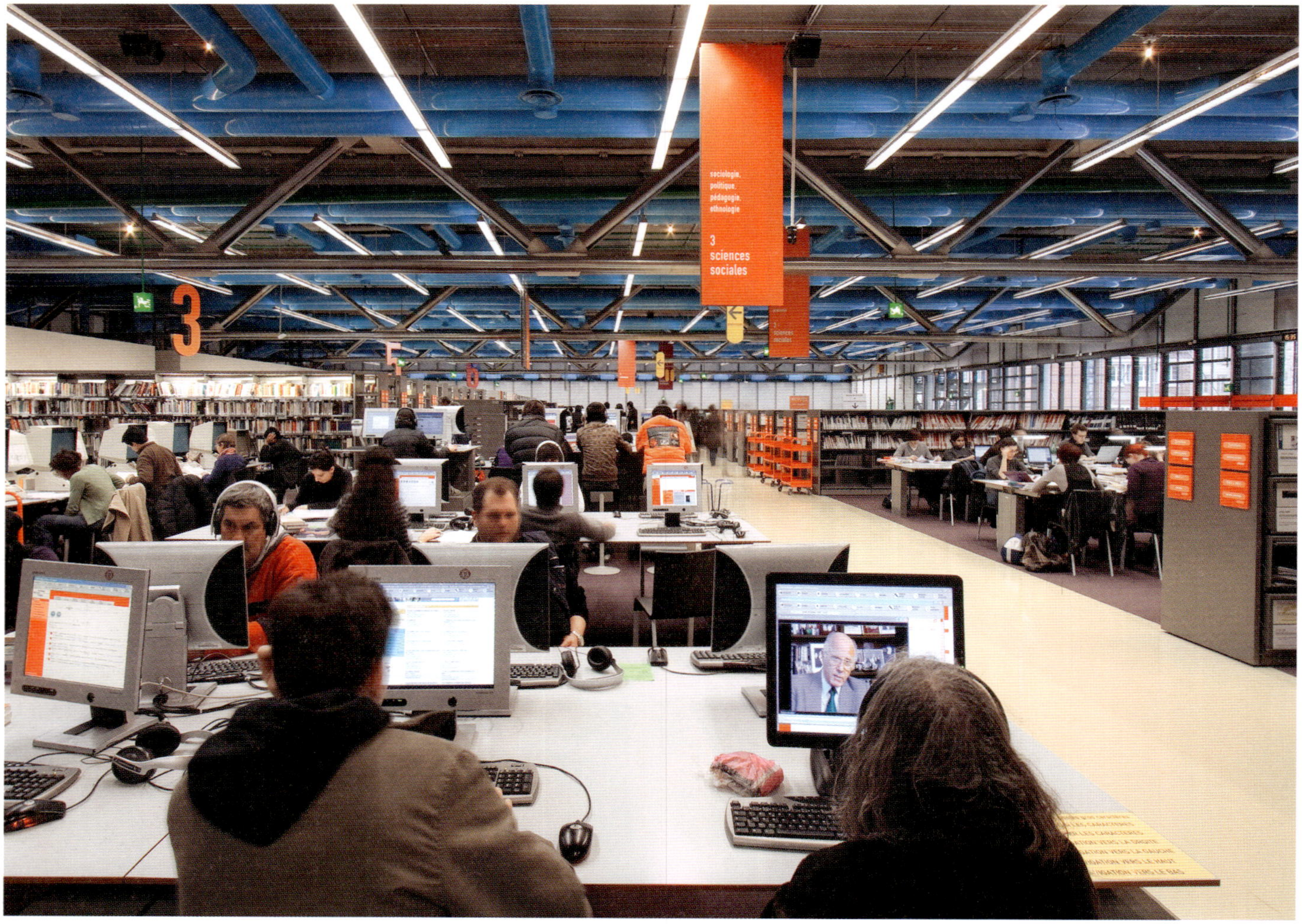

General view of the BPI on level 2.

The BPI: Public Information Library

In the 1960s, to counteract a perceived decline in reading, the state decided to create a library right in the centre of Paris, to be located in the area opened up by the coming removal of the "belly of Paris," the food markets of Les Halles. In 1969, Georges Pompidou chose to integrate this project into the neighbouring future Centre Beaubourg. It was to be the genesis of a unique type of library, the *Bibliothèque publique d'information*, and it was a huge success from day one.

Free, open access to all, including the visually impaired, no registration required, the BPI broke with the traditional model of libraries by offering free access to its collections and by making its main mission one of making information available to the public. Here readers are treated as autonomous adults, and the librarian's role is to welcome them, to facilitate access to the information they seek. Contrary to most libraries, the BPI's mission is not to collect and conserve, but rather to offer a continuously updated selection of French and foreign collections of documents on general information and current events in an encyclopaedic approach, aiming to satisfy all public needs ranging those of neophytes to specialists.

Dynamic content

Today, the BPI remains faithful to its initial mission and to the two key criteria, which are to be as up-to-date as possible and useful. It aims to offer knowledge in its latest available state,

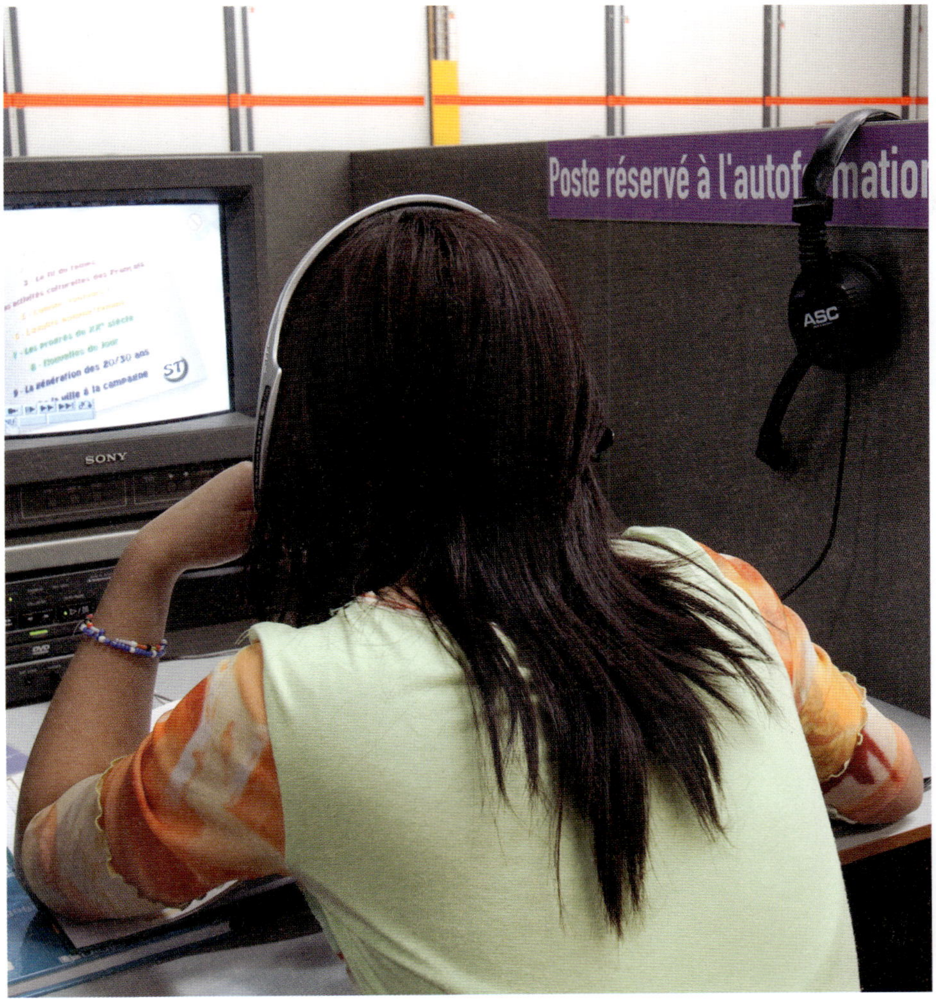

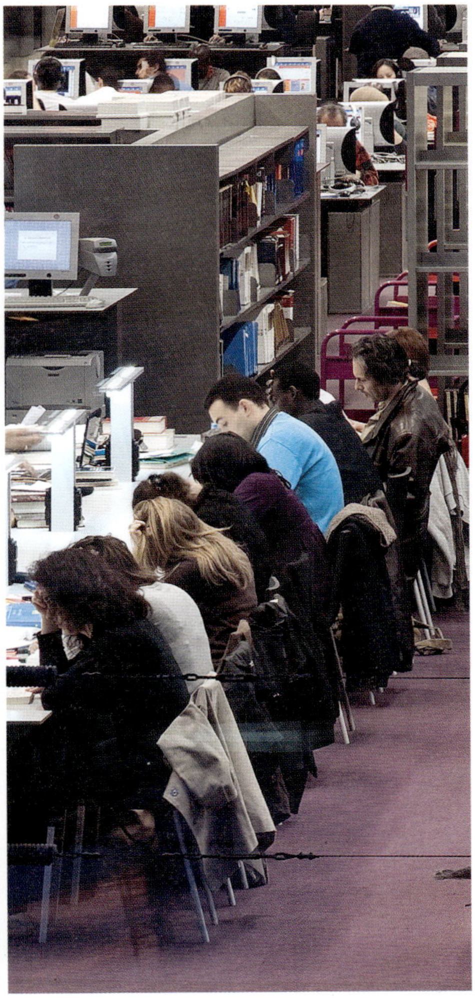

Self-learning workstation (left).
A place facilitating concentration where all modes of access to knowledge are utilised (right).

while adding to a knowledge base, making this knowledge directly and easily available, including all forms of expression (books, periodicals, sound and audiovisual recordings in the latest formats, digital resources and self-learning applications...). This is why the BPI is recognised for its know-how in the continuous updating of a balanced, easy-to-grasp knowledge base, privileging the validity and relevance of information. When new materials or basic documents are acquired, this process is always linked to the process of "weeding out" everything that has become obsolete, whether dated content, outmoded interpretations, worn copies, technologically-outdated media or films whose use rights have expired.

In the case of the BPI, the constraint of a space that is entirely open to the public and lacking any conservation areas exerts a dynamic influence on the collection. Thousands of physical documents enter and leave every year, such that 12% of the collections are always less than three years old, whereas the digital content is continuously updated.
The fact that readers cannot borrow documents guarantees the comprehensiveness and coherence of the information available, thereby strengthening the specifically cognitive role of the BPI.

Reading the world

This cognitive role is not limited to the documents made available. The BPI offers a rich and intense

BPI key figures

1.5 million entries per year (5,000 per day)

10,400 square metres (111,945 square feet) of reading rooms

2,200 seats

400 computer, audiovisual and microfilm workstations

380,000 continuously-renewed documents in all media:

340,000 books

15,000 music CDs

7,000 maps and plans

3,800 periodical titles

2,500 documentary and animated films

2,250 sound documents

2,000 music partitions

2,000 selected websites

1,000 electronic documents (CDs and databases)

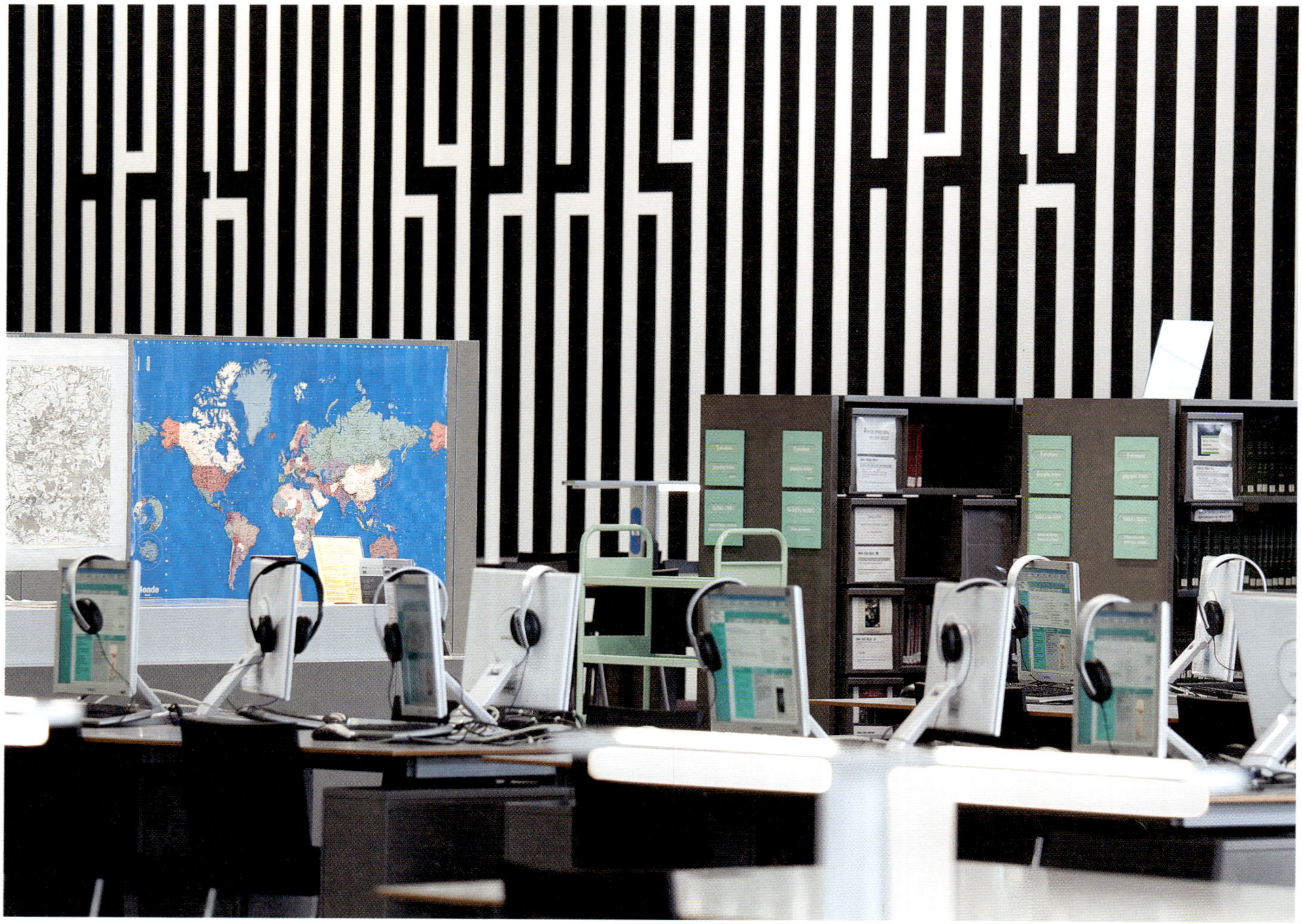

Level 3 entrance to the BPI. In the background, one of the works installed by the MNAM inside the library: Tania Mouraud, *Wysiwyg (What you see is what you get)*, 1989.

"A showcase for the avant-garde with the traffic of a hypermarket, the BPI (Public Information Library) is a functioning paradox."

Le Monde de l'éducation, April 1979

range of cultural activities, through exhibitions, encounters, colloquia, performances (slam contests, for example), public readings, and in domains as varied as literature, music, creation in all its forms, social issues, digital culture, not to forget documentary cinema, which takes on the stature of an international event, i.e. the Cinema of the Real Festival. These activities are hosted inside the BPI or in the auditoriums of the Centre Pompidou, and even outside the walls, in partnership with other French institutions. The BPI is also increasingly focused on its role as knowledge mediator, so important in an age when the superabundance of information requires qualified assistance provided to readers.

Diverse forms of mediation are deployed, ranging from teaching workshops to "Bibliosésame," the personalised service answering remote requests, by way of an active presence in the main social networks. Convinced that libraries in the age of the knowledge-based society, relying on the expertise of their librarians, must become media in sync with current events taking place in the world and capable of putting them into perspective, the BPI is developing its activity of the production of "intermediate content" more and more (micro-bibliographies, abstracts, etc.), which are part of a range of directional tools. It is no accident that it has adopted "Reading the world" as its programme and motto.

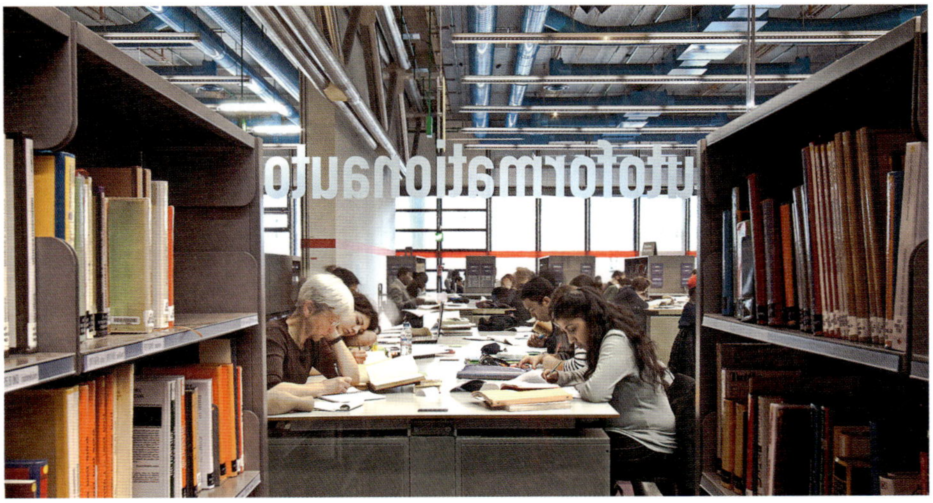

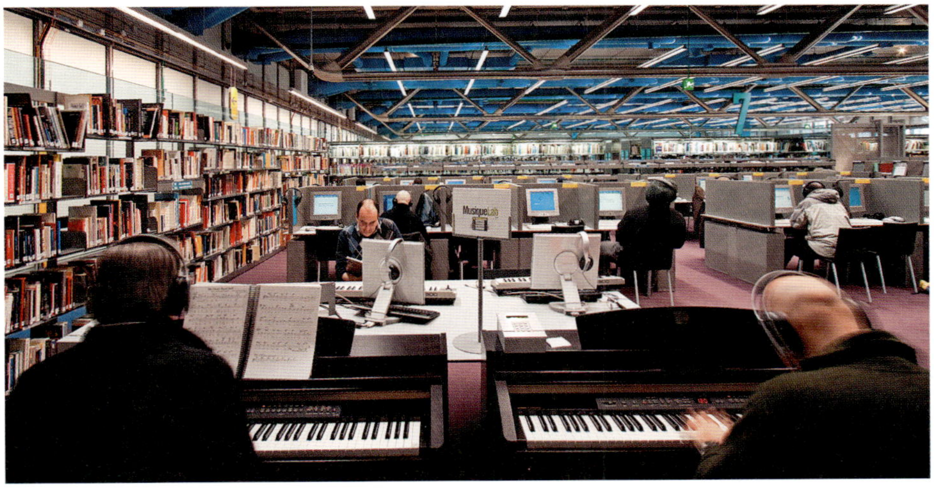

"It's truly a wonder! All the knowledge of the world is gathered here, in every language. You can learn just about anything here, from how to knit a necktie to how to build a nuclear power plant, and about geography and history, birds and flowers, cities, the arts and all humanity's past and present. What a work tool! And so easy to use! Upon entering, you ask for the catalogue, search directly in the stacks for the book you are seeking, take it to a table, sit down and read. No intermediaries, no waiting, not a minute wasted. You are at home, and all human knowledge is within reach. O Beaubourg! You will be forgiven for many things thanks to this sublime floor."

René Barjavel, "Beaubourg is the God-escalator," 5 June 1977

In the age of the Internet, the book remains indispensable (top).
Open access to pianos in the Music Area on level 3 (bottom).

A place designed for the reader inside the Centre Pompidou

The BPI is first and foremost a place whose magic owes a great deal to the architecture and to the constant presence of over 2,000 readers sharing the same intensity of concentration. Specialised areas break the rigour of a place where stacks of books and work tables dominate. Thus, the Press Area on level 2 assembles all the national dailies, a selection of foreign dailies and magazines, as well as numerous news sites accessible via Internet.
The Music Area with recorded sound documents also offers reviews, partitions and books on music. In addition, users can play or compose music on electronic pianos, listen to CDs, radio broadcasts, speeches and lectures, and even watch filmed concerts or documentaries.
A Self-Learning Area, equipped with 120 places and the latest technology, enables users to learn any of 200 languages available, or to prepare for a competitive exam, to acquire computer skills or to revise the traffic law. Users can even watch foreign television networks or relax in the café.
In keeping with the spirit of the Centre, the BPI has operated very successfully for thirty years as a space of liberty, open to all, to all ideas and all forms of expression and where it is a pleasure to work amongst others while pursuing one's passion for learning.

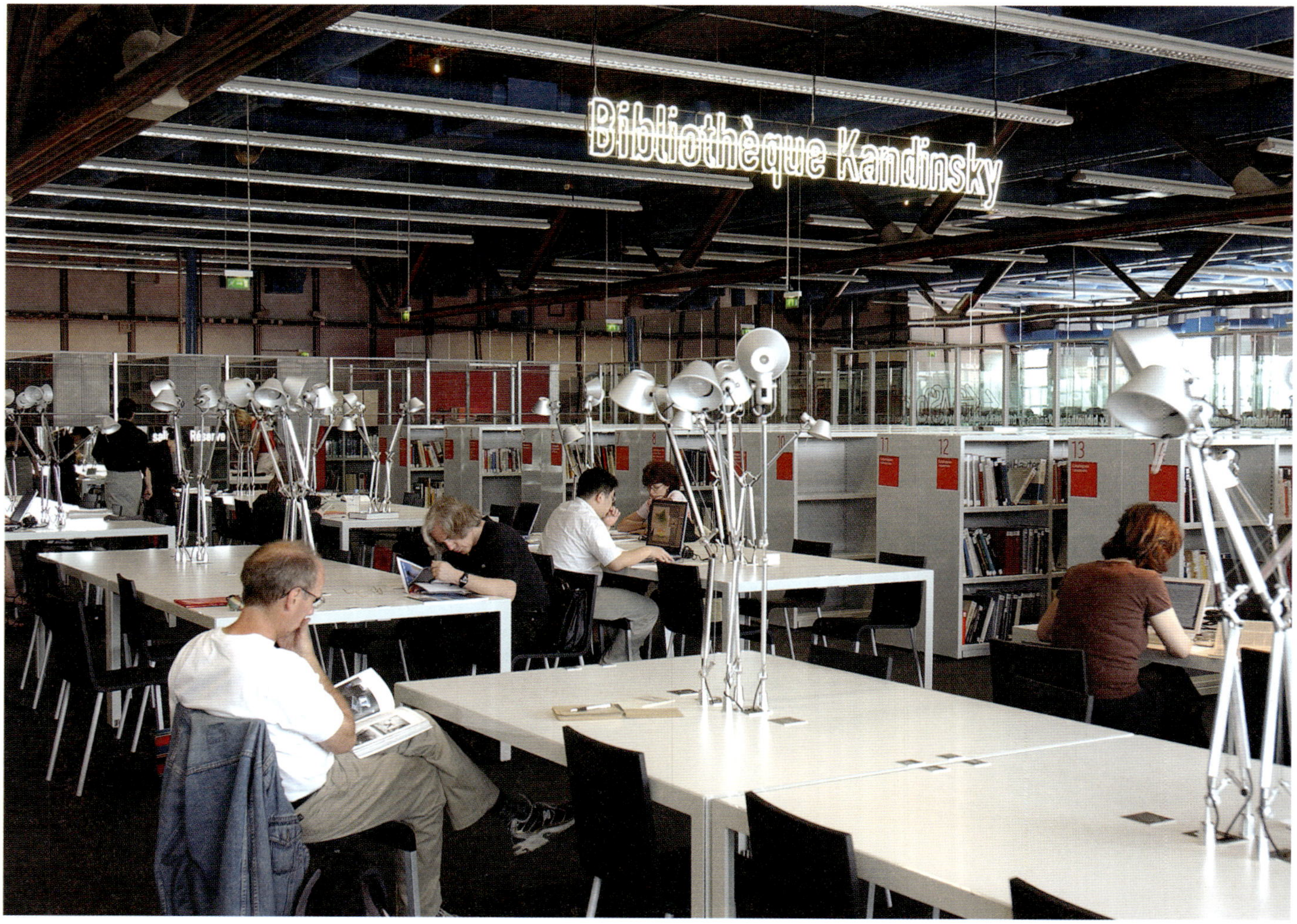

The reading room of the Kandinsky Library, on level 3, where a portion of the books is openly accessible.

The Kandinsky Library

Visitors will discover not the Kandinsky Library itself, as it is only accessible to experts and researchers, but a portion of its exceptionally rich collections on view in the Museum's display cases and integrated into temporary exhibitions. This includes books, photographs, letters, magazines and much more, all in all a broad assortment of documents that provide essential background for viewers to situate works in their context and to illustrate the collections.

Located on the 3rd floor of the Centre Pompidou, the Kandinsky Library is a legacy library whose mission has not changed since the Centre was created: to gather the greatest possible amount of documentation on the subject of the creation of modern and contemporary art. It functions as the museum's brain, providing the curators' essential working material for conceiving and designing exhibitions and preparing displays. The genesis of this collection and its dynamic came from the merger of the curators' library of the Musée National d'Art Moderne – Palais de Tokyo and the documentation service of the Centre National d'Art Contemporain. The former, though modest, notably contained Brancusi's archives. The latter, located in Rue Berryer in Paris in 1969, was focused primarily on current trends and the living arts, both in France and abroad. Its main activity involved collecting information from artists and data on their practices.

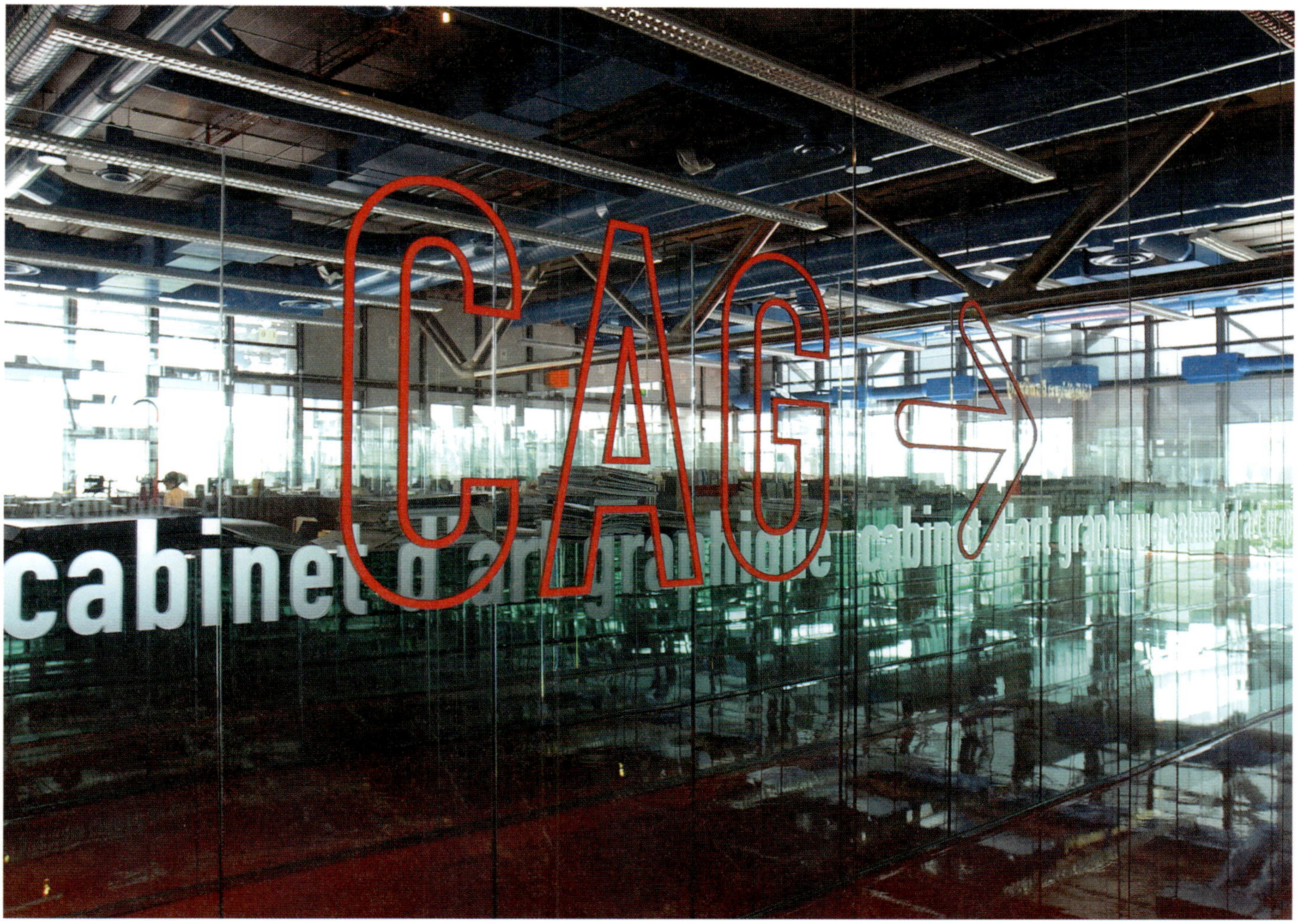

Next to the consultation room of the Kandinsky Library is the Cabinet of Graphic Art.

Information gathering was done by means of questionnaires, through photojournalism sessions in their studios and galleries, and by clipping relevant articles from the press.

"General Documentation" at the "BK"

When the Centre Beaubourg project was germinating, the idea of associating it with a centre for documentation with the fruit resulting from this earlier merger was immediately integrated into the development program. At its opening, it had to offer the greatest possible body of documentation to the Centre's teams in order to give them references required for information, identification and selection, and finally building the collection.
In 1992, yet another layer of sedimentation settled in, this time through the merger of the Musée National d'Art Moderne and the Centre de Création Industrielle. The latter possessed a documentation department covering the fields of architecture, design, urbanism, construction techniques and much more.
In 2000, what had previously been named the "Documentation Générale du MNAM" was dubbed the "Bibliothèque Kandinsky" (the Kandinsky Library), a name chosen because it synthesises all the figures that the library – like the Centre – seeks to embody: artist, theoretician, professor, foreign refugee and donor. It represents one of the Museum's largest collections and archives.

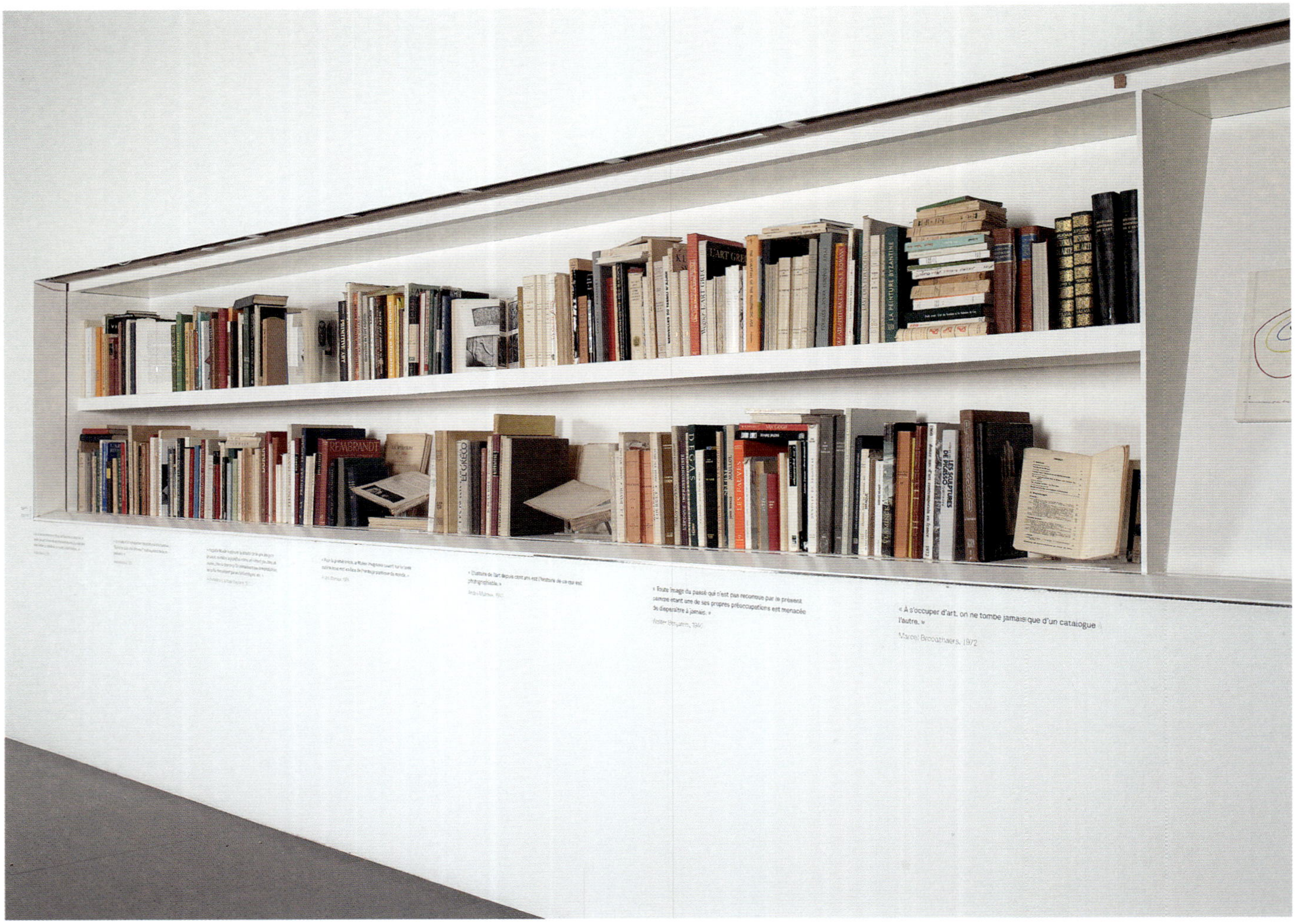

In the inaugural exhibition of the Centre Pompidou-Metz, "Masterpieces?" (12 May 2010-12 September 2011), the "Masterpieces to Infinity" section (12 May 2010-17 January 2011) comprised artworks, books, periodicals and documents on loan from the Kandinsky Library (here a part of the André Malraux library). This section questioned the persistence of the concept of the masterpiece throughout the 20th century, in the age of the reproducibility of images.

The Centre's grey matter

Today, the "BK" possesses the complete archives of numerous artists, collectors, art dealers and critics. These papers, which often include artists' private correspondence and family photographs, make it possible to relate this information with the artists' works on view in the museum's permanent galleries, temporary exhibitions and publications. The "BK" also houses ten libraries of artists and writers. André Malraux's library, for example, enables the museum to show how his books, which he literally cut into pieces, served as the raw material for his own works, including the famous *Musée imaginaire*. In addition, there are myriad documentary photographs of works and exhibition displays – including 250,000 glass plates from the Marc Vaux collection, who photographed all the artists' studios from 1920 to 1970, and from Giacometti to Jean-Pierre Raynaud. Rounding out its collections is a beautiful catalogue of 5,000 artists' books, including the series of illustrated books by Vollard and Kahnweiler, and books on art history. In the field of contemporary art, the Library continues to gather all the artists' "ordinary" day-to-day documentation: exhibition flyers, invitation cards, catalogues, etc. Artists have left their mark in the constitution of the collections with some of them coming personally to add to them regularly, a tradition going back to the 1970s. The young Christian Boltanski, for example, was employed during this period to assist in sorting this massive and continuous flow of information! In addition to all this, the library contains a catalogue of 7,000 magazine titles from across the globe, which can either be consulted or displayed. Standing out among these collections is the one of Paul Destribats, acquired in 2006. Dedicated to poetry and the visual arts, its 1,000 titles include virtually the entire European and American production of periodicals on the avant-gardes of the 20th century (Constructivism, Futurism, Dadaism, Surrealism, etc.) in which the greatest artists of the period participated. This makes the "BK" the richest collection in existence on the first half of the last century. Finally, the Kandinsky Library

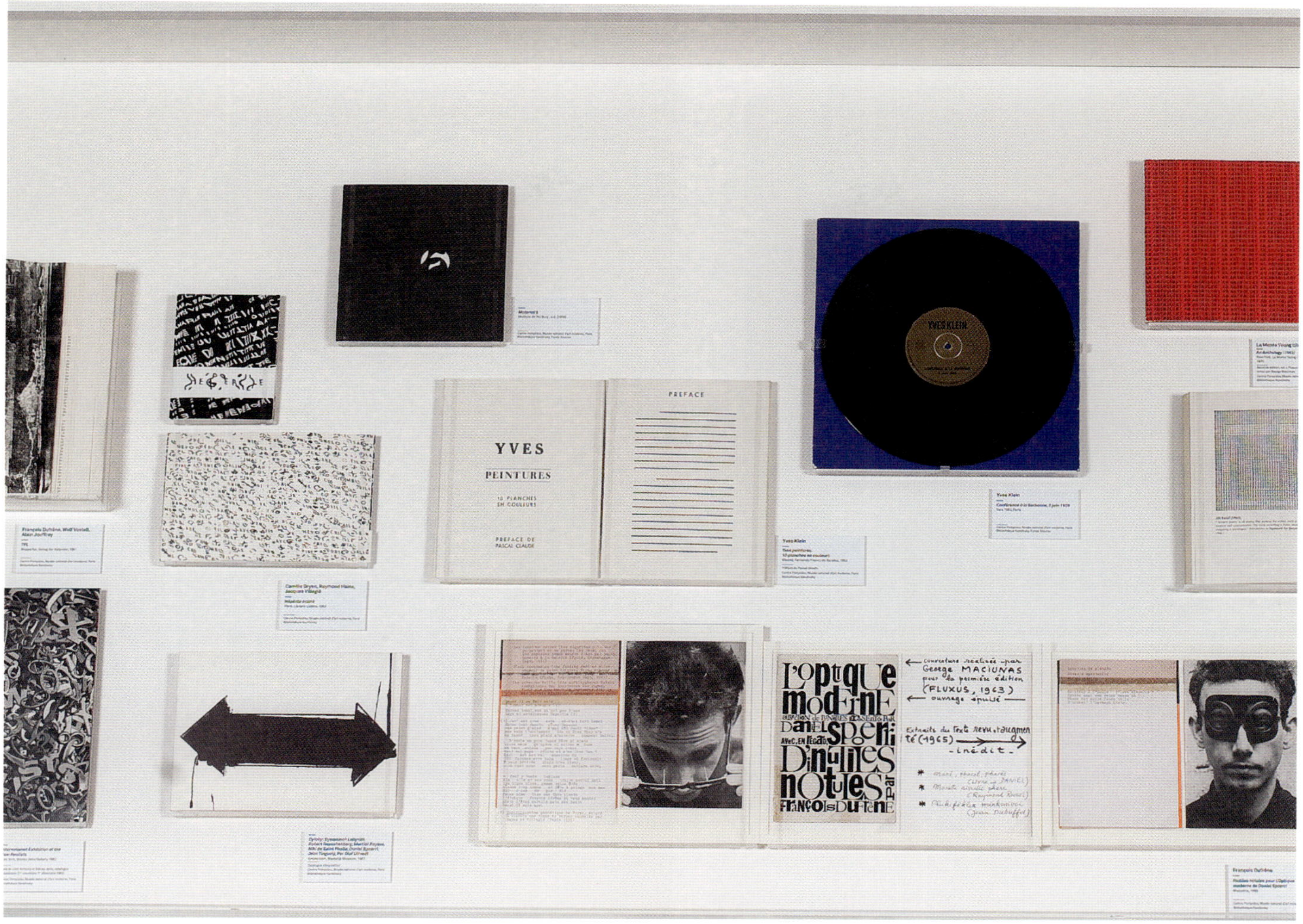

Detail of the long display case of the "Masterpieces to Infinity" section of the first exhibition of the Centre Pompidou-Metz.

constantly produces its own documentation, and namely a collection of films on art, shot in the studios of both renowned and up-and-coming artists. The collection is further enriched by films on art and by its archives of sound recordings of interviews with artists.

An international reference

This highly international collection, carefully built over time, whose scope goes well beyond the visual arts to encompass all avant-gardes in the broadest sense of the term, is the world's leading library in its domain. Its breadth and quality make the Kandinsky Library one of the primary international research tools and a resource for the writing and exhibition of the history of art in the 20th and 21st centuries. The 5,000 artists, designers and architects present in the collections of the MNAM receive priority documentary attention. The Centre Pompidou is one of the rare museums to possess such depth of documentary resources for its collections, whose accessibility is facilitated by an online catalogue and a portal (http://bibliothequekandinsky.centrepompidou.fr) with links to numerous digital resources, selected from among the Kandinsky Library's rarest documents.

"When looking after art, one never simply falls from one catalogue onto another."

Marcel Broodthaers, 1972

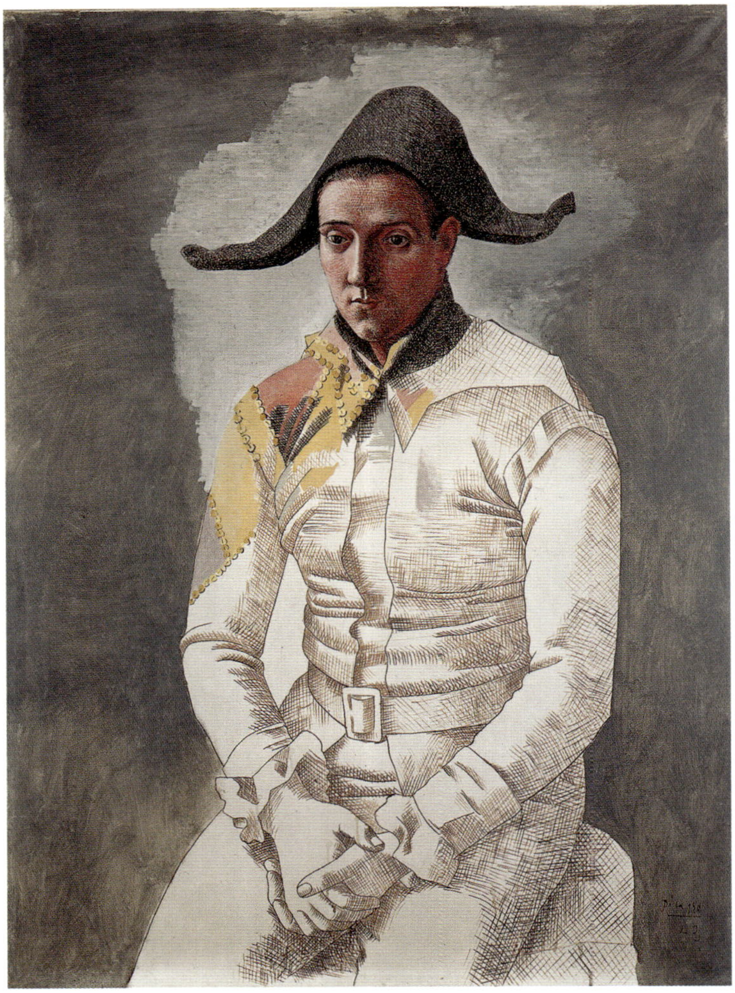

Pierre Soulages (1919-), *Peinture*, 19 June 1963, oil on canvas, 260 x 202 cm (left).
Pablo Picasso (1881-1973), *Harlequin (The Painter Salvado as Harlequin)*, 1923, oil on canvas, 130 x 97 cm (right).

The Musée National d'Art Moderne

The permanent collections of the Musée National d'Art Moderne-Centre de Création Industrielle occupy two entire levels of the Centre Pompidou, organised according to the principle of a long and luminous north-south circulation, opening onto spaces of varying dimensions. Just as on the day of the Centre's inauguration, visitors still enter on level 4, devoted to contemporary art from 1960 to today. From here they can access the upper level, dedicated to the modern period, which begins with works from 1905, the date chosen for the beginning of the collections.

The constantly expanding ensemble is impressive in that it covers all the artistic currents beginning with the Fauves and no less than eight disciplines: painting, sculpture, graphic arts, photography, experimental cinema, new media, design and architecture, without overlooking the collections comprising the Kandinsky Library.
In less than 40 years, these collections have seen spectacular growth, increasing from about 17,000 works in 1977 to 44,000 in 2000 and over 65,000 today. They have become a global reference for the art of the 20th century, rivalling in excellence the Museum of Modern Art in New York, its historic counterpart.
They are characterised by vast monographic groupings of works unique in the world, by an often exhaustive representation of the major movements of modernism – of course with a few gaps – and a decisive place given to contemporary trends since 1970; an identity that reflects their history.

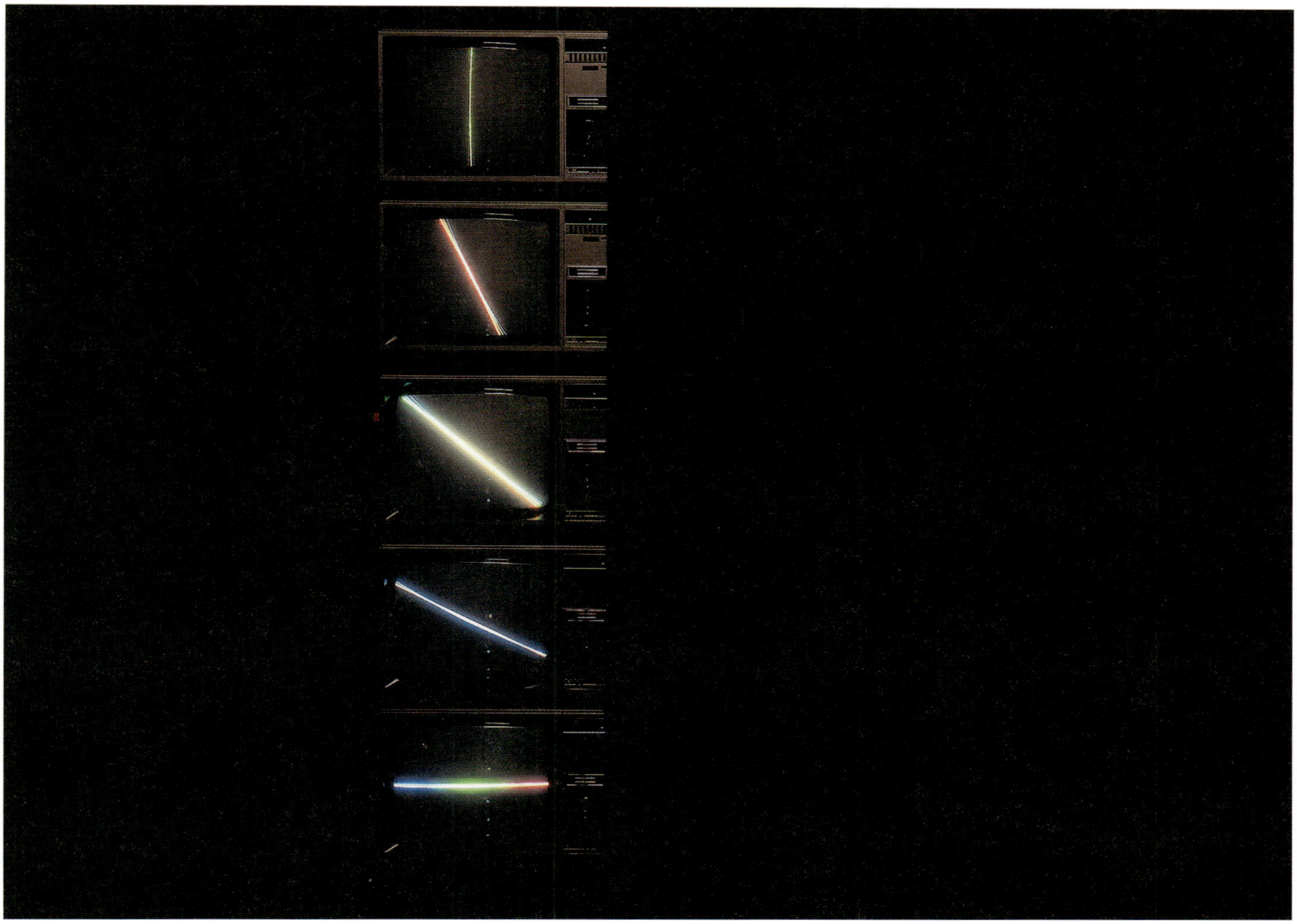

Nam June Paik (1932-2006), *Moon is the Oldest TV*, 1965-1992, TV screen installation, edition 1/1, 12 to 17 black and white televisions, silent, 12 to 17 magnets.

The inception of the Musée National d'Art Moderne

The history of the Musée National d'Art Moderne began 30 years before the opening of the Centre Pompidou, on 9 June, 1947, with its inauguration in the Palais de Tokyo. The new museum combined the collections of two institutions: the Musée du Luxembourg, dedicated since 1818 to living artists and often criticised for its conservatism, and the Musée du Jeu de Paume, which since 1922 had housed contemporary foreign schools.
These two museums ignored all the avant-gardes and independent art of their period. In these national collections there were only a few works by Braque, four by Delaunay, two by Léger, one by Kandinsky and one by Dalí. Only Bonnard, who embodied the French tradition, was properly represented. In the 1930s, an insistent movement of artists and critics began demanding the creation of a new museum to enable Paris to catch up with other cultural capitals that had taken the lead. Le Corbusier even imagined a "museum of unlimited growth," a project that would later be abandoned.

The MNAM – Palais de Tokyo, French-style modernity

In 1945, Jean Cassou, the first director of the Musée National d'Art Moderne, set to work filling in the gaps in the museum's collections. He succeeded in building the initial modern collection thanks to the close relationships he wove with French artists.

New Media and Film

A space in the museum is dedicated to the New Media and Film collections, which represent over 2,000 video and audio tapes, installations and multimedia works, CD-ROMs, artists' websites, experimental films and artists' films created at the edges of the film industry. These movies, which cover over a century of creation, have been digitised to enable their viewing onsite on computer screens in the New Media and Film Area. Whether as a media of creation or a record of performances, these "new media" interest artists from all countries working in all disciplines - the visual arts and cinema, but also dance, music, architecture, theatre, etc., across a conceptual field astonishingly vast in scope. The list of creators present in the collections is enormous, but to mention a few: Doug Aitken, Claude Closky, Jean-Luc Godard, Gary Hill, Pierre Huyghe, Mike Kelley, Chris Marker, Bruce Nauman, Nam June Paik, Walid Ra'ad, Pipilotti Rist, Bill Viola and many more. As the other collections of the museum, these are among the most important in the world.

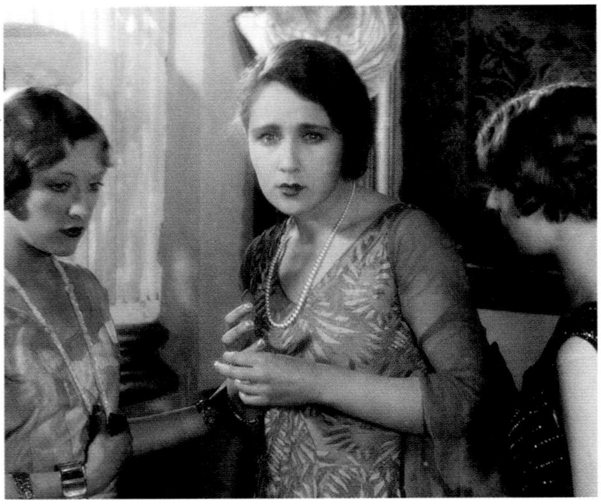

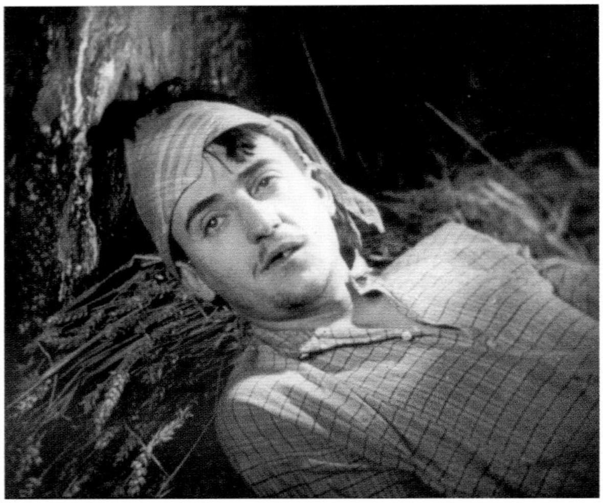

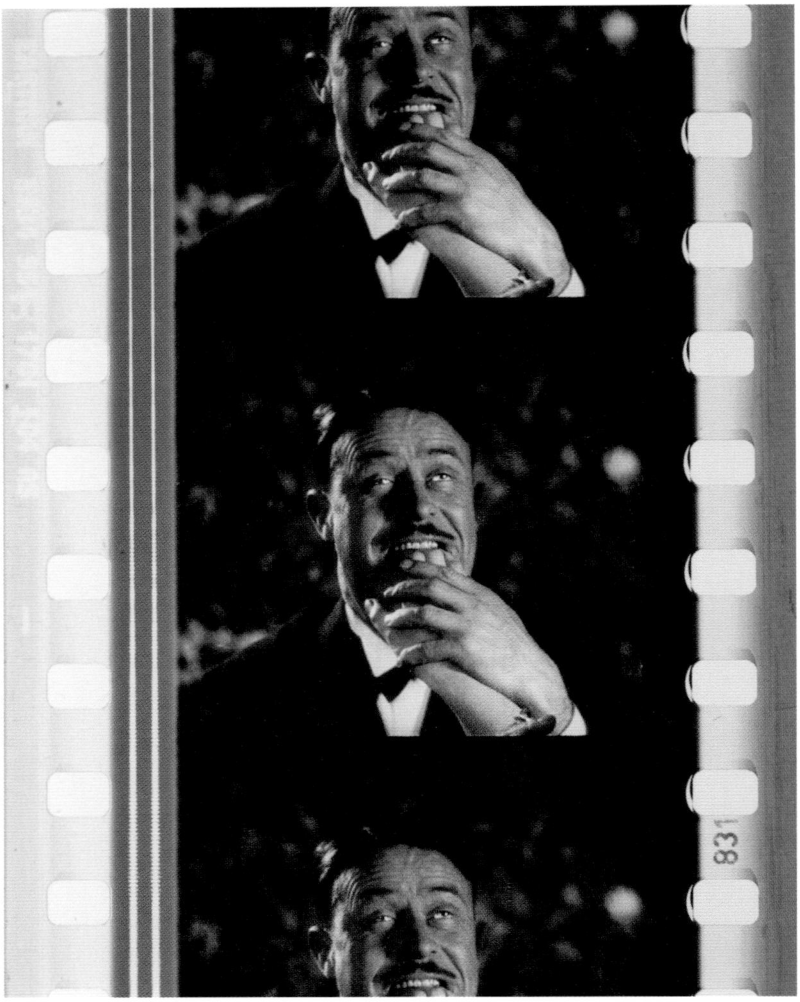

Luis Buñuel (1900-1983), *L'Âge d'or (The Golden Age)*, 1930, 35 mm black and white film with sound, length: 63 min (left page).
Man Ray (1890-1976), *Le Violon d'Ingres (Ingres's Violin)*, 1924, silver salts proof enhanced with graphite and India ink, glued on paper, 28.2 x 22.5 cm (right page).

The numerous artists called upon to contribute included: Picasso, who gave eleven canvases from his personal collections, among which *L'Aubade*; Braque, whose *L'Estaque, l'embarcadère*, the first Fauvist painting, was presented at the Museum's inauguration; Matisse, who donated many drawings; and, Brancusi, who would later bequeath his entire studio. Several collectors also responded with donations of their own. Lacking significant resources, the Museum struggled to adopt and implement a consistent and independent acquisition policy. Nevertheless, a few major purchases were made in the early years, such as Brancusi's *The Rooster* in 1947, Picabia's *Udnie* in 1949, Matisse's *The King's Sadness* in 1953 and Picasso's *Parade* curtain, in 1955. Thus, the collection of the Musée National d'Art Moderne was essentially founded through private acts, involving the generosity of artists, their families and collectors. These "major donations" involved collections often numbering over a hundred works by the same artist, entire studios that gave the museum its very specific physiognomy: Pevsner in 1962; Kupka, Dufy and Rouault in 1963; Delaunay and González in 1964; Braque in 1965; Calder in 1966; Laurens in 1967...
The pace was frenzied.
The Museum also elicited the interest of major collectors such as Paul Rosenberg, Raoul La Roche, Baroness Gourgaud for Léger, Marie Cuttoli and Henri Laugier for Picasso's collages, André Lefèvre for Cubism and Heinz Berggruen for Klee. Hence the Museum's solid historical footing and the basis of its depth of field, on a scale well beyond the reach of any other museum of modern art. For the 20th century, neither the MoMA in New York, whose collections were assembled by art historians aiming to present an overview of all avant-gardes, each one illustrated by at least one masterpiece, nor the Tate Gallery in London, possesses such monographic collections. Around a core group of major works, visitors could observe the entire path of an artist unfold, see the actual memories of the works including: studies, models, projects, archives, etc.
If the collection of major French artists of the first half of the century was without peer, younger generations of contemporary artists continued to be overlooked, and those not working

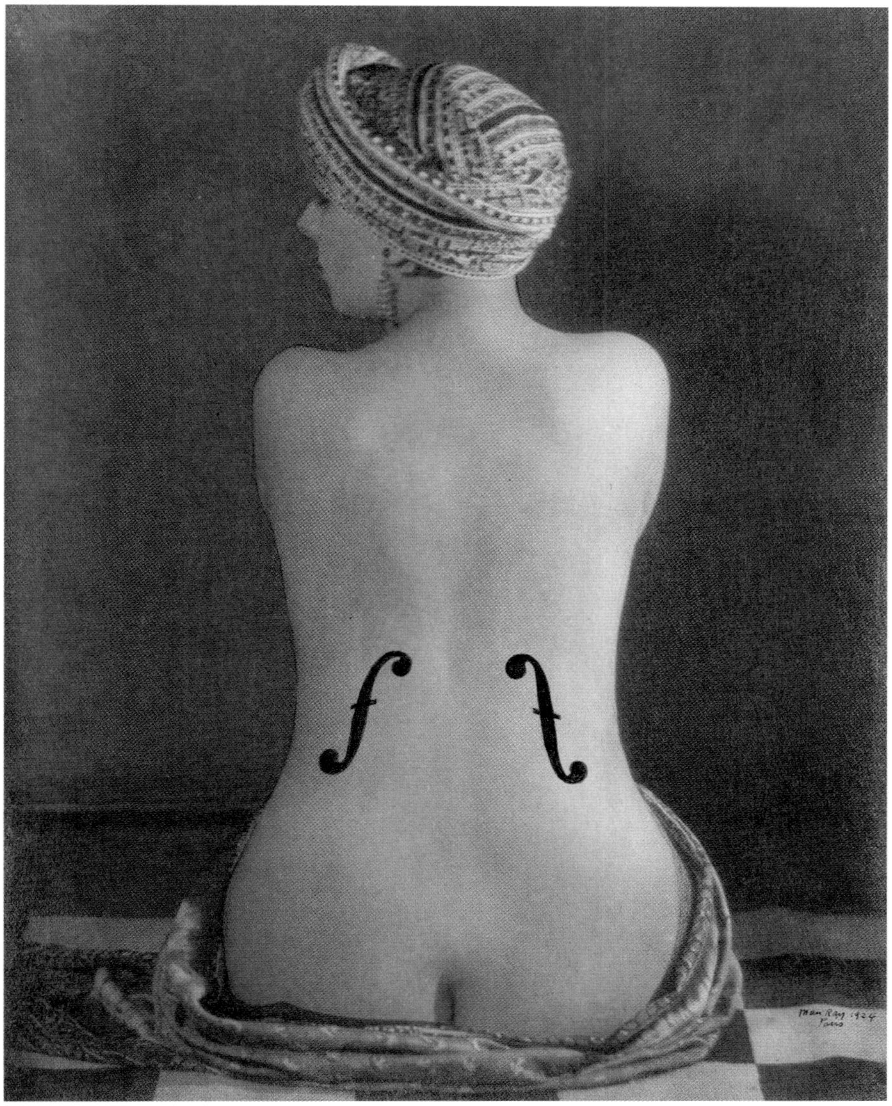

"A museum that is part of a major cultural complex cannot ignore the responsibility incumbent upon it, the one of fostering and situating all forms of creation. The Musée National d'Art Moderne had a duty to assume, as best it possibly could, a livelier responsibility with a broader scope in which the present is expressed and the past is decanted."

Pontus Hulten, first director of the Musée National d'Art Moderne at the Centre Pompidou, Introduction to *100 New Works, 1974-1976*, 1977

in France even more so. The Centre National d'Art Contemporain (CNAC) was designed to serve as a showcase for living art. Settled in the Rue Berryer, in Paris, the CNAC presented cutting-edge French and international art through its exhibitions, while developing a policy of sharing with European institutions and building its own collection of works by Balthus, Bacon, Rothko, Giacometti, Dubuffet, de Kooning, etc.

Prefiguring the Centre Beaubourg, openness to contemporary art and the international scene

Despite their extraordinary richness, on the eve of the launch of the Centre Beaubourg project, the collections of the Musée National d'Art Moderne still had significant gaps and had fallen seriously behind the times: neither Surrealism nor Dadaism were properly represented given their importance, Futurism, the various German currents and American painting were virtually absent, as were specific artists such as Duchamp, Ernst, Miró, Dubuffet and Fautrier. The collections gained a new lease on life in 1974, with the Centre Beaubourg project. The MNAM was to be transferred there to form a single department, along with the CNAC, at whose head was appointed Pontus Hulten. For the very first time, a French museum was endowed with a significant and independent budget for acquisitions, thereby ensuring it had the real freedom and resources to design and implement an ambitious

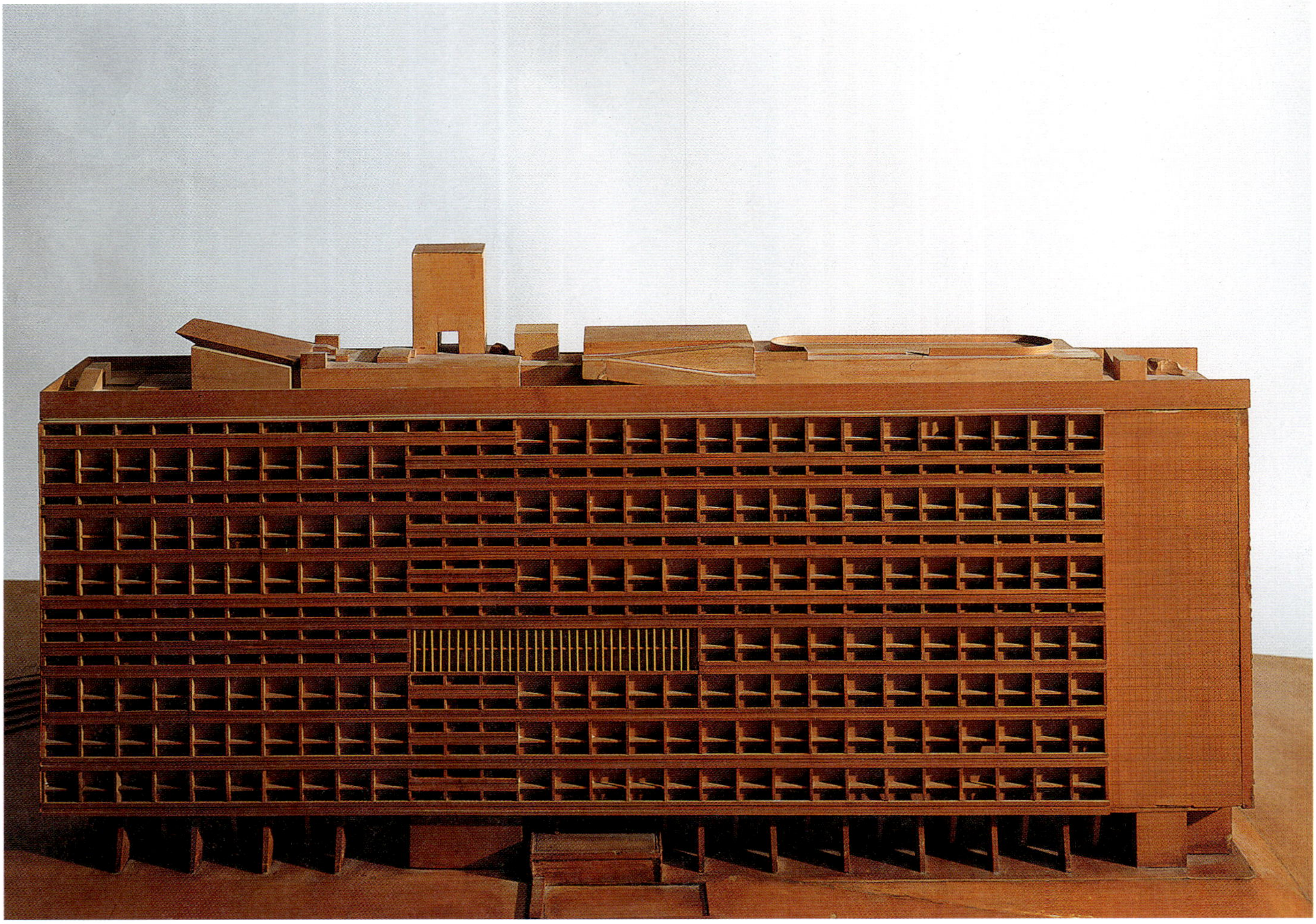

Le Corbusier (pseudonym of Charles-Édouard Jeanneret) (1887-1965), *Unité d'habitation, Berlin-Tiergarten*, 1957-1958, study model, wood (solid and veneer), 55 x 122 x 90 cm.

long-term purchasing policy.
The museum began collecting works by contemporary artists and developing its international dimension. Its most glaring gaps were filled. Major figures of modern art were at last presented in the collection, including de Chirico, Magritte, Malevich, Mondrian and Arp, as well as many key contemporary artists, such as Beuys, Warhol, Johns, Klein and Pollock. Donations continued to pour in with the works of Magnelli in 1972, Ernst in 1975, Lipchitz in 1976, Fontana in 1977, Albers in 1979 (completed in 1999).
In parallel, the Museum "lightened" its collection by transferring some works to the Louvre and by leaving huge portions of the collections at the Palais de Tokyo: the post-Impressionists, the Nabis, and all works prior to Fauvism (i.e. 1,377 drawings, 735 paintings and 228 sculptures), which were later integrated into the collections of the Musée d'Orsay. In 1977, at the opening of the Centre Pompidou, visitors discovered a totally transformed MNAM.

The MNAM-CCI, an artists' and collectors' museum

The collections continued to grow at an astounding rate, according to the three main guidelines defined by Pontus Hulten, and to which the subsequent directors of the Museum remained faithful. These were to complete the historic heritage of the first half of the 20th century, to enrich the presence of subsequent generations and to follow current French and international trends. Part of the budget would always be allocated to design, photography and video art, which are integral parts of the mission of a determinedly interdisciplinary MNAM.
Another wave of major donations occurred, including the extraordinary ones by Nina Kandinsky in 1981 (510 drawings, 90 paintings, 116 aquarelles and gouaches, and the entire set of objects and archives conserved in the artist's studio) and by Dominique de Ménil, notably of American artists such as Pollock, Warhol and Oldenburg.
The foundations of a truly international collection were finally in place and the importance of French art of the 1960s affirmed. A new coherent arrangement took shape, organised around New Realism and with Raynaud, Raysse, Spoerri, Takis and Arman. Works by Buren, Boltanski, de Staël, Ryman,

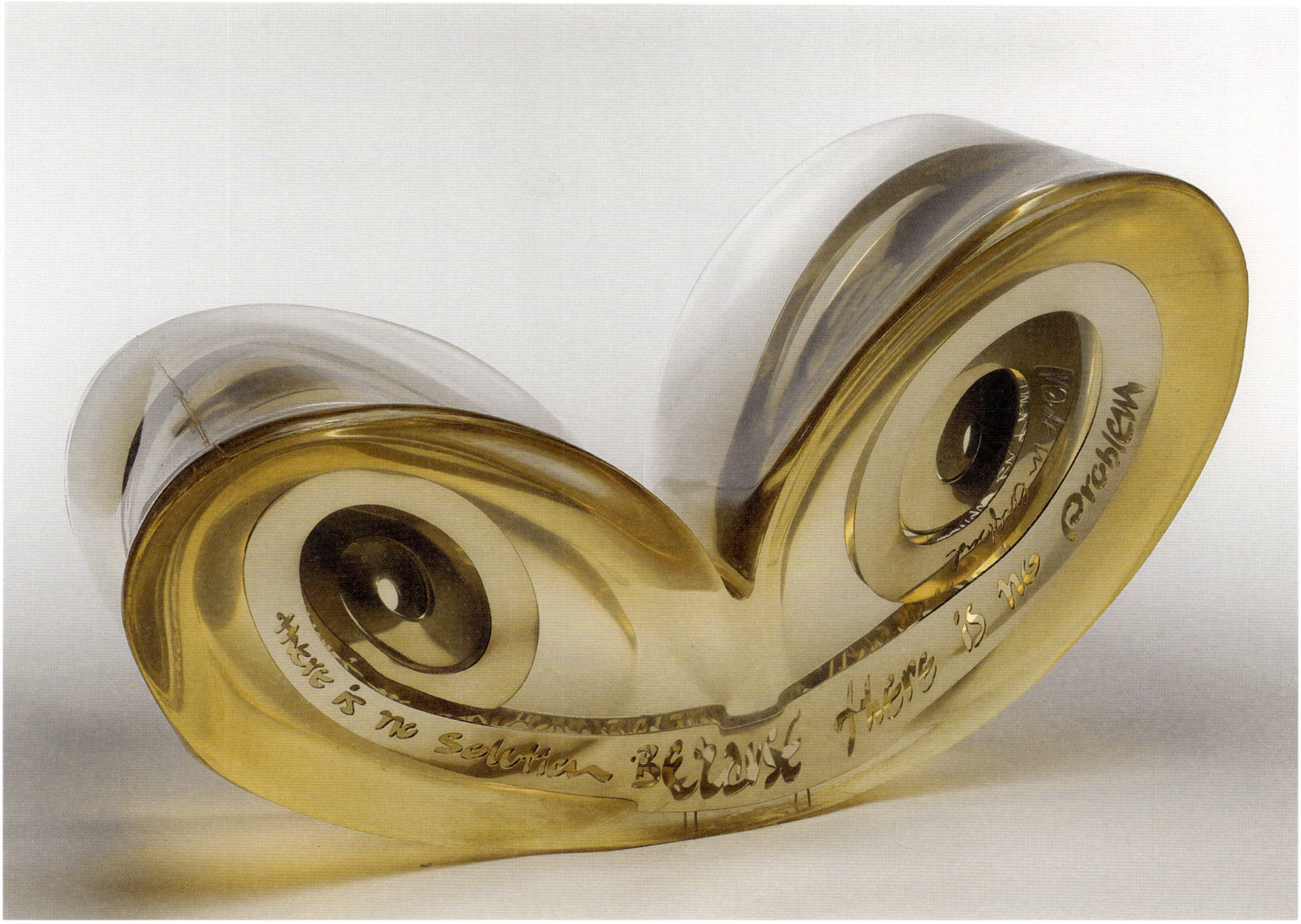

Ron Arad (1951-), *Oh-Void Chair*, 2006, "Blo-Glo" series, armchair, transparent moulded silicone, aluminium framework, 70 x 120 x 65 cm.

Carl Andre and Richard Long also came to hang on the Centre's walls. In addition, photography, video and new media benefited greatly from the push to acquire, which enabled for example the integration of virtually the entire archives of negatives of Brassaï and Man Ray. To keep up with the increasingly competitive market for contemporary art, the Museum relies on the "*dation*" or payment-in-kind system set up by the state, which enables legatees to donate works in payment of inheritance taxes. In this way, the collection has been enriched with masterpieces by Braque, Matisse and Gris, as well as the essential core of the estates of several artists: Dubuffet in 1986, Giacometti in 1987, Chagall in 1988, Vieira da Silva in 1993, as well as those having belonged to dealers and amateurs-connoisseurs. Every single gallery of the Museum has been enriched by these successive arrivals. The entire Museum was transformed by the Cubist donation of Louise and Michel Leiris in 1984, so great was its impact on the major groupings of works by Braque, Picasso, Léger, Masson, Klee and Derain. And the various donations made by Daniel Cordier alone total over 500 works.

Interdisciplinary approach and movement

This uninterrupted expansion has impacted all the "traditional" disciplines of the museum, including photography, video and experimental cinema, which enjoy an unusually prominent place in the collections since the Centre Pompidou's opening, and to which

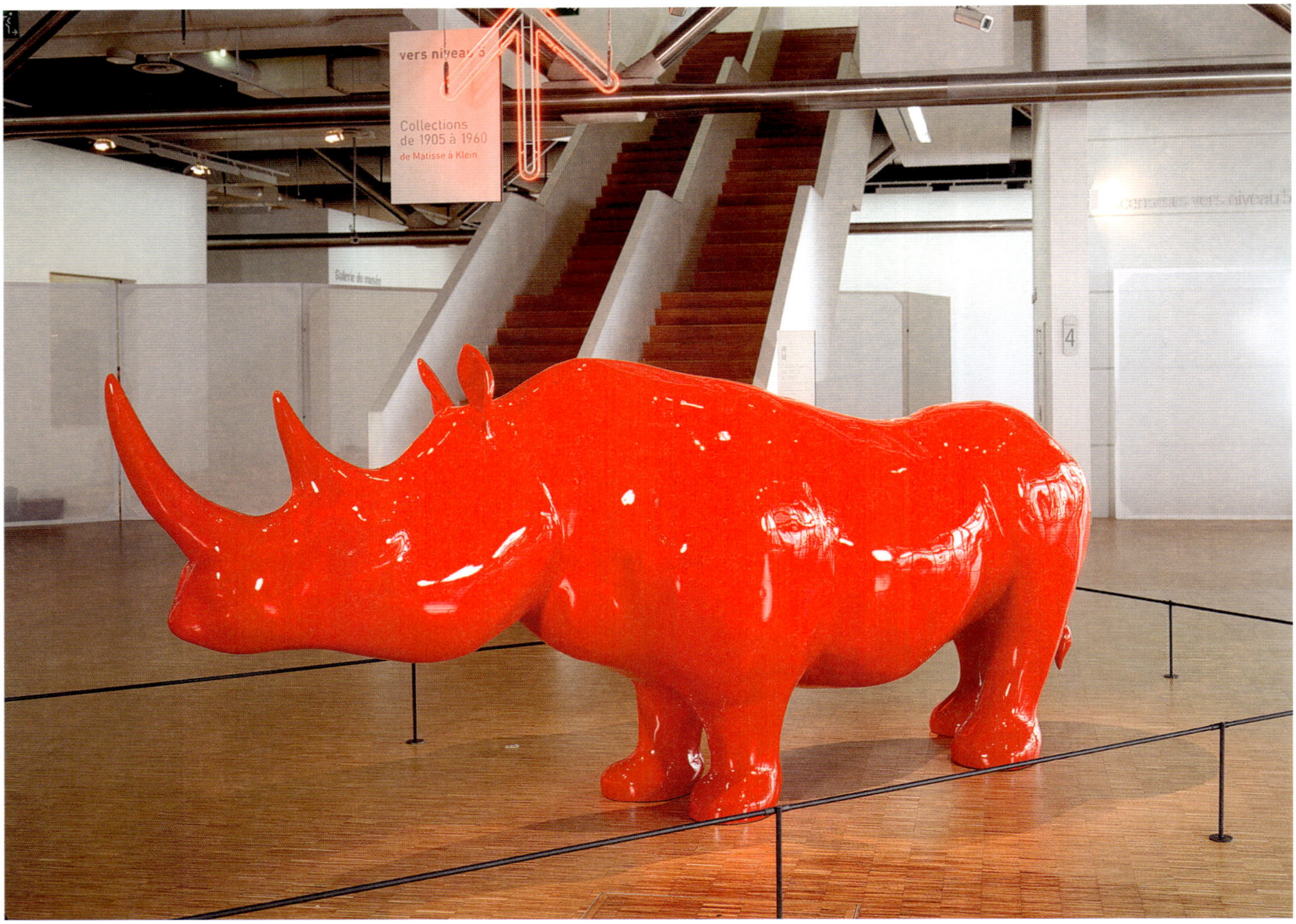

Xavier Veilhan (1963-), *The Rhinoceros*, 1999-2000, resin, polyester paint, varnish, 110 x 415 x 140 cm.

architecture and design were added in 1992. It was on this date that the Musée National d'Art Moderne was merged by administrative decree with the Centre de Création Industrielle in order to cover an even broader range of creative endeavour. The CCI is first and foremost an institution dedicated to research and analysis of the contemporary world and of industrial design. When it joined the Museum, the acquisition teams began constituting collections for these domains, with a determination to achieve chronological simultaneity and intellectual affinities enabling the optimal blending of the collections. In a few years, architects' drawings, plans, models, edited furniture, prototypes and everyday objects were gathered under the three main management teams constantly steering and shaping the museum. Priceless monographic collections focused on major architects and designers have been integrated into the Museum's collection, including Eileen Gray, Jean Prouvé, Charlotte Perriand, Jean Nouvel, Rem Koolhaas, Ettore Sottsass and Philippe Starck. This extensive collection has been achieved largely thanks to the generosity of the architects and designers themselves, as well as that of their legatees. Major pieces of historical significance such as the *Modulor* by Le Corbusier have been acquired, while particular care and attention has been paid to the youngest architects and designers. The Museum's patrimony has radically – and swiftly – transformed. The new disciplines, displayed in the largest galleries of level 4, have established a fruitful dialogue with the ensemble of the Centre's collections. Today, while research on the art of the 20th century continues, the artist is emphasised more. The Museum remains faithful to its mission of open examination of contemporary trends, though eschewing blind faith, and pursuit of its aim to represent the French and international scenes, by facing the globalisation of art head on.
A dedicated team is always on the lookout for the most recent trends and practices, scouting contemporary and future-oriented creation, spotting new technologies, identifying the emerging artists in France and abroad and acquiring their works.
To reflect this constant enrichment of its collections, and to renew the interest of visitors, the galleries are reorganised

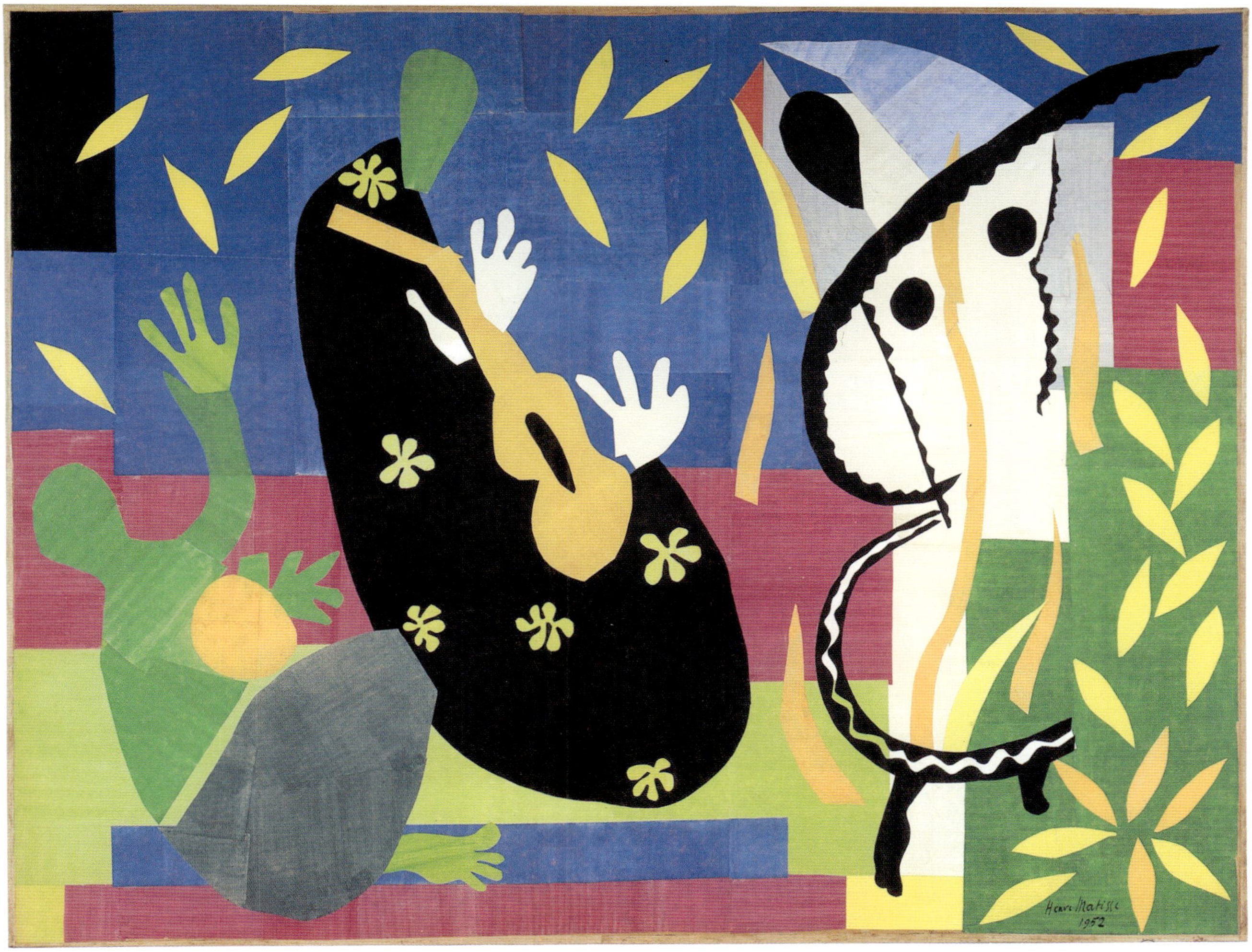

Henri Matisse (1869-1954), *The King's Sadness*, 1952, collage, 292 x 386 cm.

and re-hung biennially, floor by floor. Elements of the collections also frequently circulate on loan to exhibitions in France and abroad, and of course to the new Centre Pompidou-Metz. In perpetual transformation, the Museum is a place of living creation, fully engaged with its time. It offers a home for artists' encounters while fulfilling its role as an institution dedicated to preserving this major historical heritage, which is its mission, and as the source for a large part of the programming of the Centre Pompidou. The permanent collections have been enriched to the point that they equal the drawing power of the exhibitions – not the case 30 years ago – as one of the major attractions of the Centre and one of its best tools for sharing and for ensuring its continued influence.

The Breton Wall

Eskimo goggles, an Australian boomerang, a fossilised nautilus, The *Double World* by Picabia, a Mexican funerary doll, rocks picked up from the bed of the Durance River and entitled by Breton *Souvenir of an Earthly Paradise*, a box of butterflies, beetles and other stuffed animals, works by Duchamp, a Navajo tomahawk, a witch's mirror, a Papuan shield, *The Head* by Miró, a mace from the Salomon Islands, an Egyptian amulet, *Black Pollen* by Degottex, a Spanish chest of drawers... and, in the centre, the photograph of Elisa and the *Still Life with Cherries* by Douanier Rousseau—the Breton Wall is an exact replica of the writer's studio, originally located in the Rue Fontaine in Paris. Entering the collection of the Musée National d'Art Moderne in 2003 as payment of inheritance taxes, it is the high point of an almost 30-year relationship, based on the generosity and commitment of the artist's widow and his daughter, Aube Breton-Eléouët, with the museum.

A policy of regular purchases from the Breton collection began in 1975. Some twenty works entered the museum in this way, including *Chimera* by Ernst, *The Suspended Ball* by Giacometti and Dali's *William Tell*. Upon her mother's death, and as payment in kind for inheritance taxes, Aube Breton-Eléouët offered the entire wall (over 250 objects) to the Museum, where it had already been deposited and on display since 1999. Thus this unique testimony to the Surrealist movement was saved from dispersion. The transfer was accompanied by a gift of three major works: *Hitler* by Brauner, *Spanish Dancer* by Miró and "Poster for Arcane 17" by Matta.

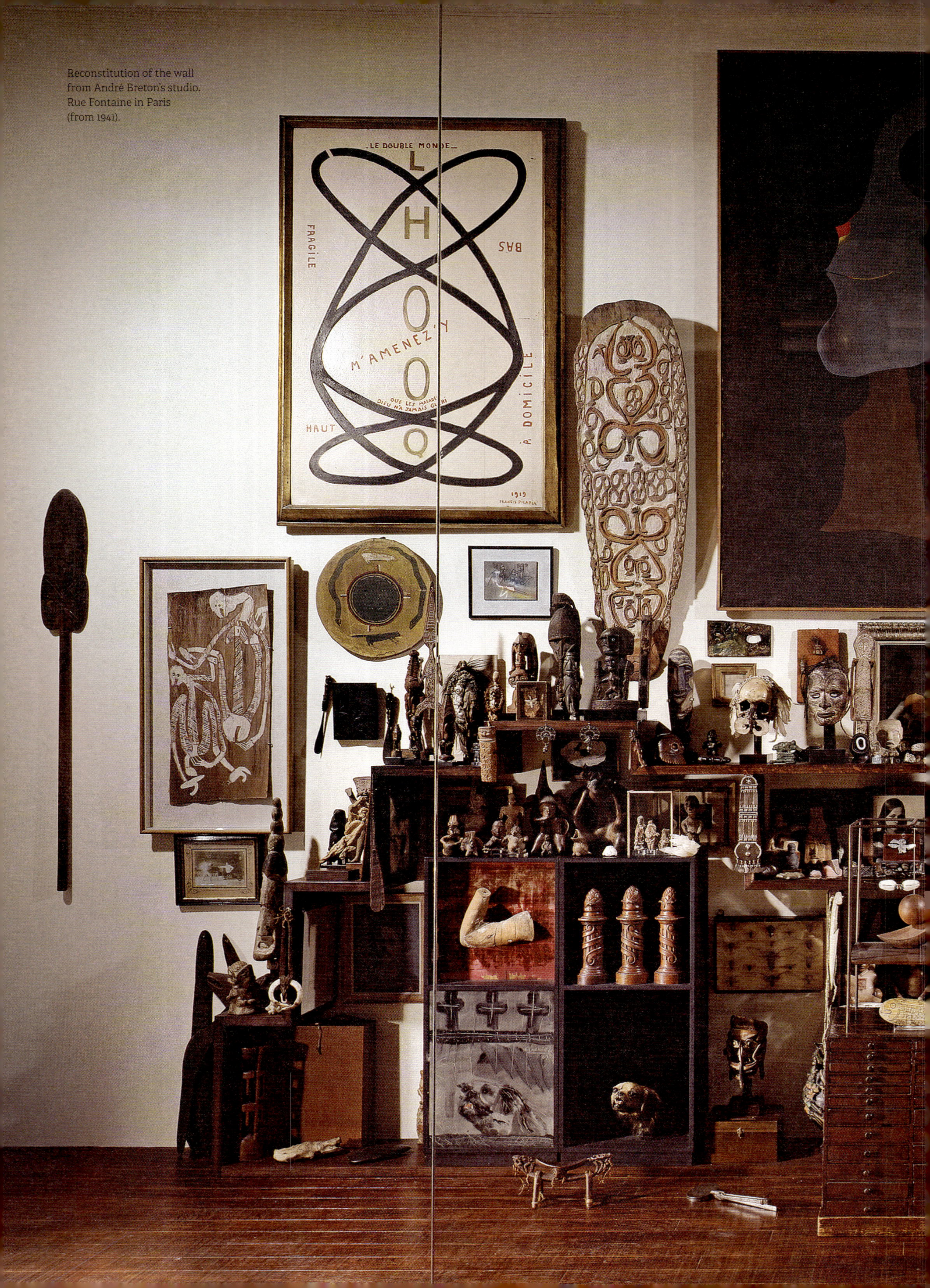

Reconstitution of the wall from André Breton's studio, Rue Fontaine in Paris (from 1941).

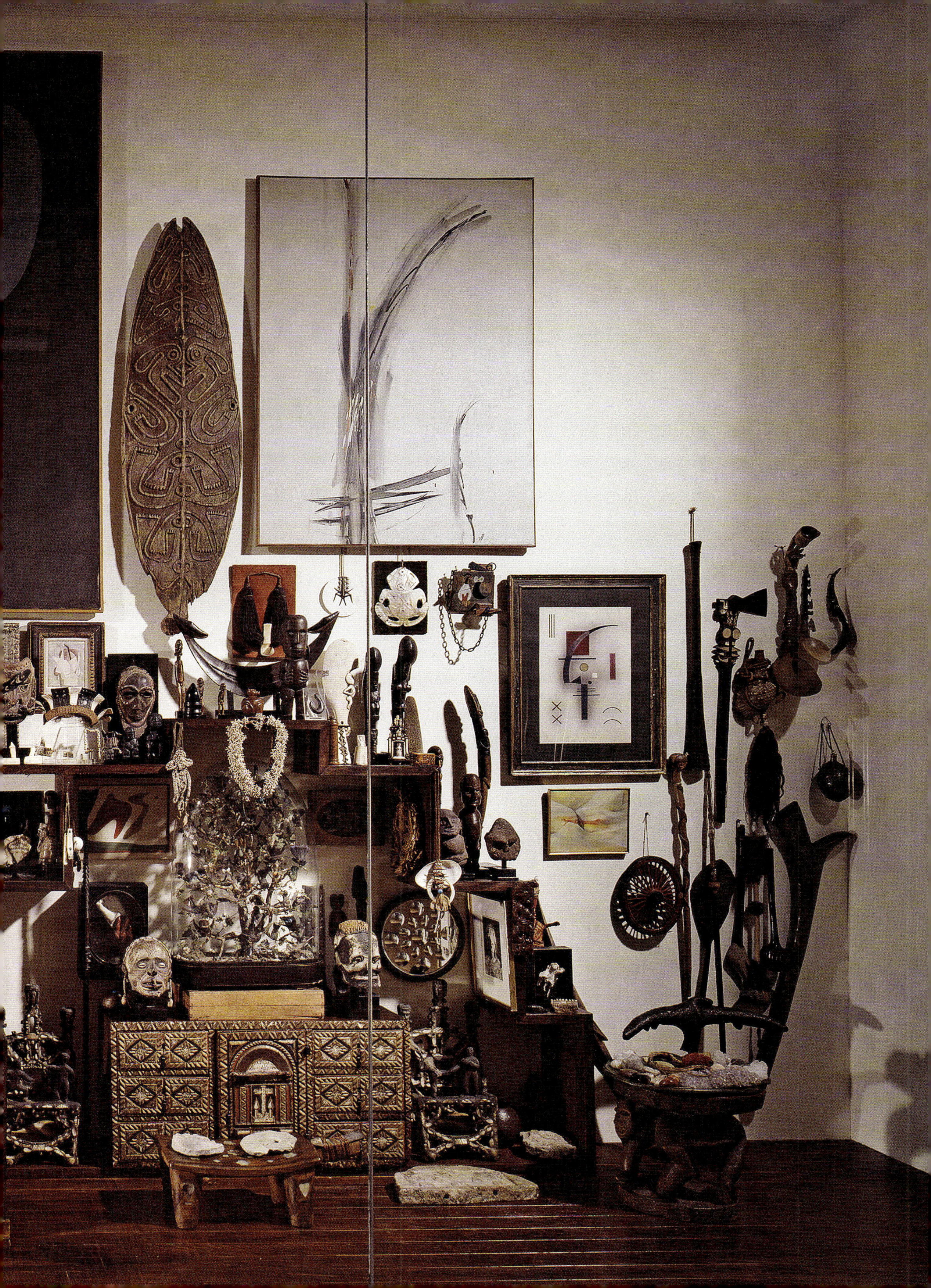

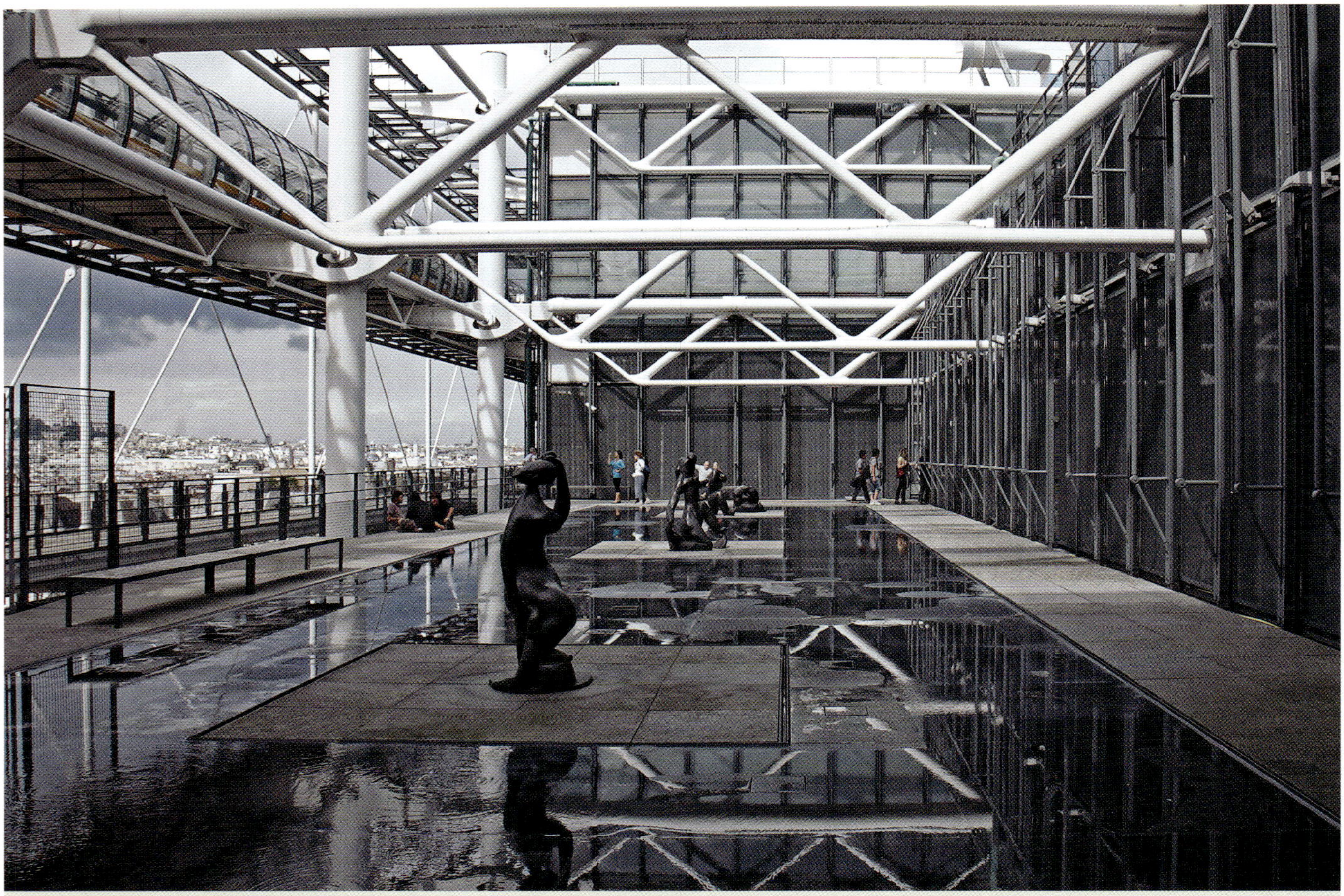

On level 5 of the Centre Pompidou, the Musée National d'Art Moderne also exhibits in open air, on a terrace where reflecting pools encircle the sculptures.
Left page, top: in the foreground, profile view, *Baigneuse (Bather)*, 1947, by Henri Laurens; Bottom: *Capricorne*, 1948/1964, by Max Ernst.
Right page: *Signal*, circa 1998, by Takis.

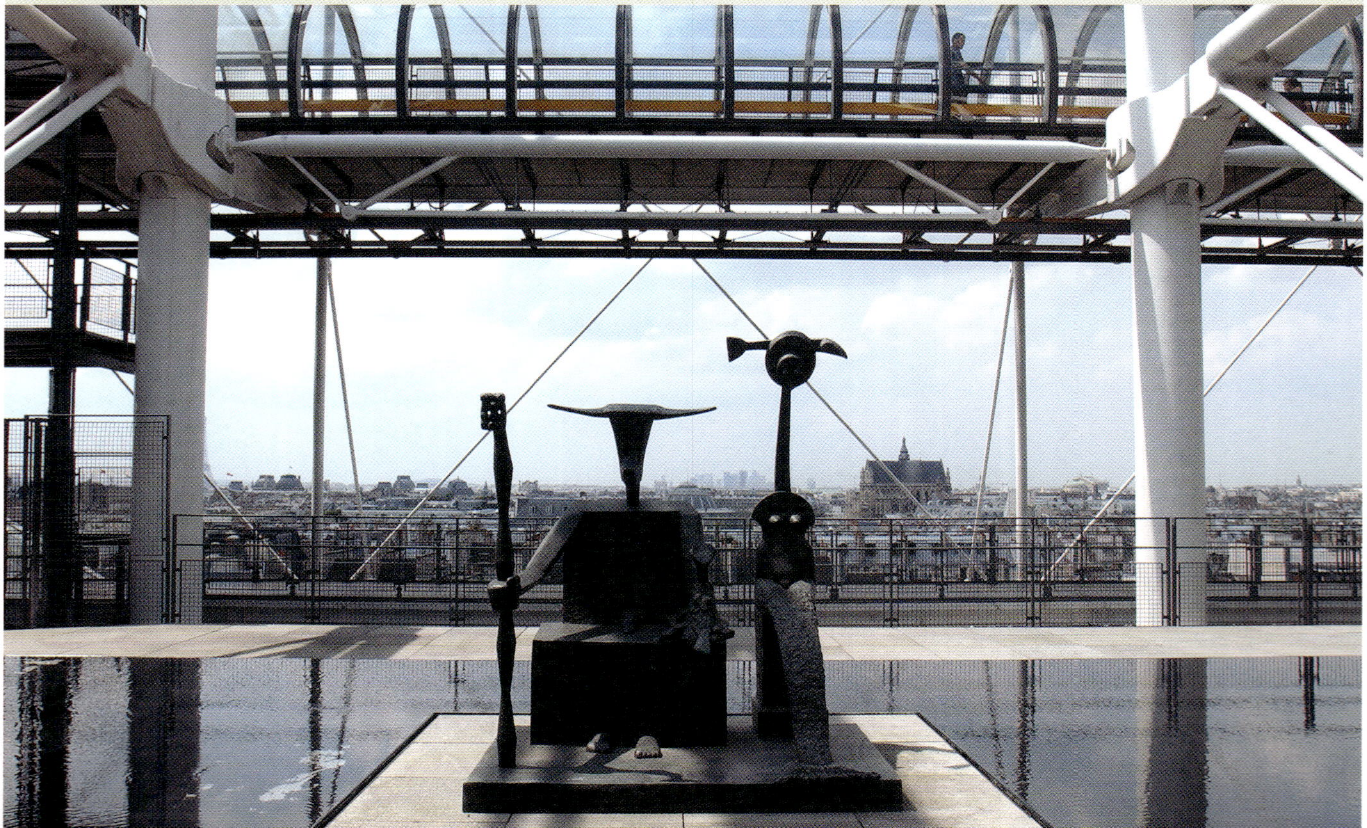

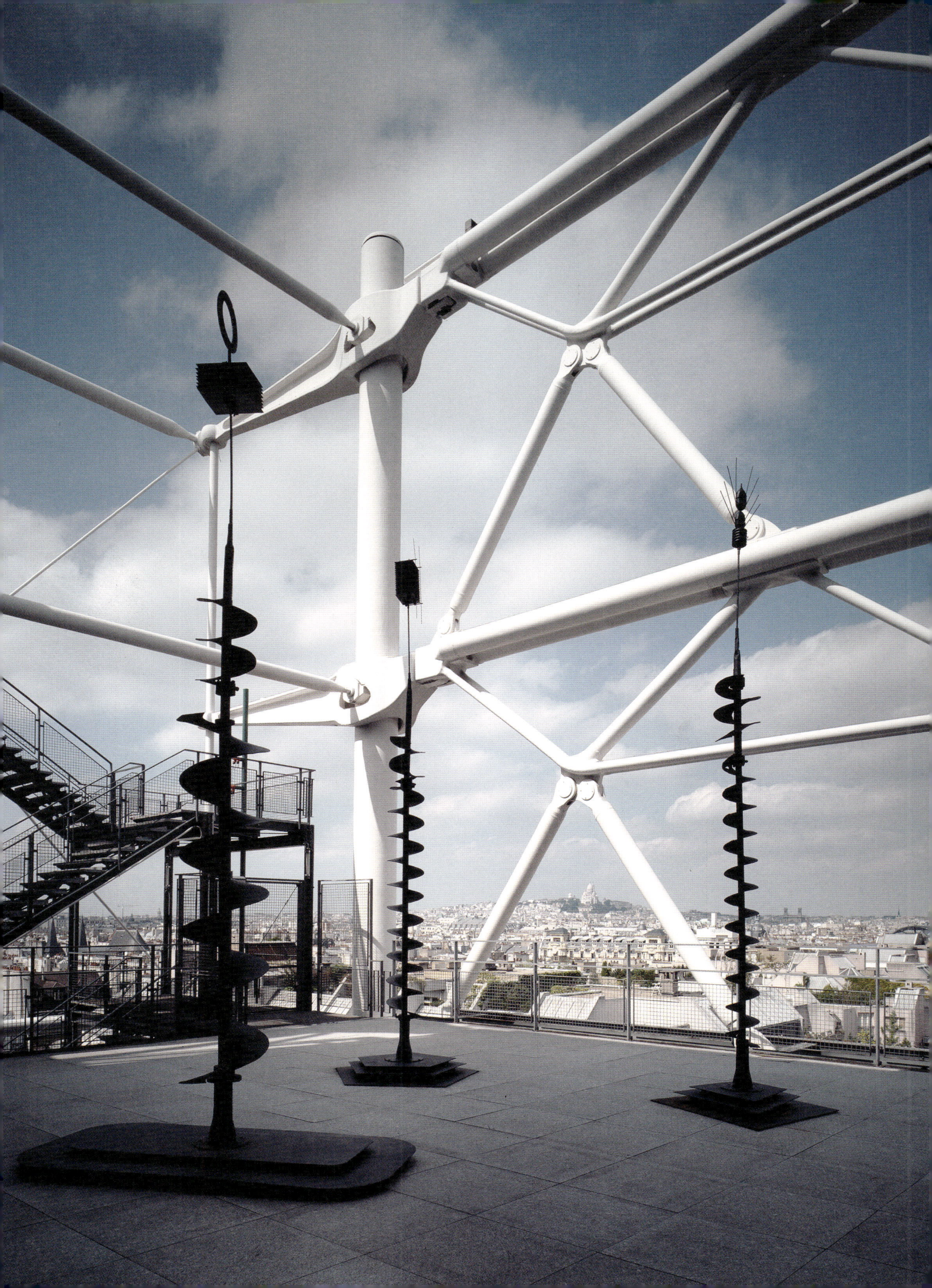

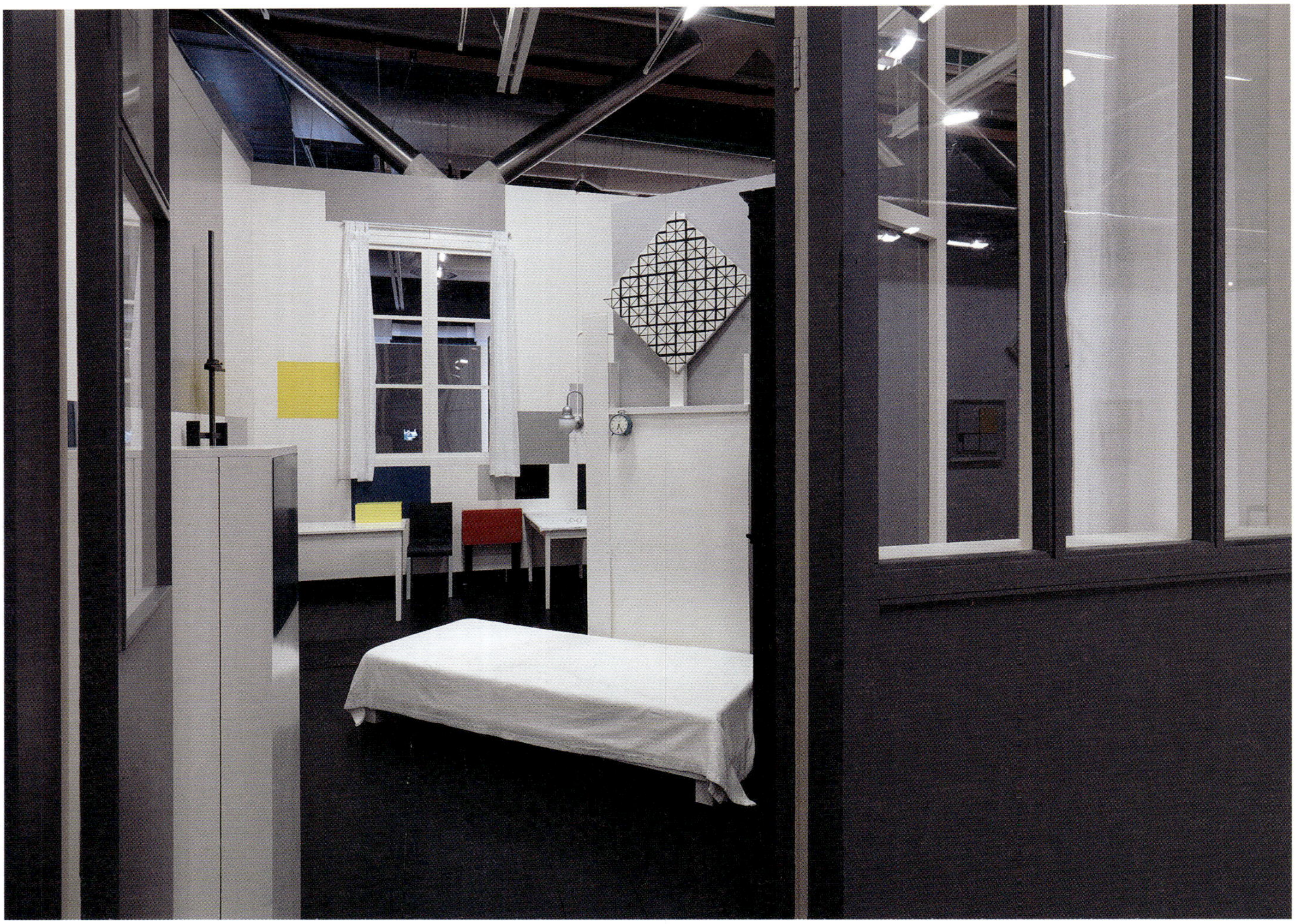

"Mondrian / De Stijl," Galerie 1 / 1 December 2010-21 March 2011. Reconstitution of Piet Mondrian's studio

Exhibitions

The building's top floor is dedicated to the major temporary exhibitions which are part of what makes the Centre Pompidou an international institution of reference and one of the most visited museums of modern and contemporary art in the world. These exhibitions are aimed at the broader public. Along with its historical exhibitions, thematic exhibitions are one of the components of the Centre Pompidou's identity and often privilege a societal and multi-disciplinary approach, by presenting the major issues of our contemporary world through the view of artists, as was notably the case with "Dreamlands" in 2009.

The richness and density of the programming are astonishing: one-person shows of living artists and major historical retrospectives, contemporary and cross-disciplinary themes, and openness to globalised art. The Centre is in fact both "a museum and a centre of creation," in keeping with Georges Pompidou's formula, and the exhibition programming is divided between the heritage approach and the determination to show the best of the contemporary scene, a skilful temporal dosing, while also highlighting the Museum's collections. Through its exhibitions, the Centre Pompidou also supports the French art scene and affirms its influence in the world. The Centre's inaugural exhibition, a Marcel Duchamp retrospective, symbolised this positioning because, through a key figure for contemporary artists, it proposed a new approach

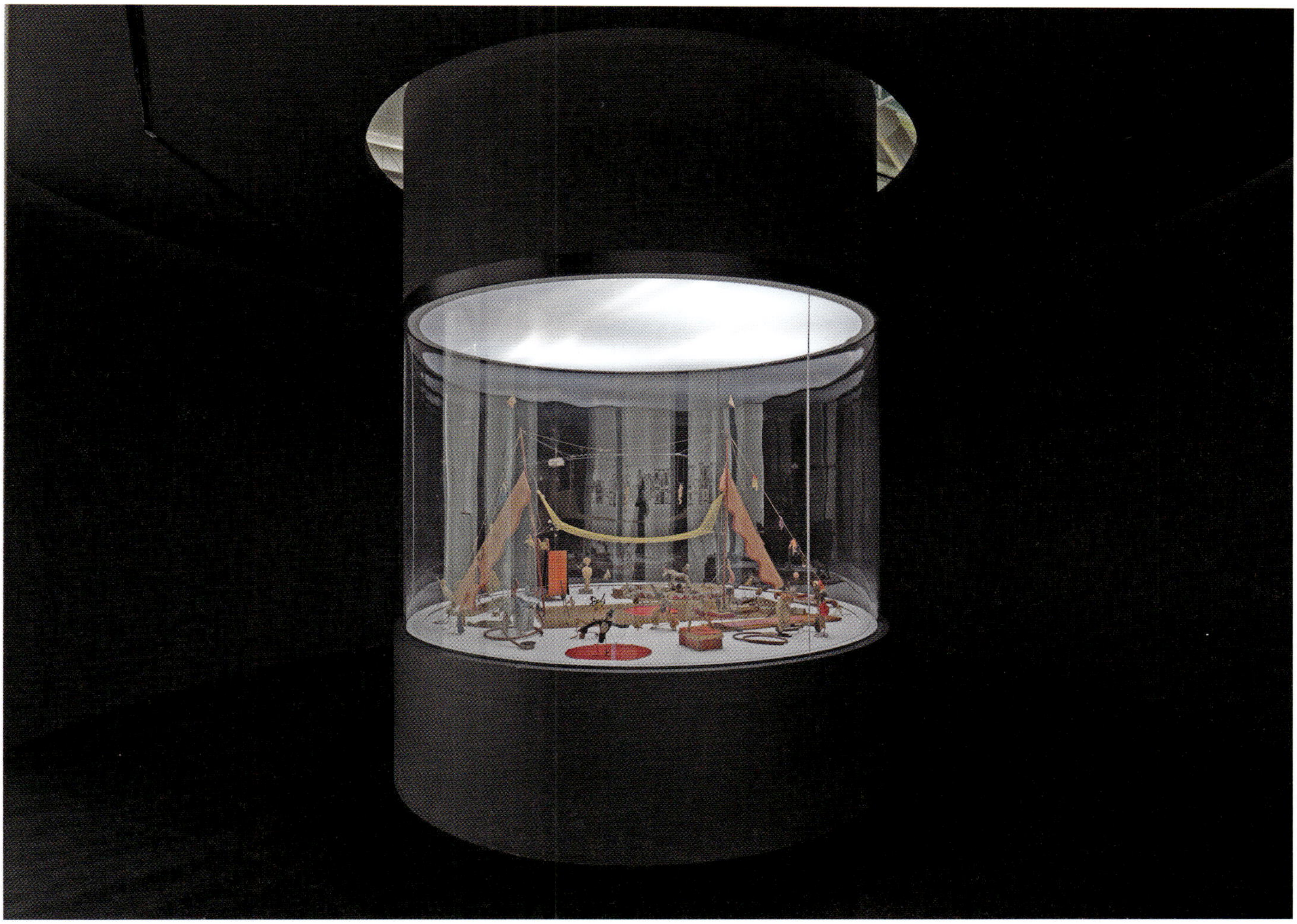

Alexander Calder, *Le Cirque (The Circus)*, 1926-1931, New York, Whitney Museum of American Art, "Alexander Calder. The Parisian Years, 1926-1933," Galerie 2 / 18 March-20 July 2009.

to historical avant-gardes at the same time as it reclaimed the emeritus personage of this "French-born American artist" (the formula used in American museums) for France. The Centre was simultaneously hosting three other contemporary exhibits: a one-man show on Gerhard Richter, a group exhibition on the figure of Ben, and a show on new artists.

Two complementary Galleries

The vast floor is divided into two spaces, each presenting two shows per year. Gallery (Galerie) 1 (over 2,000 square metres) alternates historical and thematic exhibitions. Some are monographic shows, such as "Kandinsky" or "Calder," dedicated to major French or foreign artists – garnering the largest number of visitors – others are thematic and collective, assessing entire periods or founding movements in the history of art of the 20th century, such as "Dada," "Traces of the Sacred" or "Futurism in Paris."
Gallery (Galerie) 2 (nearly 900 square metres) is used for holding one-person shows on contemporary artists – from Sophie Calle to Louise Bourgeois and Lucian Freud – and historical exhibitions.
All in all, nearly half of the contemporary exhibitions are monographic, the format artists prefer, and an important place is given to architecture and design. Each exhibition is an occasion for lectures, meetings, performances and film cycles.

The 10 exhibitions with the highest affluence since 2000

Kandinsky (2009): 702,905 visitors
Soulages (2010): 502,028 visitors
Miró (2004): 475,601 visitors
Calder (2009): 473,800 visitors
La révolution surréaliste (2002): 450,000 visitors
Nicolas de Staël (2003): 431,492 visitors
Giacometti (2007): 423,701 visitors
Mondrian/De Stijl (2010-2011): 401,021 visitors
Dada (2005): 377,269 visitors
Yves Klein (2006): 375,792 visitors

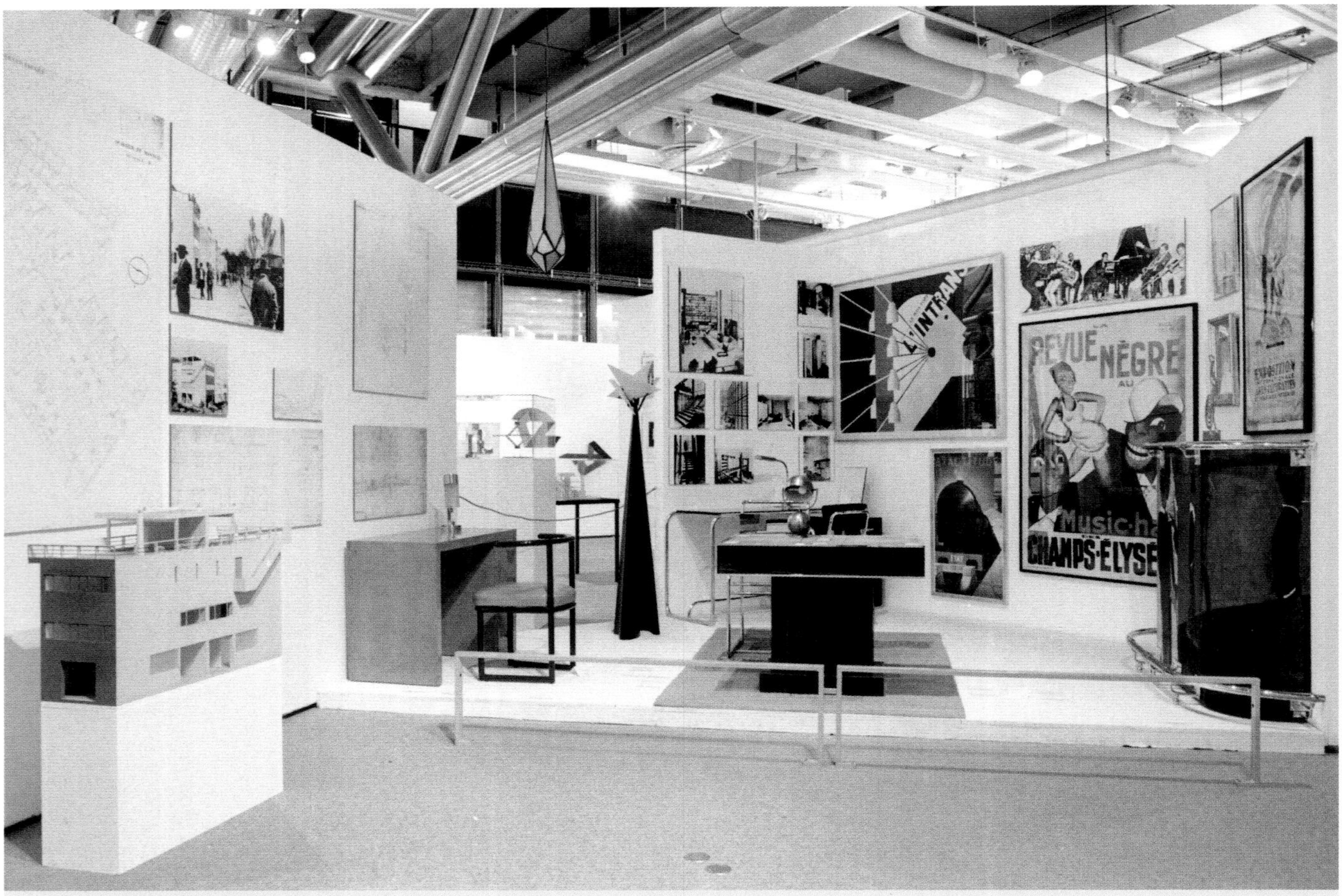

"Paris-Berlin," level 6 / 12 July 1978-6 November 1978 (top).
The Crocodrome of Zig et Puce, by Jean Tinguely, Bernhard Luginbühl and Niki de Saint Phalle, Forum and level -1 / 18 June 1977-2 January 1978 (bottom).

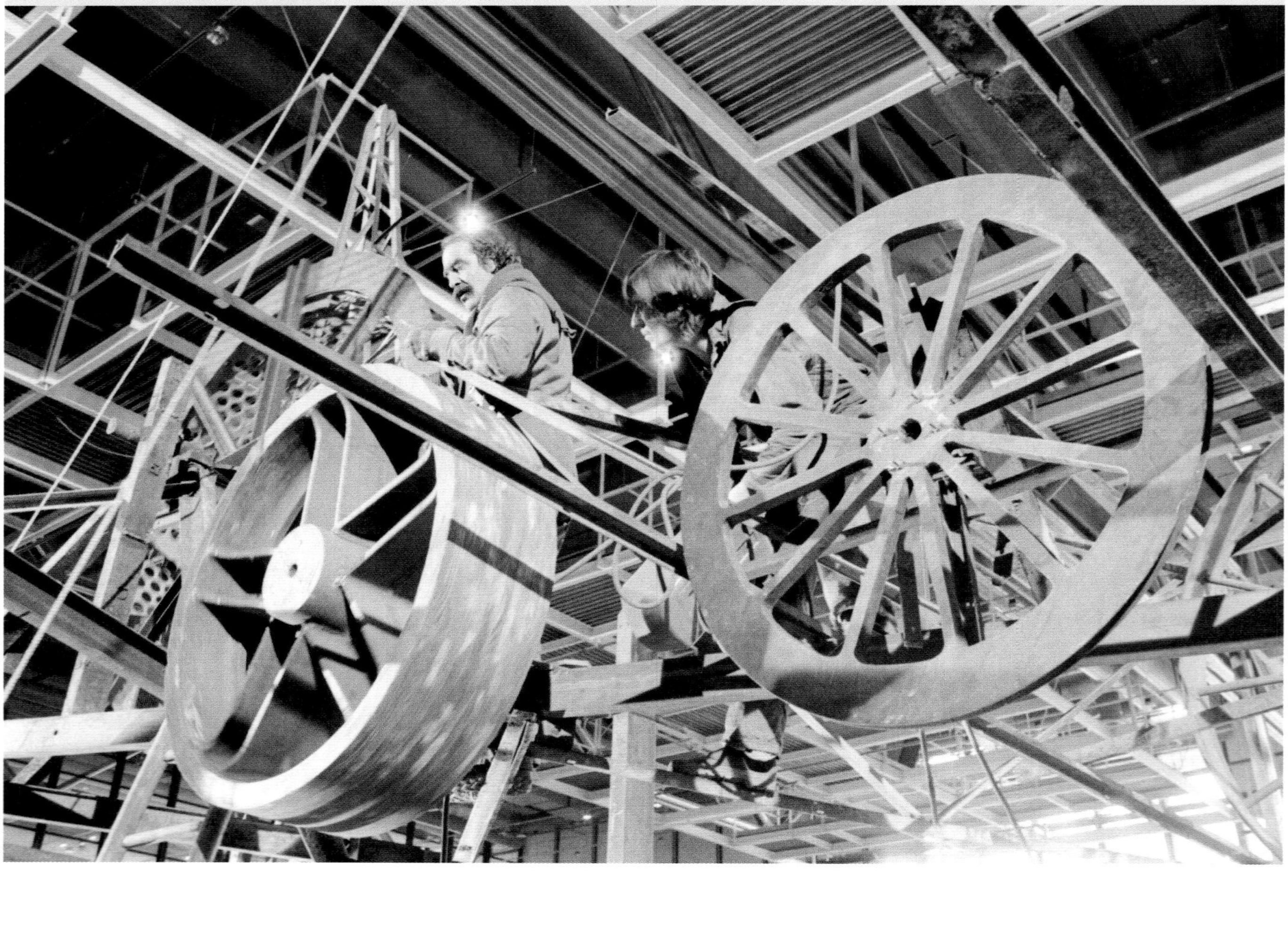

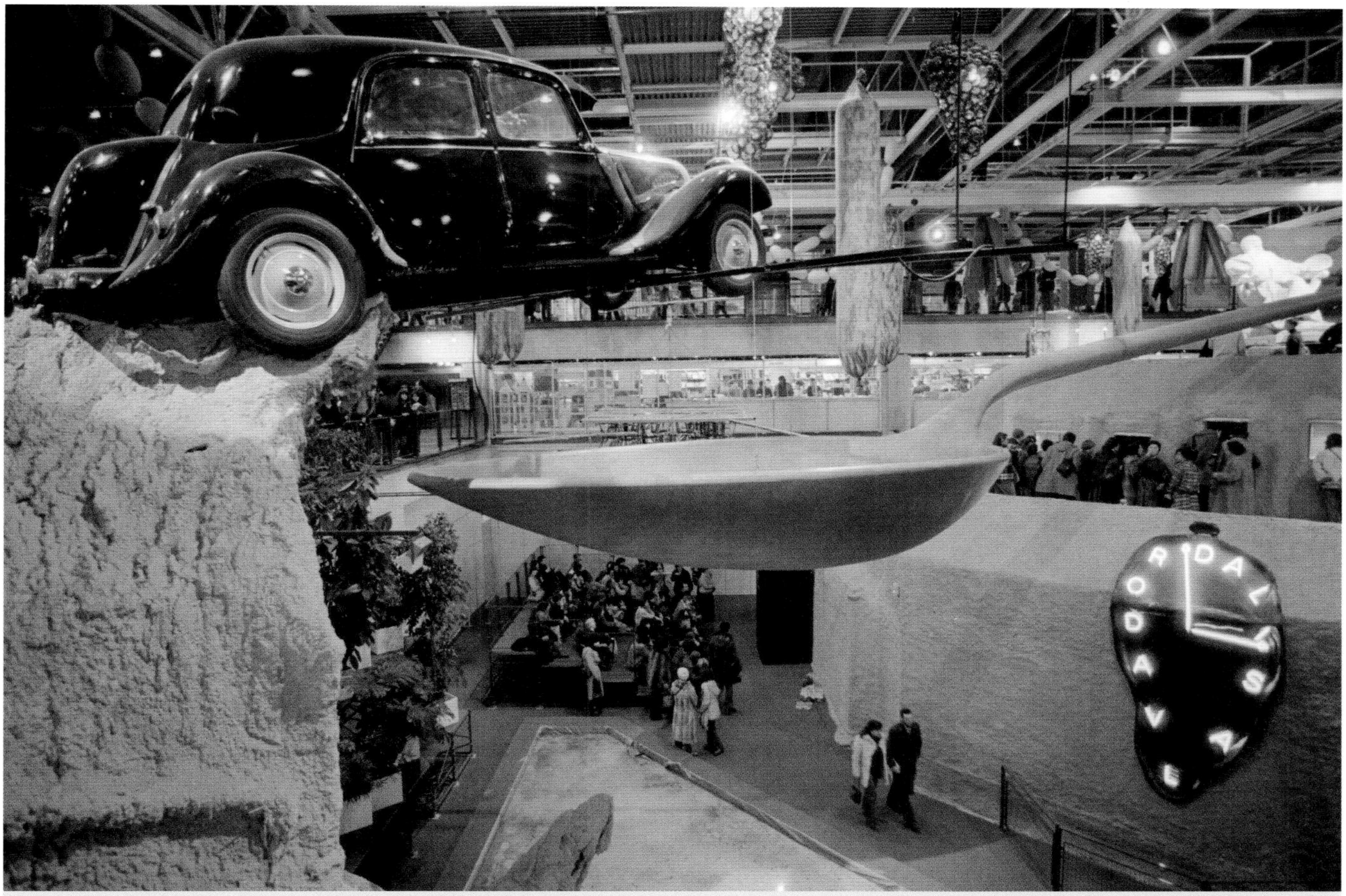

"Dalí, the Heroic Kermis," Forum, level -1 and level 6 / 19 December 1979-20 April 1980.

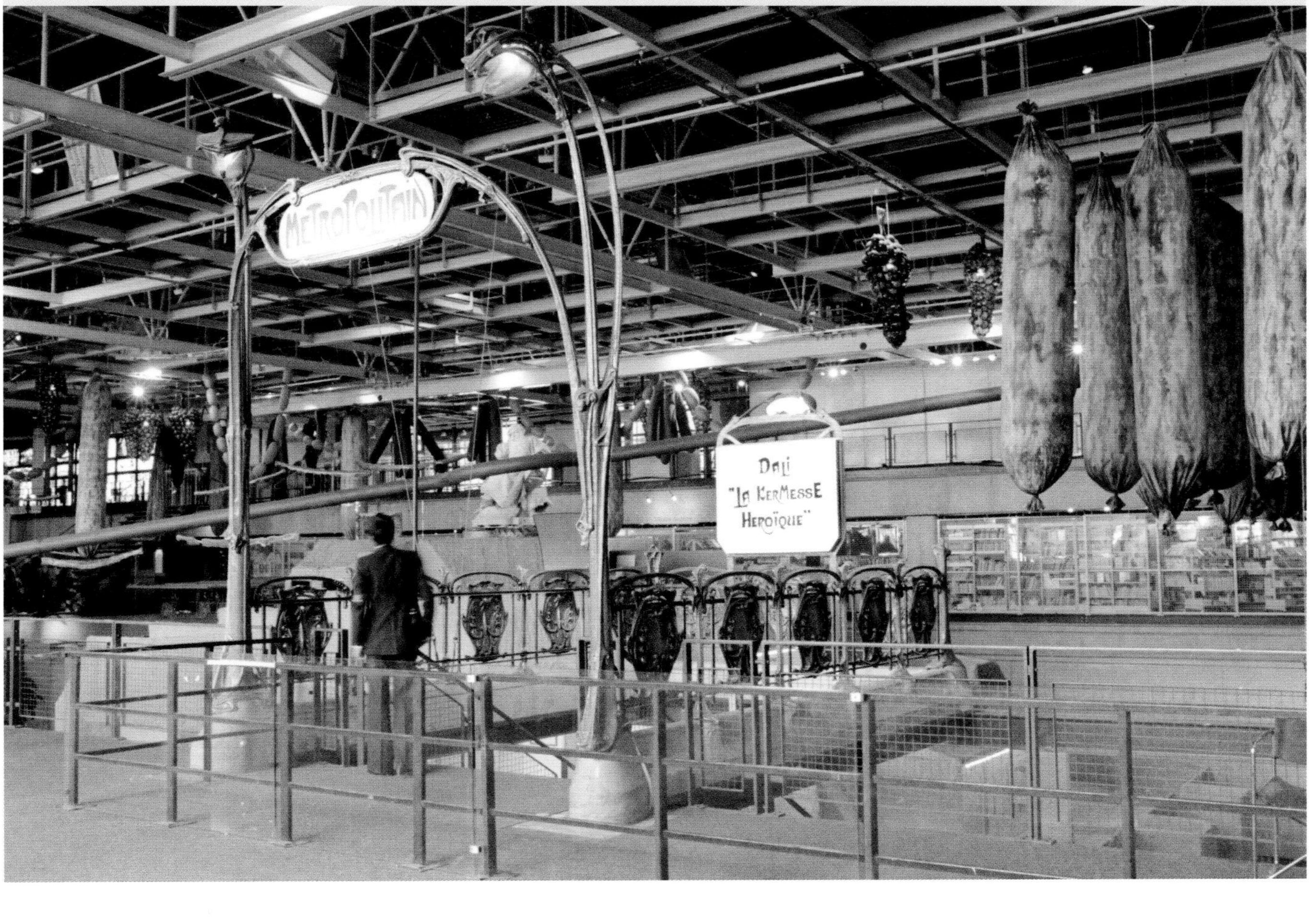

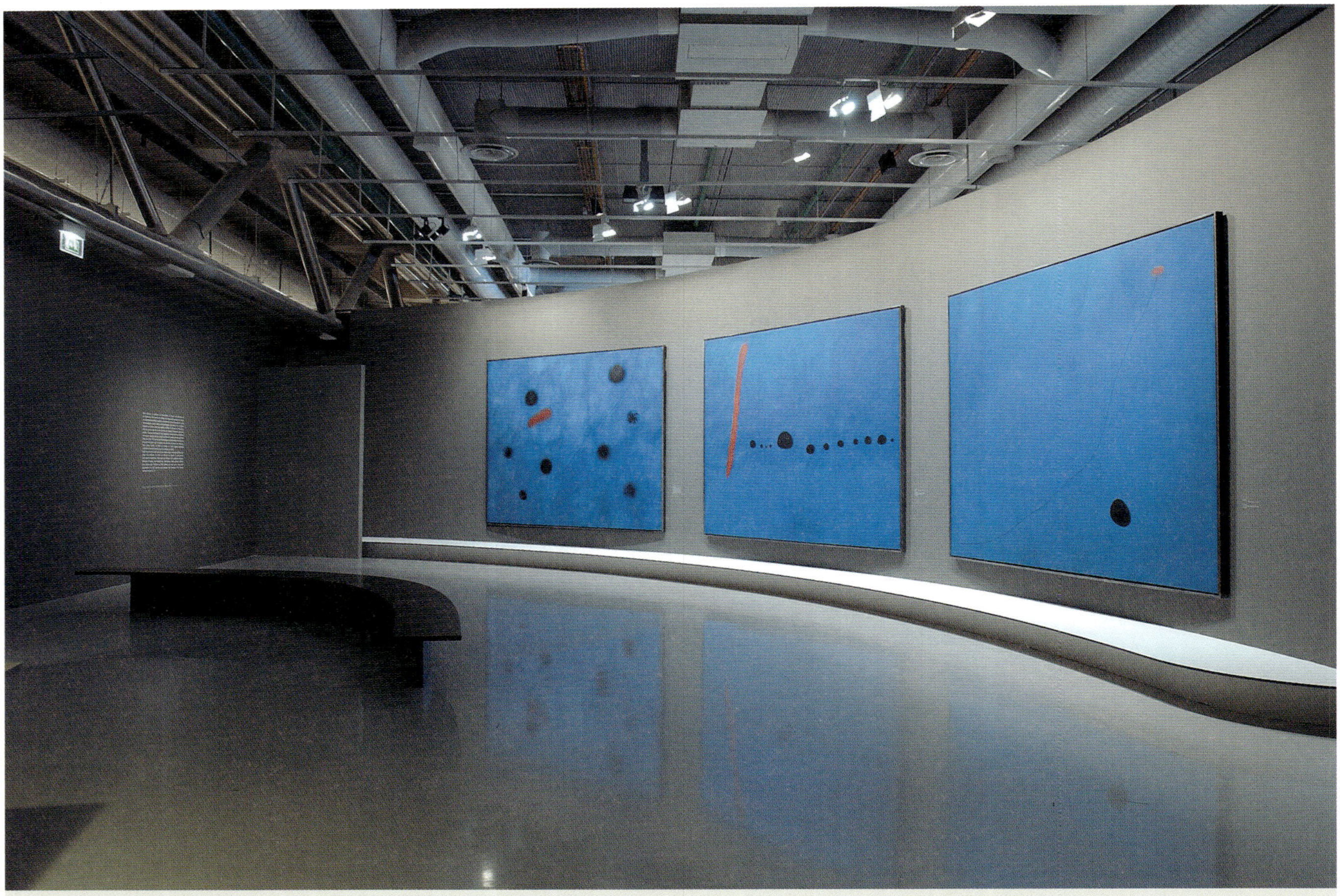

"Joan Miró, 1917-1934. The Birth of the World," Galerie 1 / 3 March-28 June 2004 (top).
From left to right: *Blue I*, 1961; *Blue II*, 1961; *Blue III*, 1961. "Africa Remix. Contemporary Art of a Continent," Galerie 1 / 25 May-8 August 2005 (bottom).
In the foreground: *Waiting for Bus*, 2003, by Dilomprizulike.

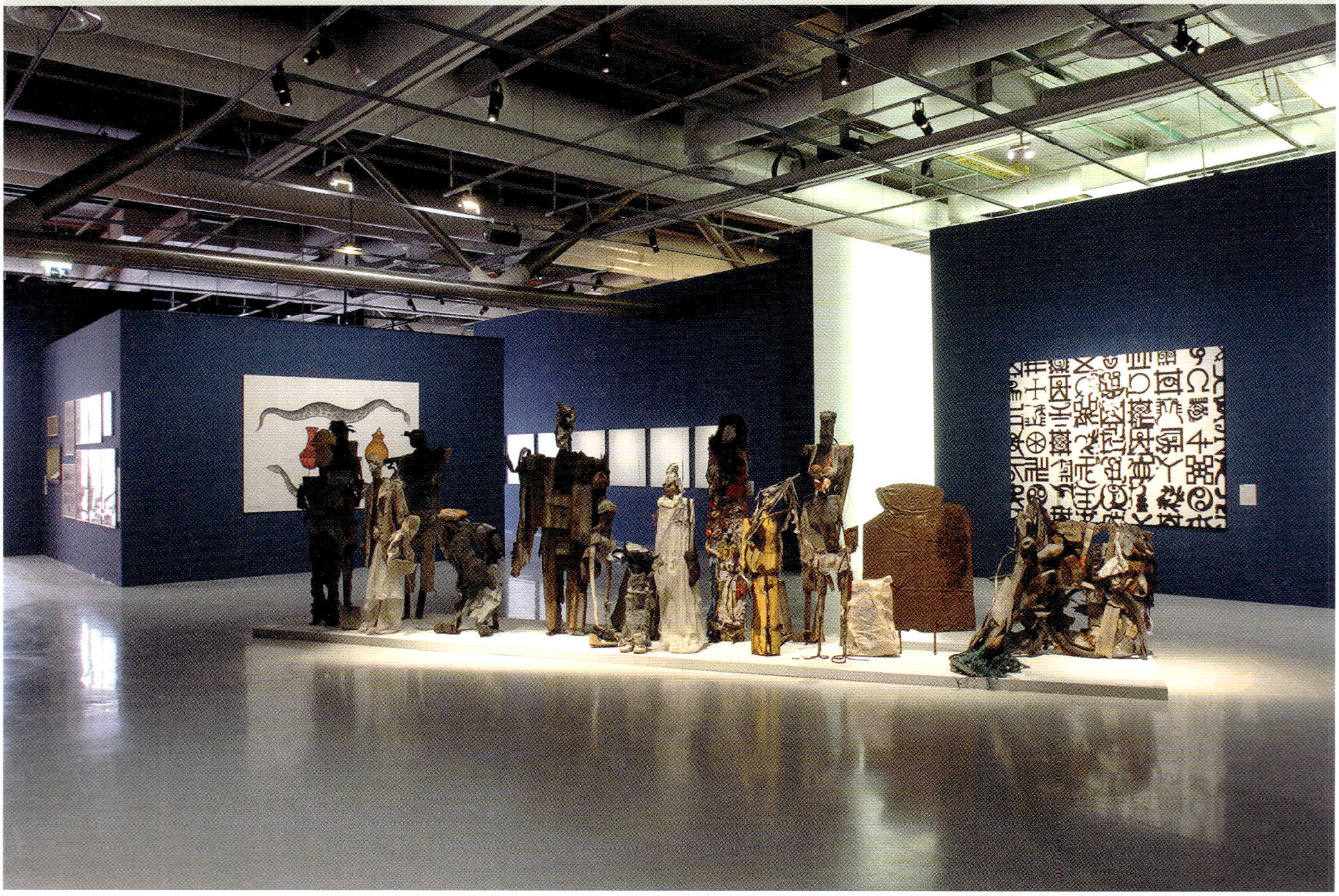

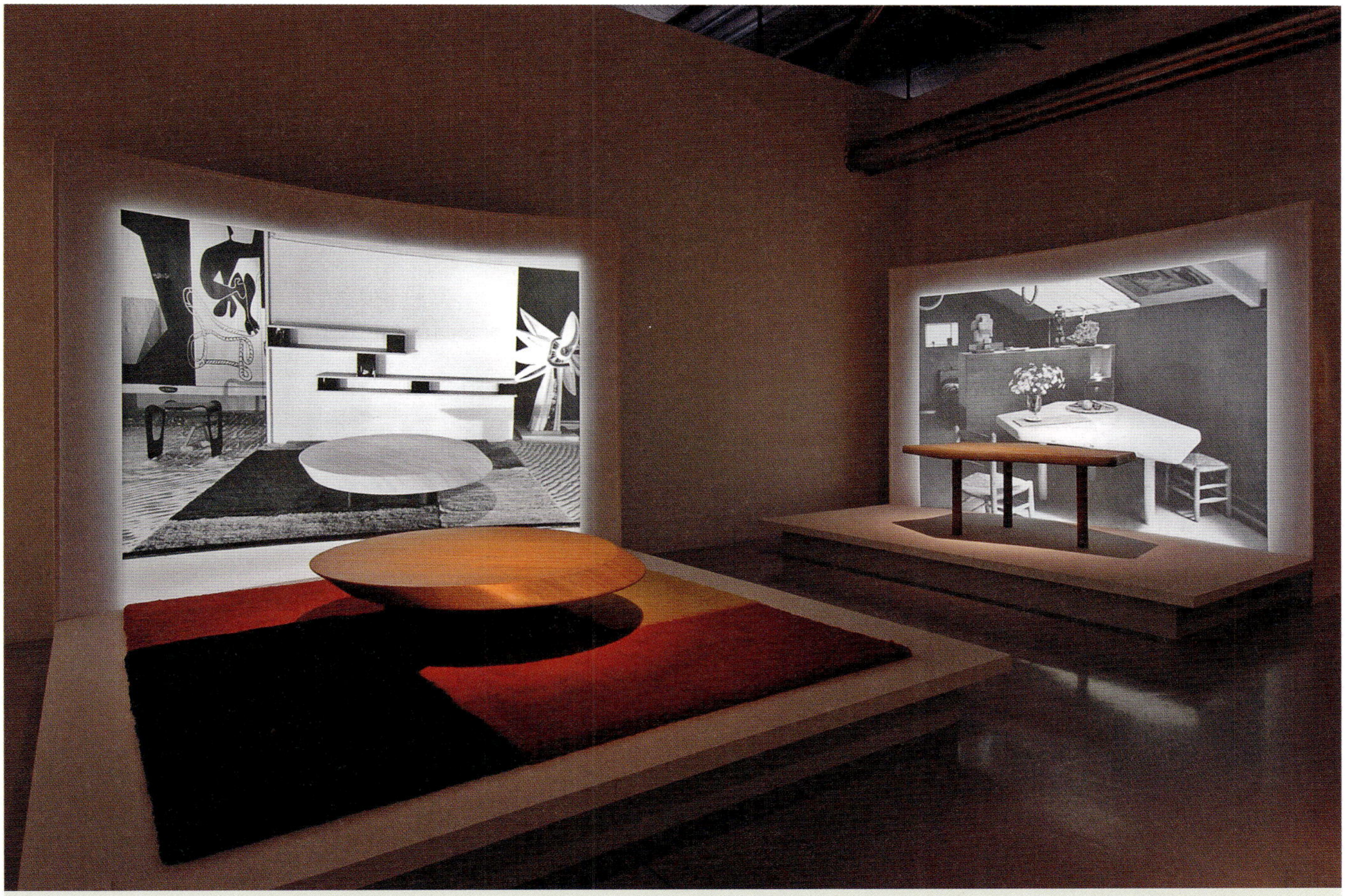

"Charlotte Perriand," Galerie 2 / 7 December 2005-10 April 2006 (top). In the foreground, on the left: *Table tapis*, 1984; on the right: *Table en forme*, 1938.
"Dada," Galerie 1 / 5 October 2005-9 January 2006 (bottom). In the foreground: *Fountain*, 1917-1964, by Marcel Duchamp.

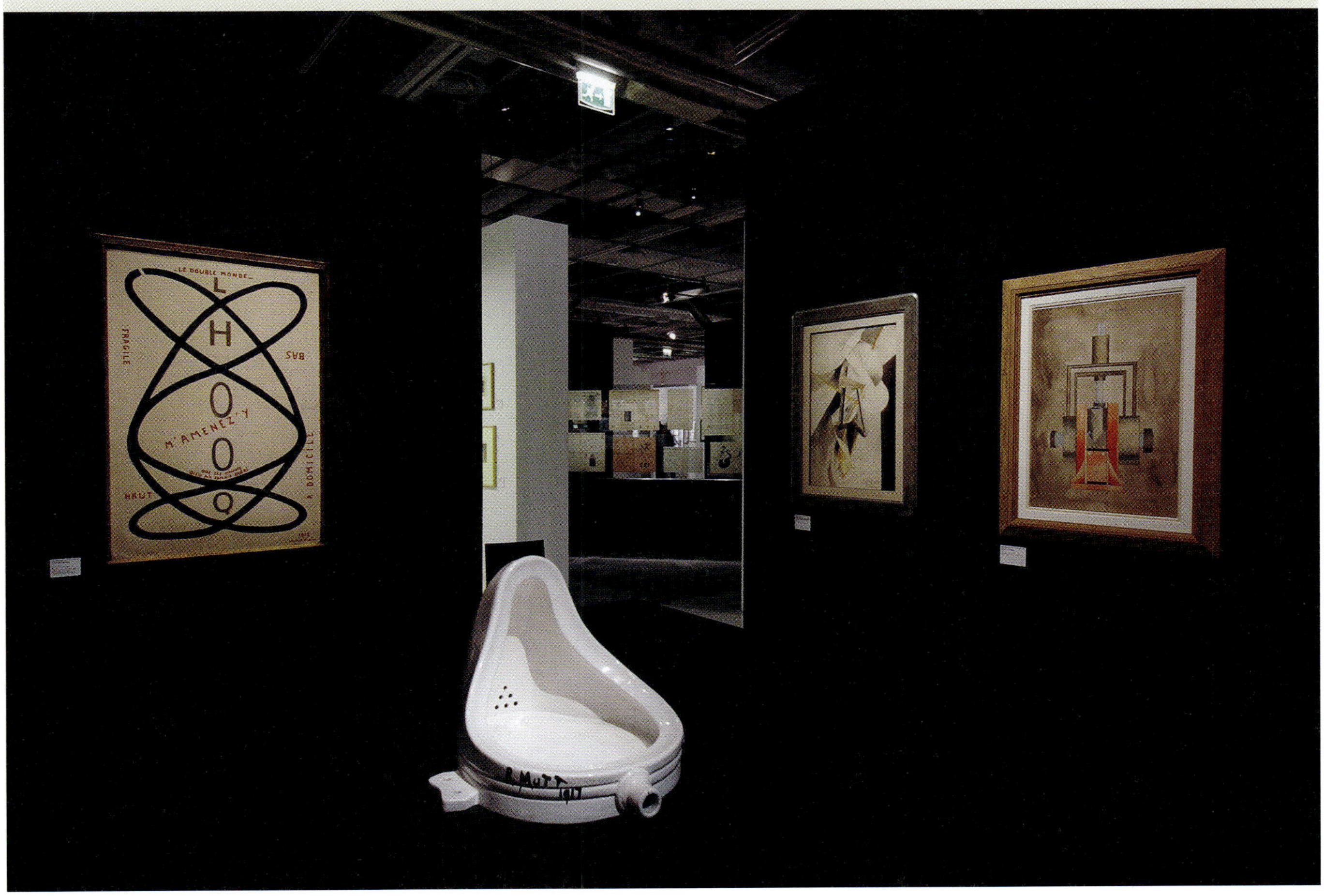

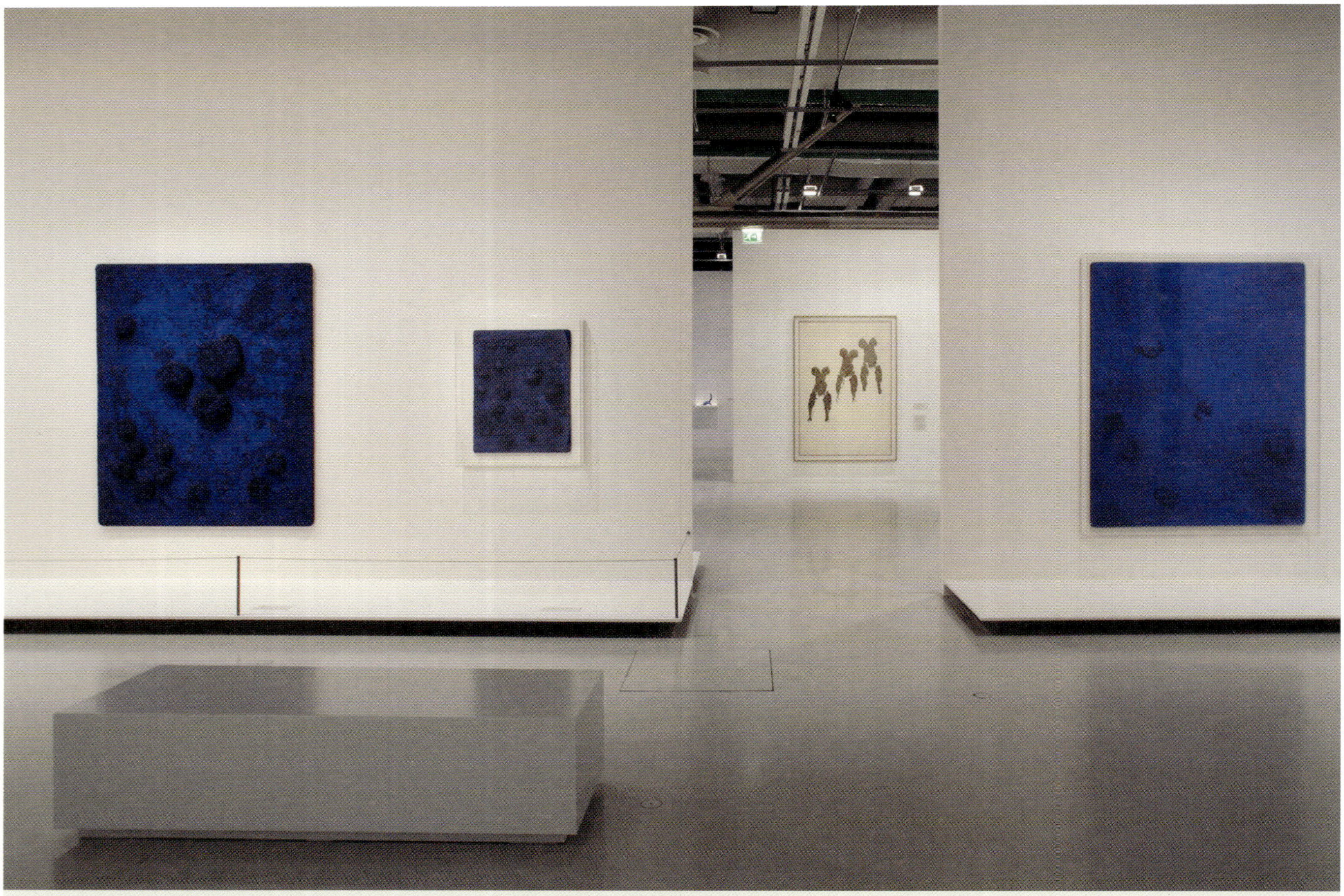

"Yves Klein. Body, colour, Immaterial," Galerie 1 / 5 October 2006-5 February 2007 (top).
Louise Bourgeois, *Passage dangereux (Dangerous Passage)*, 1997, in the exhibition "Louise Bourgeois," Galerie 2 / 5 March-2 June 2008 (bottom).

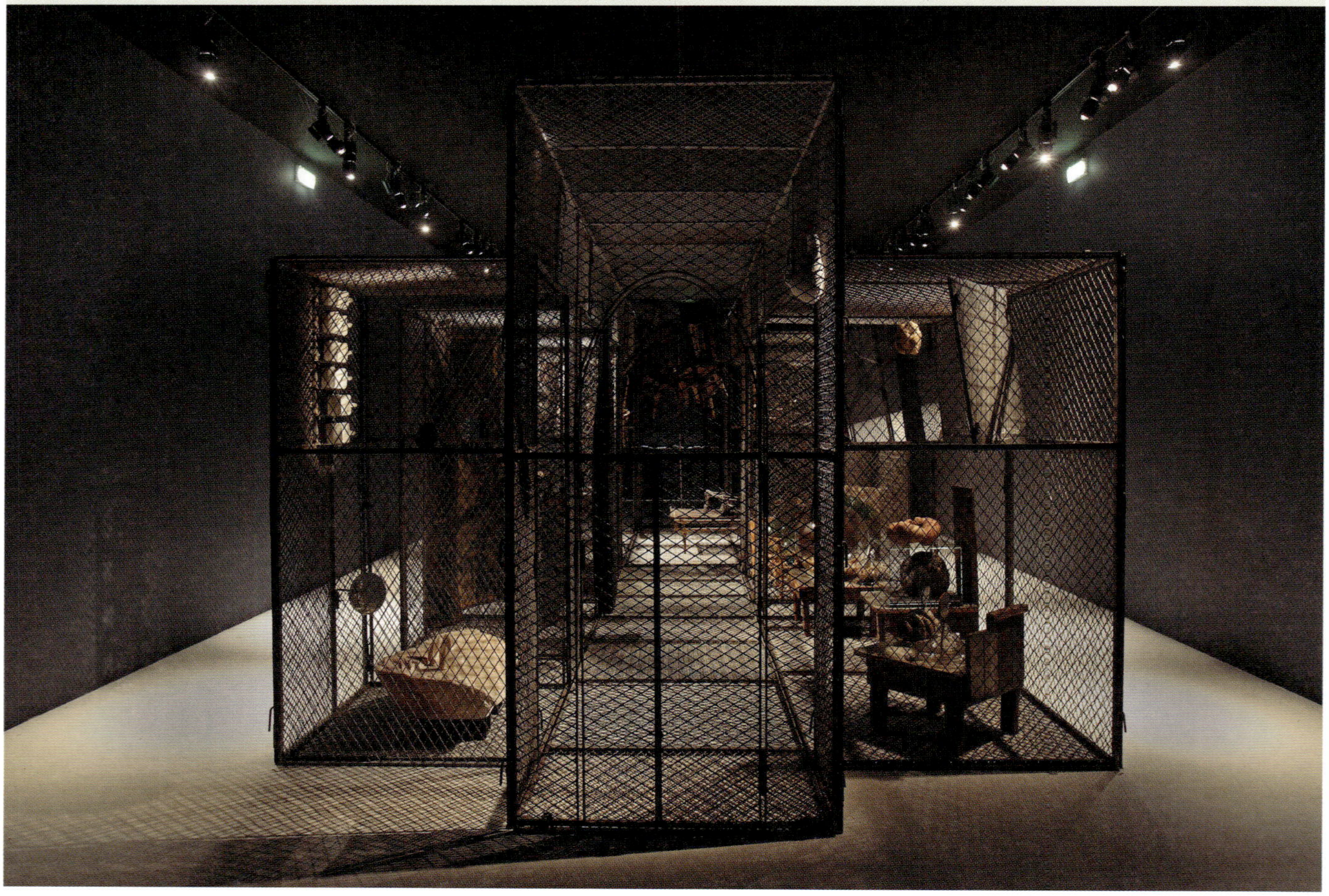

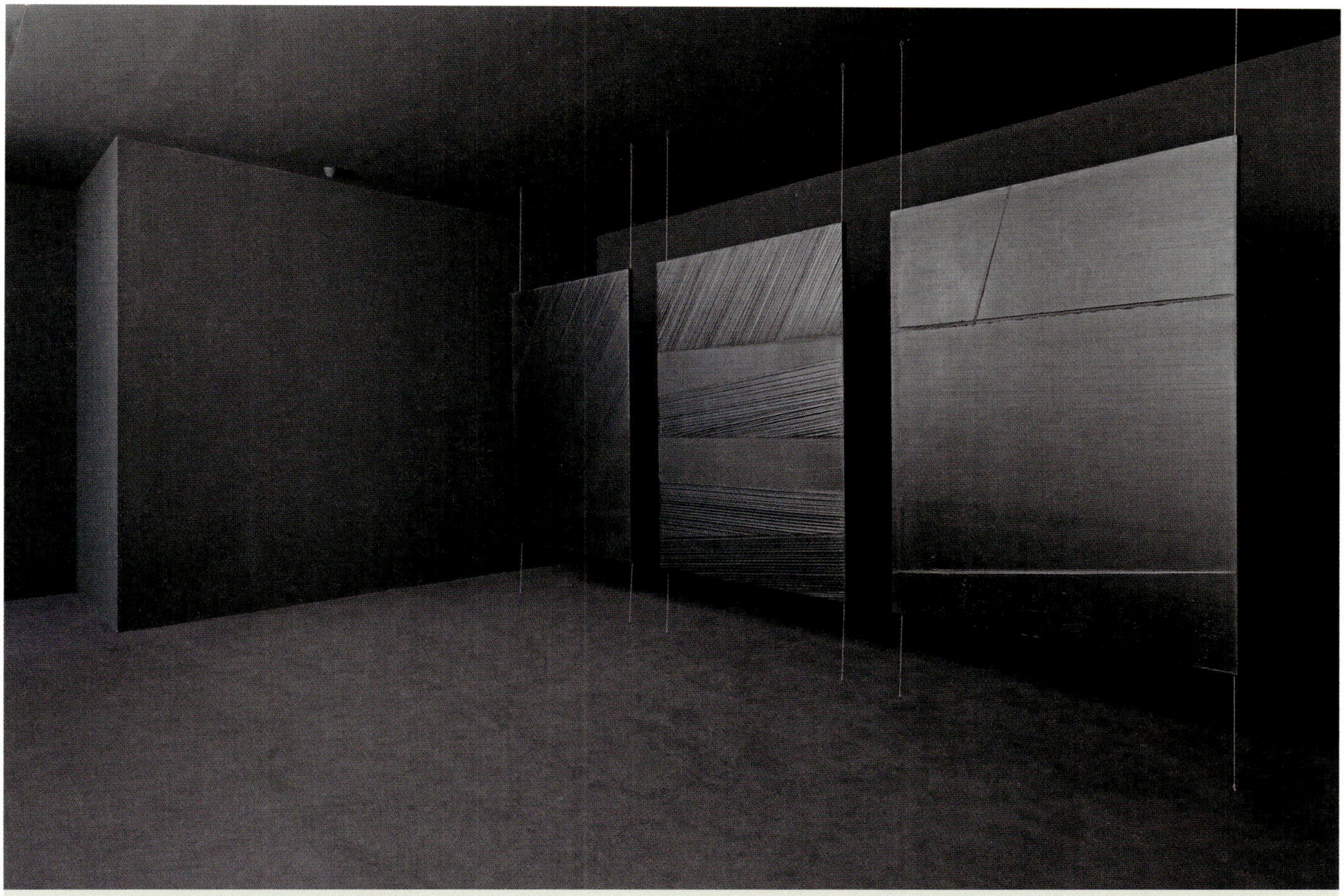

"Soulages," Galerie 1 / 14 October 2009-8 March 2010 (top).
From left to right: *Peinture 222 x 157 cm, 7 February 1991; Peinture 222 x 157 cm, 28 December 1990; Peinture 222 x 157 cm, 19 February 1991.*
"Dreamlands. From Amusement Parks to Cities of Tomorrow," Galerie 1 / 5 May-9 August 2010 (bottom). In the foreground: *Love it! Bite it!*, 2009, by Liu Wei.

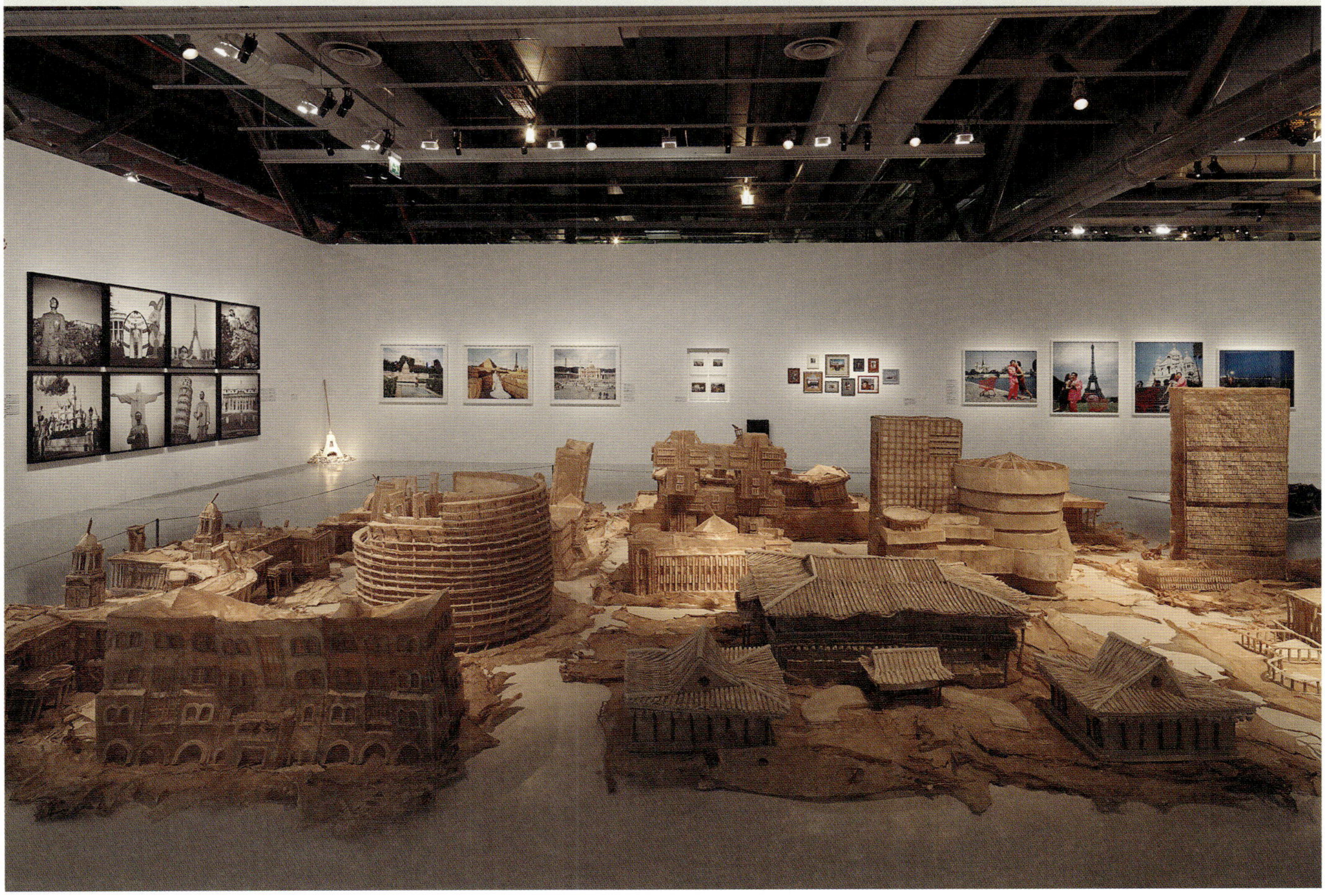

The most beautiful view of Paris

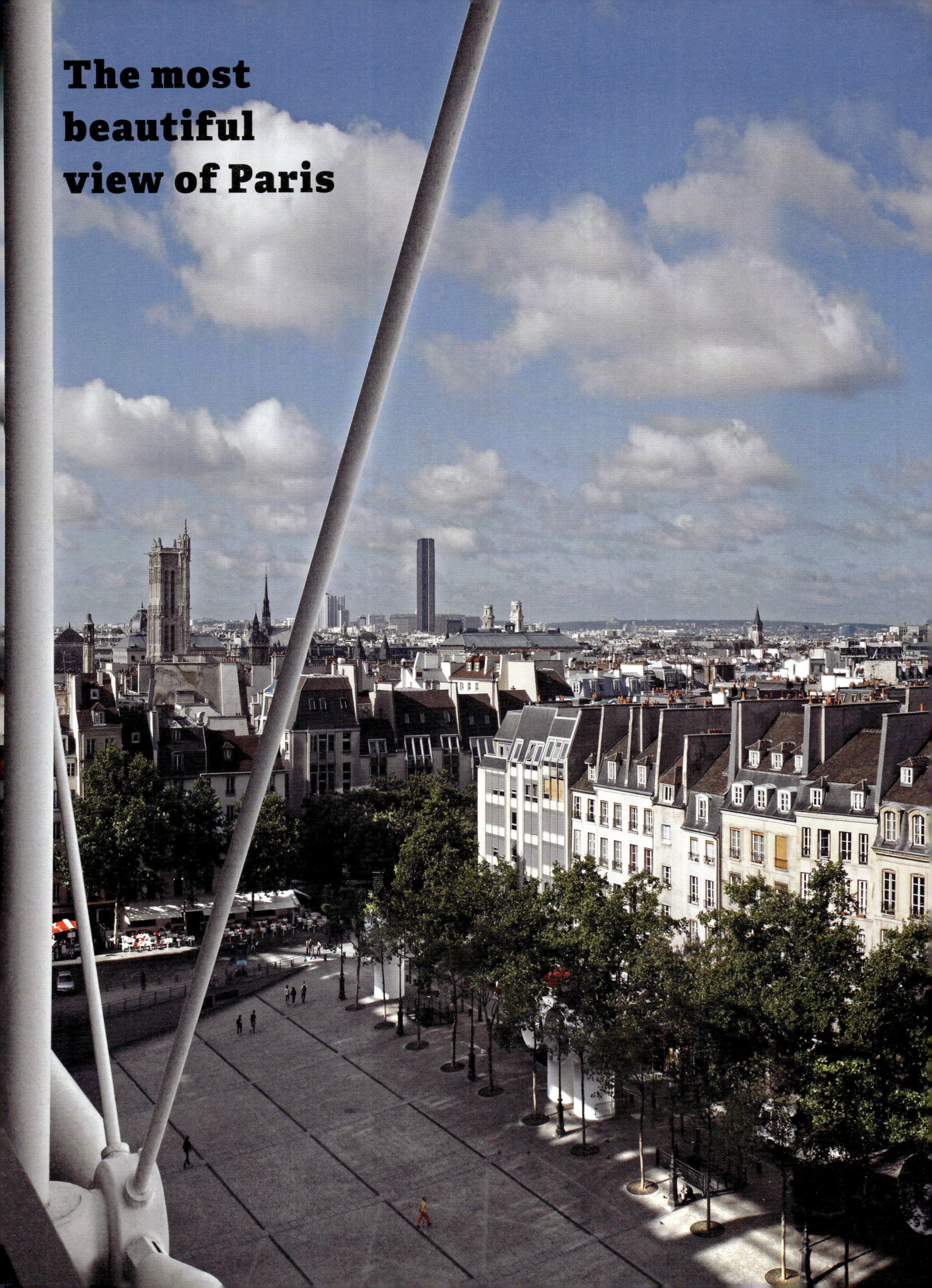

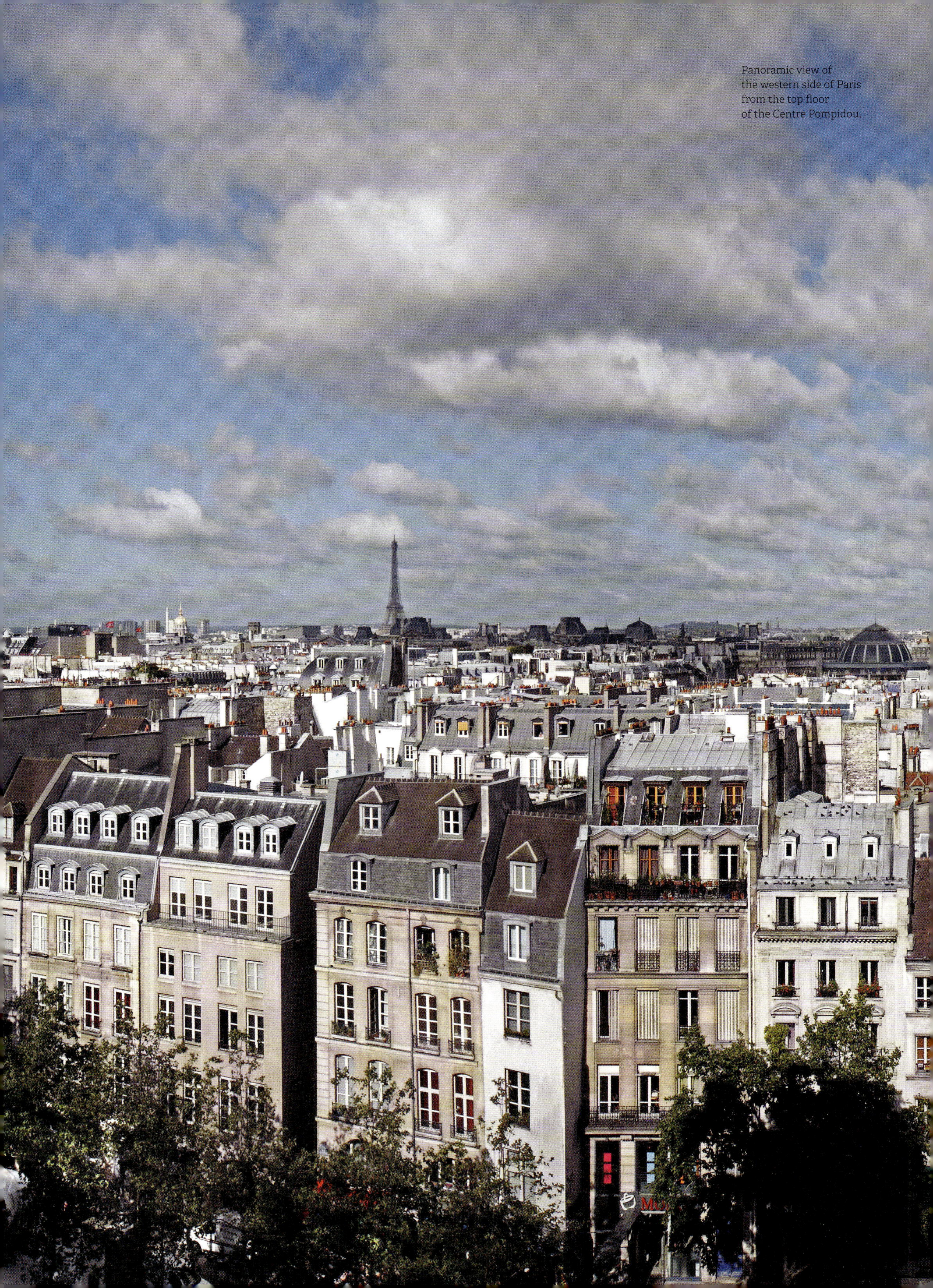

Panoramic view of
the western side of Paris
from the top floor
of the Centre Pompidou.

The "ceiling of Paris"

Most Parisian buildings were built during the 19th century, in compliance with the regulations of Baron Haussmann. One of the constraints governing their construction was a height limit: they could not exceed 6 or 7 storeys or a maximum of 20 metres (at the end of the 19th century, construction techniques made it possible to erect the first skyscrapers). This limit is still in force today, with the authorised maximum height in the districts at the centre of Paris set at 25 metres. It can only be exceeded for exceptional buildings, such as the Centre Pompidou. This standard created what is referred to as the "ceiling of Paris." Seen from above, it seems as though a sea of zinc covers the city. Only a few important monuments pierce this ceiling:

Eiffel Tower: 300 metres (excluding its antennae)
Montparnasse Tower: 210 metres
Sacré-Cœur: 83 metres (with the hill of Montmartre, 200 metres)
Pantheon: 83 metres
Saint-Jacques Tower: 52 metres
Arc de Triomphe: 50 metres
Centre Pompidou: 42 metres
Cathedral of Notre-Dame: 35 metres
Church of Saint-Eustache: 35 metres

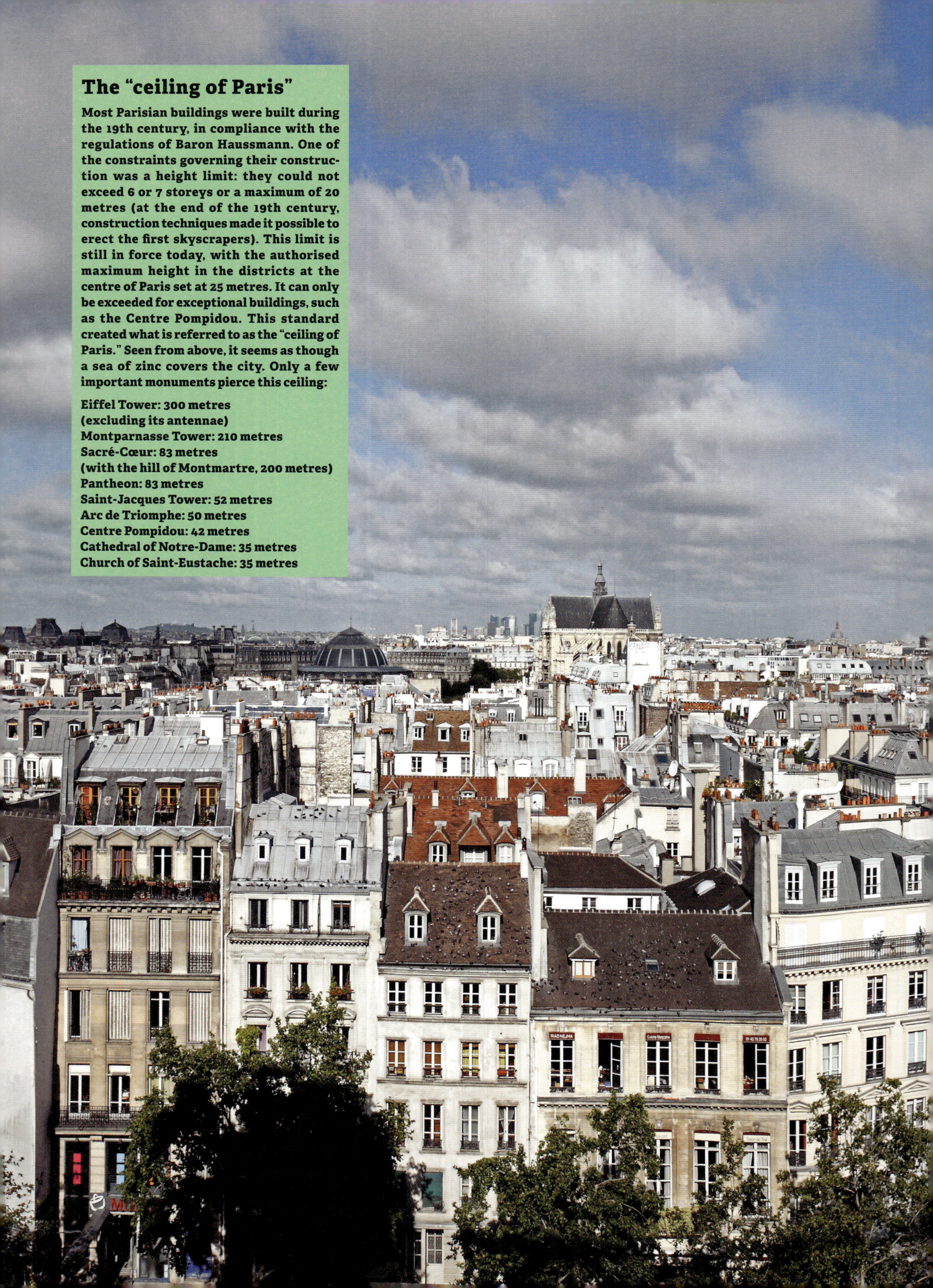

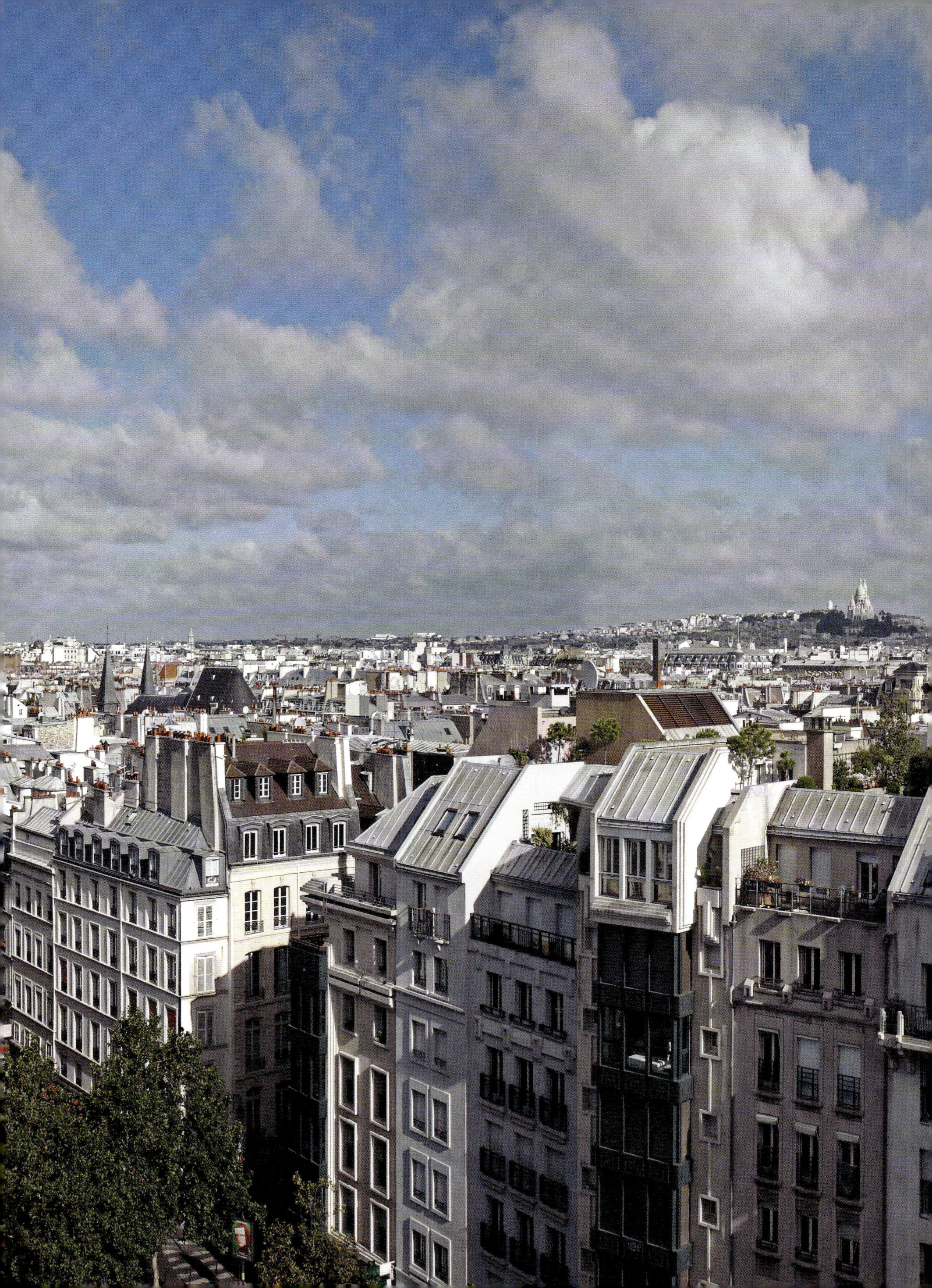

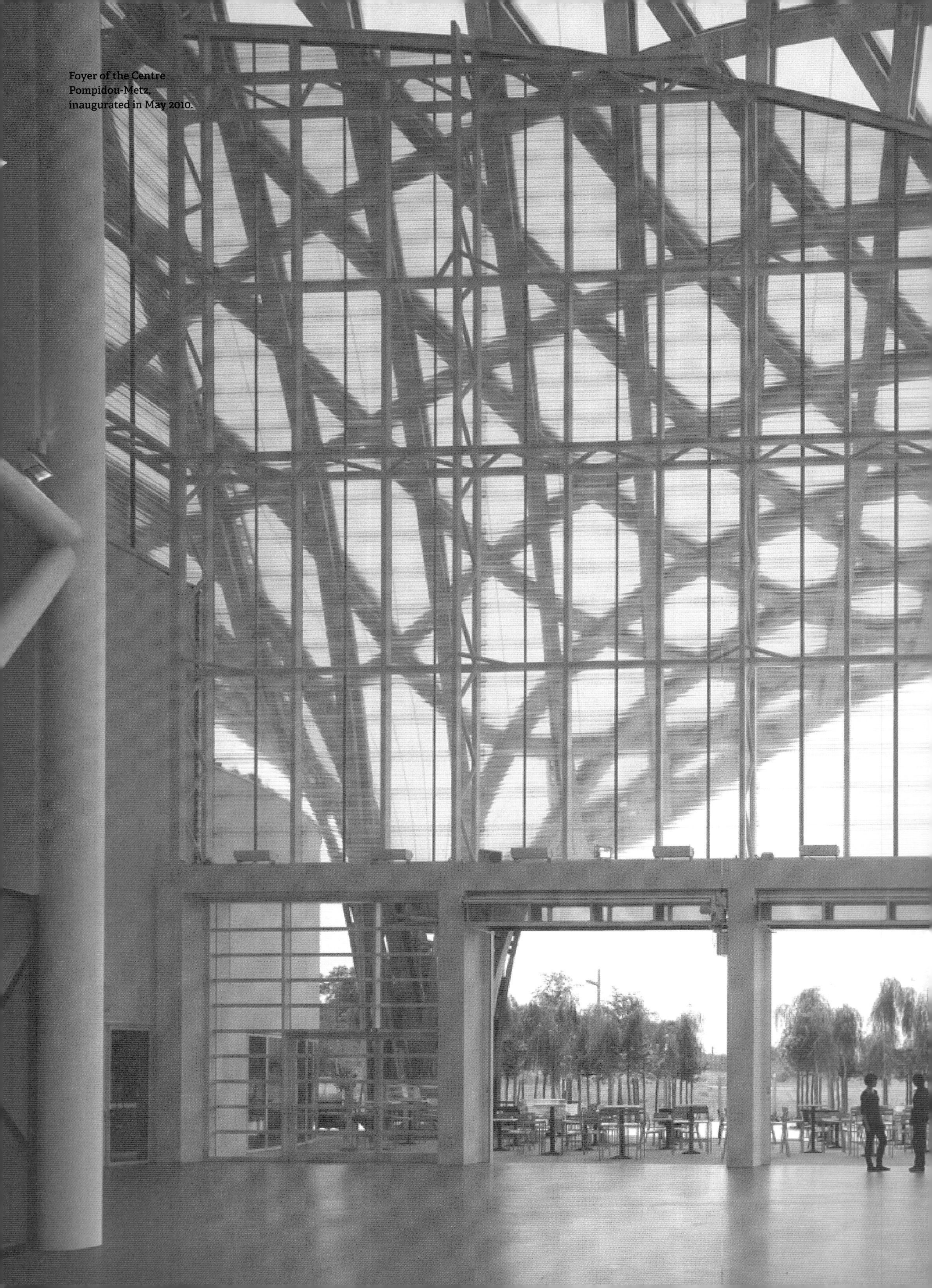

Foyer of the Centre
Pompidou-Metz,
inaugurated in May 2010.

the other Centres Pompidou

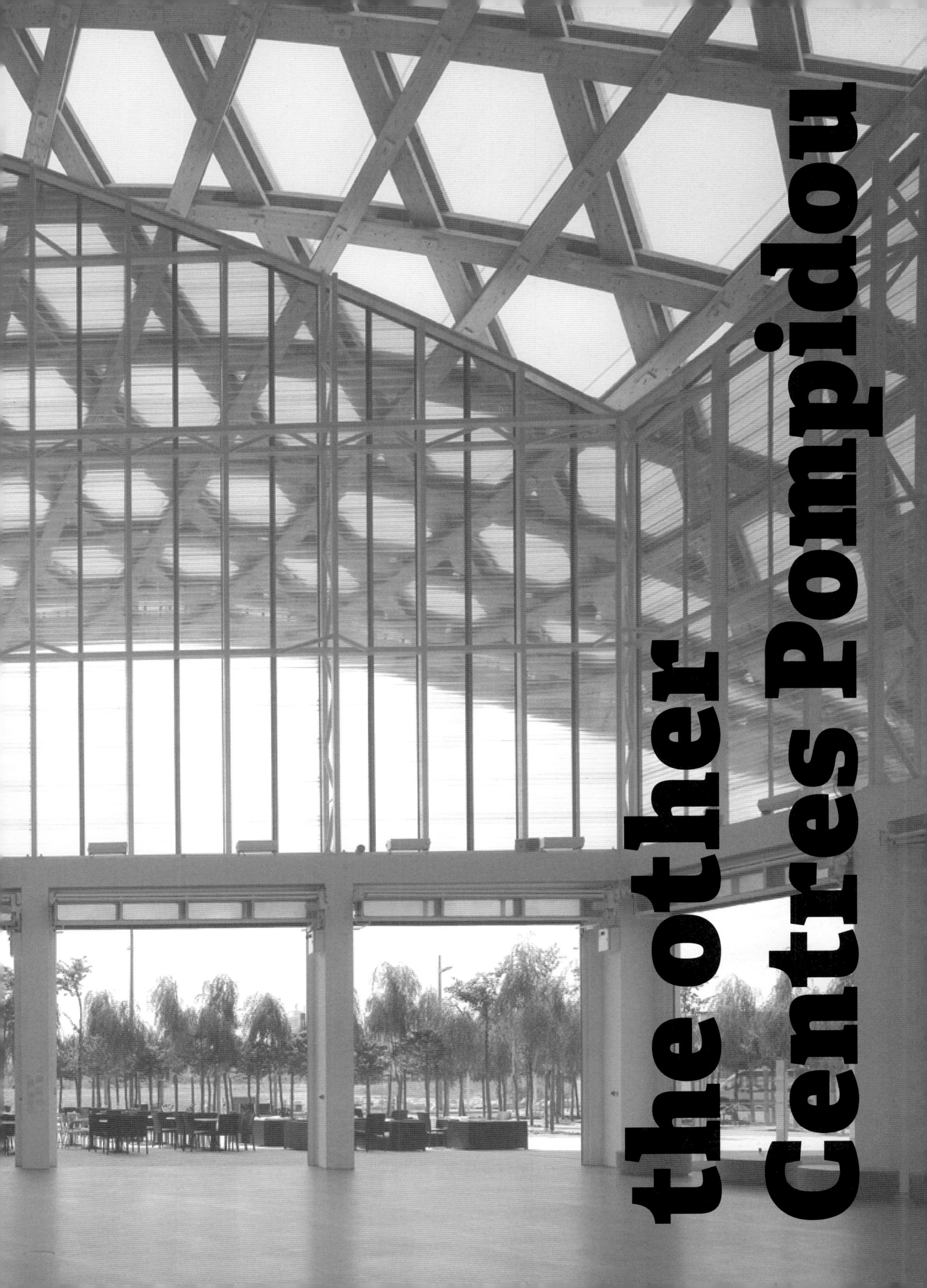

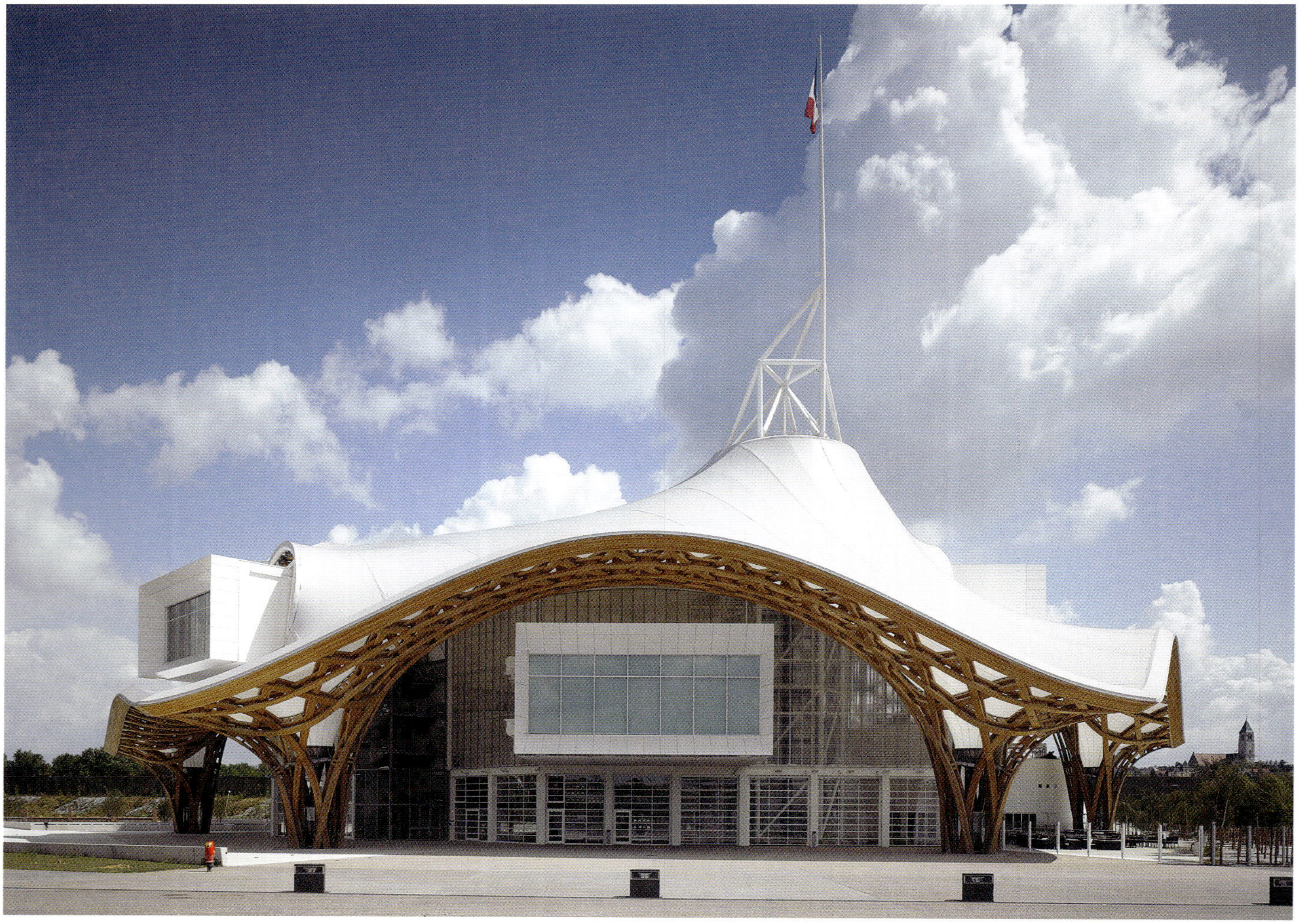

Exterior view of the Centre Pompidou-Metz, designed by architects Shigeru Ban and Jean de Gastines.

The Centre Pompidou-Metz

Sister institution to the Centre Pompidou in Paris, the Centre Pompidou-Metz is the first example of the decentralisation of a national public cultural institution. Like its older Parisian sibling, it is an innovative cross between a museum and an art centre financed by regional authorities. As it does not possess its own collections, it draws from the 65,000 works in the collections of the Centre Pompidou and invites living artists to offer to the public constantly renewed opportunities to encounter modern and contemporary creation.

Gazing at the Centre Pompidou-Metz one perceives how it subtly evokes the filiations tying it to the Parisian Centre, through its plaza, replicating in surface area and incline the Beaubourg Piazza, and its central steeple, rising to a height of 77 metres and echoing the inauguration date of the Centre Pompidou in 1977. The Museum's interior is flooded with light that enters from large-plate glass windows, filters through the fibreglass and teflon membrane stretched over the building's blond wood framework – designed as a hexagonal Chinese hat measuring 90 metres in width – and bounces off the walls and structures painted in white. Architects Shigeru Ban and Jean de Gastines' tour de force is confirmed. Under a roof resembling a "big handkerchief placed over the volumes," according to Jean de Gastines, the Forum opens onto the Great Nave, the largest exhibition space. Its ceiling height – reaching

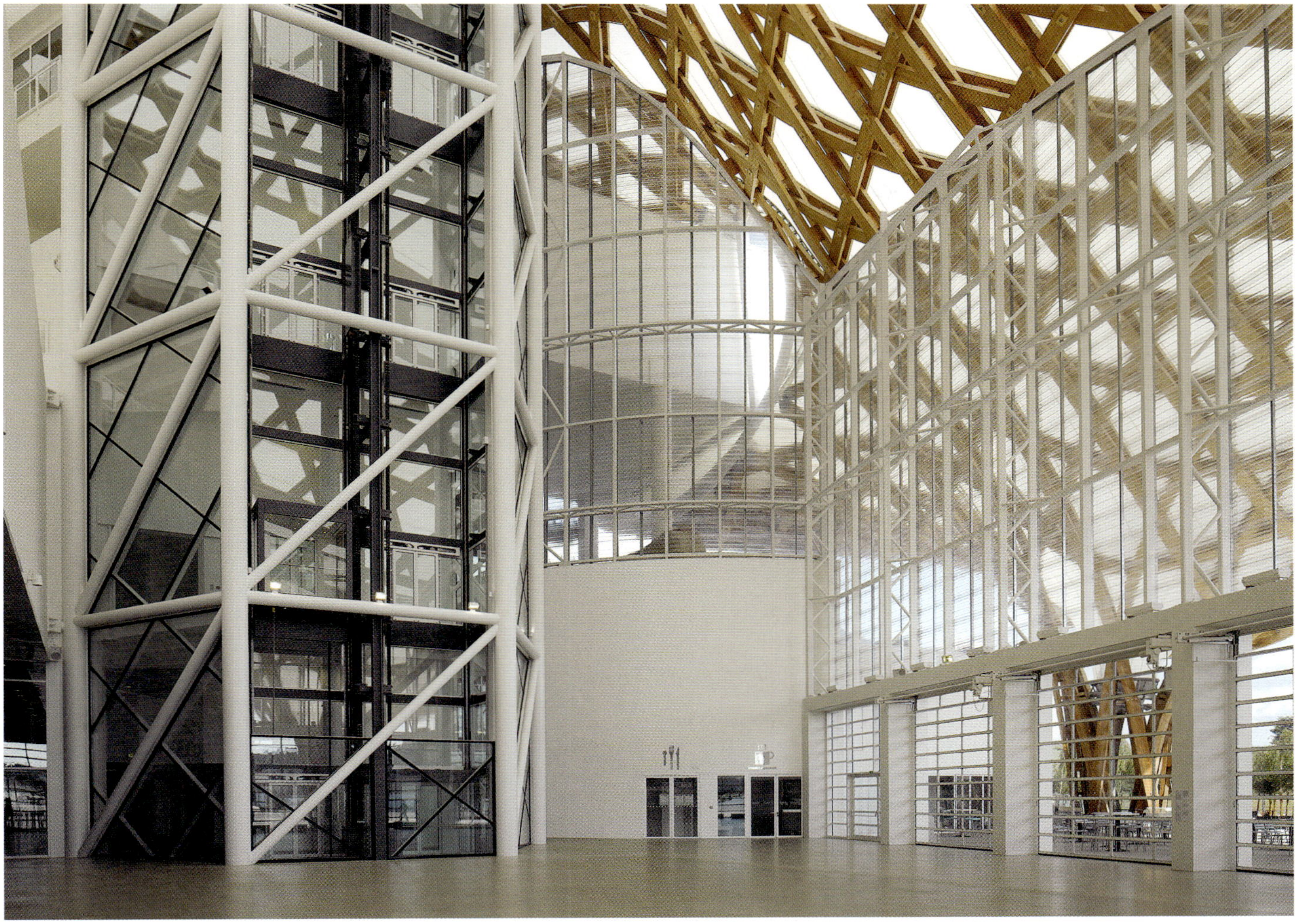

The reception area at the Centre Pompidou-Metz opens onto the three levels of the museum.

a height of 21 metres, is the highest exhibition space in Europe, just behind the Turbine Hall of the Tate Modern – and makes it possible to hang such monumental works as Pablo Picasso's *Parade* stage curtain or Robert Delaunay's large format paintings. Three galleries, in the shape of square concrete tubes, free of interior supporting pillars, overlap and intersect. Their glass extremities jutting out beyond the roof are oriented to offer "picture perfect" vantage points of the city, and notably the Cathedral of Metz.

Innovative programming

A place in perpetual motion where events unfold one after the other, the Centre Pompidou-Metz hosts three to four exhibitions per year, whose rhythm and scope vary according to the subjects and the spaces. Major thematic exhibitions on the history of art since 1905 intersect with evolving exhibitions where visitors discover several shows on the same theme, subject or artist. Monographic shows are dedicated to major figures rarely exhibited in such breadth in France, as well as emerging artists enjoying the advantages of such an exhibition space for the first time. Enhancing these exhibitions and in the spirit of the Centre Pompidou model, the Centre Pompidou-Metz proposes regular multi-disciplinary programming in various spaces – Wendel Auditorium, Studio, Forum and gardens – and, owing to a lack of an acquisition policy, develops a policy of art production and support for creation.

Key project dates

January 2003:
decision to locate the project in Metz

March 2003:
launch of the international architecture competition

15 December 2003:
the project by Shigeru Ban (Tokyo), Jean de Gastines (Paris) and Philip Gumuchdjian (London) wins the competition

November 2006:
the first foundation stone laid by Mrs. Georges Pompidou

2006-2009:
construction work on the Centre Pompidou-Metz

31 December 2009:
creation of the Public Institution for Cultural Cooperation

12 May 2010:
opening to the public

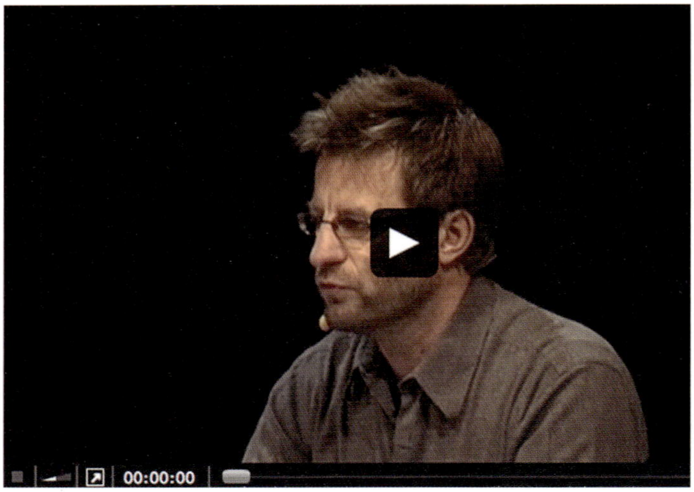

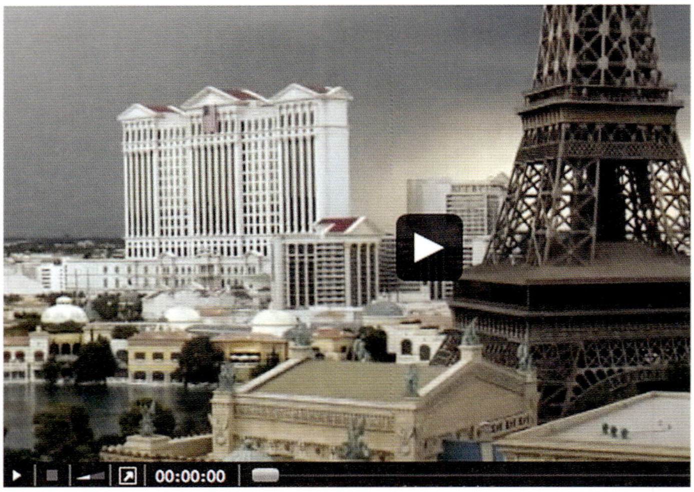

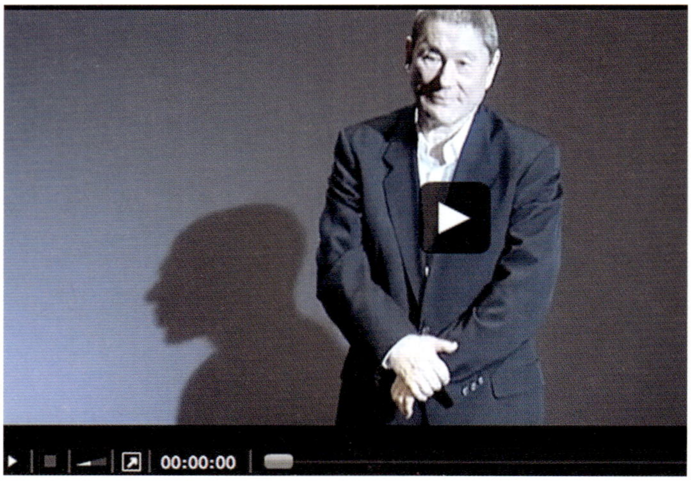

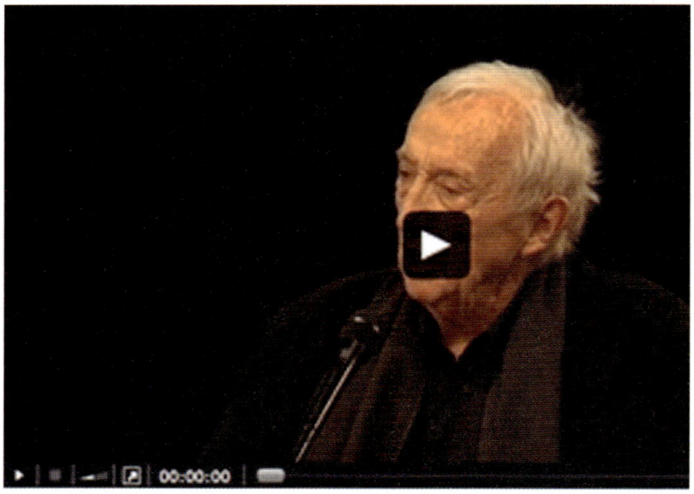

A few of the videos available on the site of the virtual Centre Pompidou (from top to bottom and left to right): Jean-Yves Jouannais, 20 May 2010, 18th conference-performance of his *Encyclopédie des guerres;* Takeshi Kitano, encounter led by Jean-Pierre Limosin, 11 March 2010, on the occasion of the inauguration of the "Takeshi Kitano, the iconoclast" retrospective, (2010); "Dreamlands. From Amusement Parks to Cities of Tomorrow" film on the exhibition (2010); Pierre Soulages colloquium, second day, last part, 22 January 2010.

The virtual Centre Pompidou

The Centre Pompidou, breaking with established models for a cultural institution's presence on the Internet, imagined a virtual Centre Pompidou. The approach is resolutely open to and focused on digital cultural content to create a new platform for its dissemination, which implies rethinking the production and the organisation of this content, and developing new tools that other cultural institutions can freely utilise and integrate.

Three main priorities are driving this vision of the future, all inspired by the identity of the Centre Pompidou. The first consists of making the virtual Centre Pompidou a reference in the domains of modern and contemporary creation, and for sharing contemporary ideas, by making available online digital resources linked to the Centre's collections, programming, production and architecture. The second touches on the website's openness and multi-disciplinary approach, because the virtual Centre Pompidou aims to be a convivial space where regular visitors of the Centre Pompidou and French and foreign Web users who have never even set foot there feel welcome. The third is the one of movement, which enables the Centre to stay abreast of the times and contemporary creation and anticipate new developments concerning the Web. The website is no longer mainly about targeting potential visitors to the physical institution. They can still find all the tools they need on the site to plan and enrich their visit. The aim is more about reaching a much wider public by means of the digital resources made available online. These include, notably: the digitised collection of the Musée National d'Art Moderne, the events database of the Centre Pompidou, digitised descriptions of the content of the collections in the Public Information Library and the Kandinsky Library, video resources, documents related to visits, texts in the galleries, guided visits and teaching packages produced by the Centre.

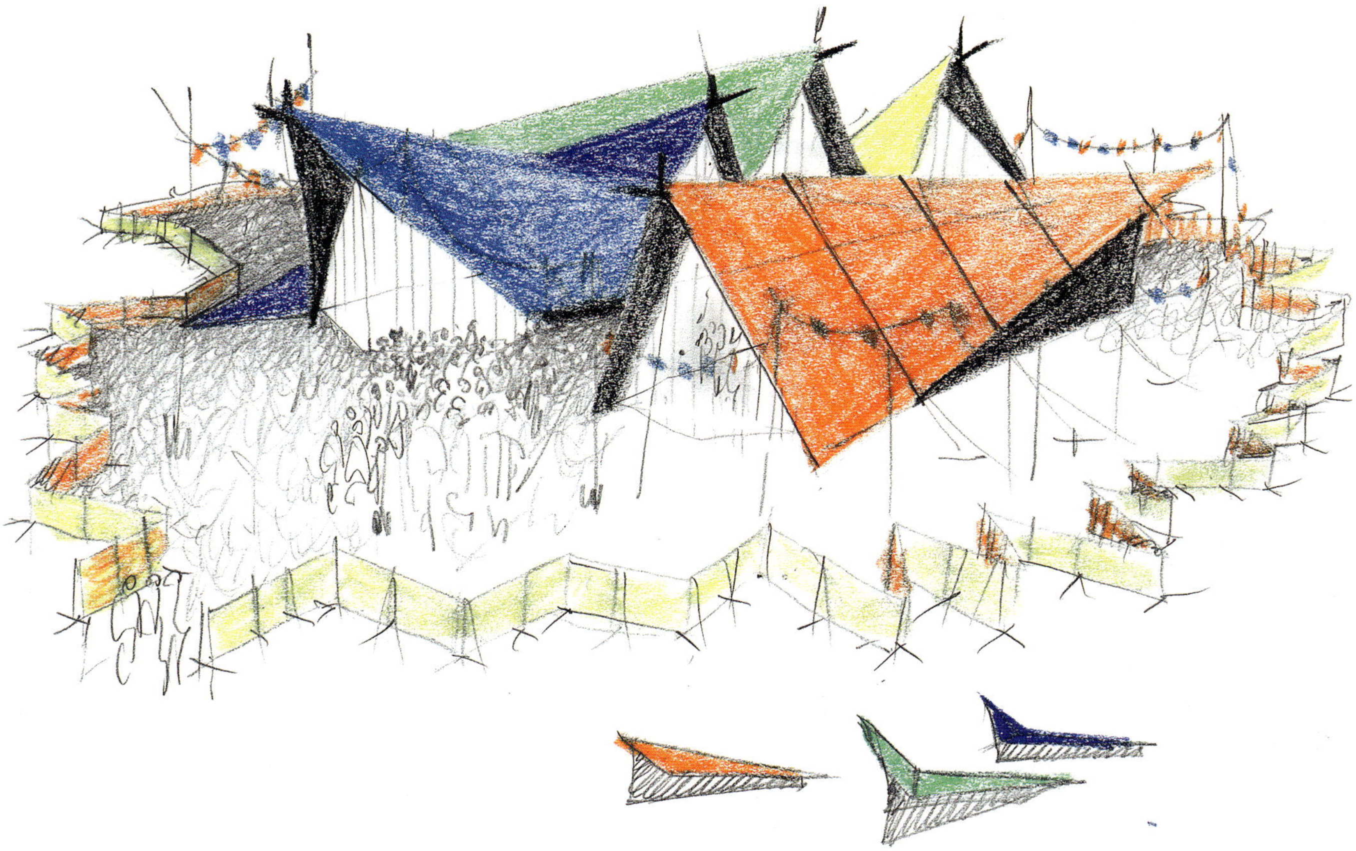

The mobile Centre Pompidou, preparatory drawing by Patrick Bouchain showing its highly colourful modular structure.

The mobile Centre Pompidou

Still faithful to its central mission of reaching out to a wider and more diverse public audience, in October 2011 the Centre Pompidou created the mobile Centre Pompidou, a travelling structure as light, from an architectural point of view, as it is solid with regard to its project of museography, and which moves about to present masterpieces from the Museum's collections outside the walls, like a bit of the Centre that leaves Paris to encounter an as yet unreached public.

Thanks to its modular, easy to disassemble, coloured canvas architecture designed by Patrick Bouchain, a specialist of travelling structures, the mobile Centre Pompidou can settle almost anywhere for a few months – notably in areas barely or poorly served by cultural institutions – thereby offering everyone the experience of discovering these works of art in person, close to home.

With a surface are of 1,000 square metres, the mobile Centre Pompidou presents, free of charge, a thematic show of works from the collection of the MNAM since 1905, organised round some fifteen major works of art. If, from the outside, the mobile Centre Pompidou resembles the cheerful overcoat of a protective harlequin, the interior is decidedly one of a museum.

The works are hung from inside of self-supporting safe-box paint railings, which are independent, air-conditioned, secure and white, like the ones at the Centre Pompidou, and in front of which visitors can settle in to contemplate the works at their leisure.

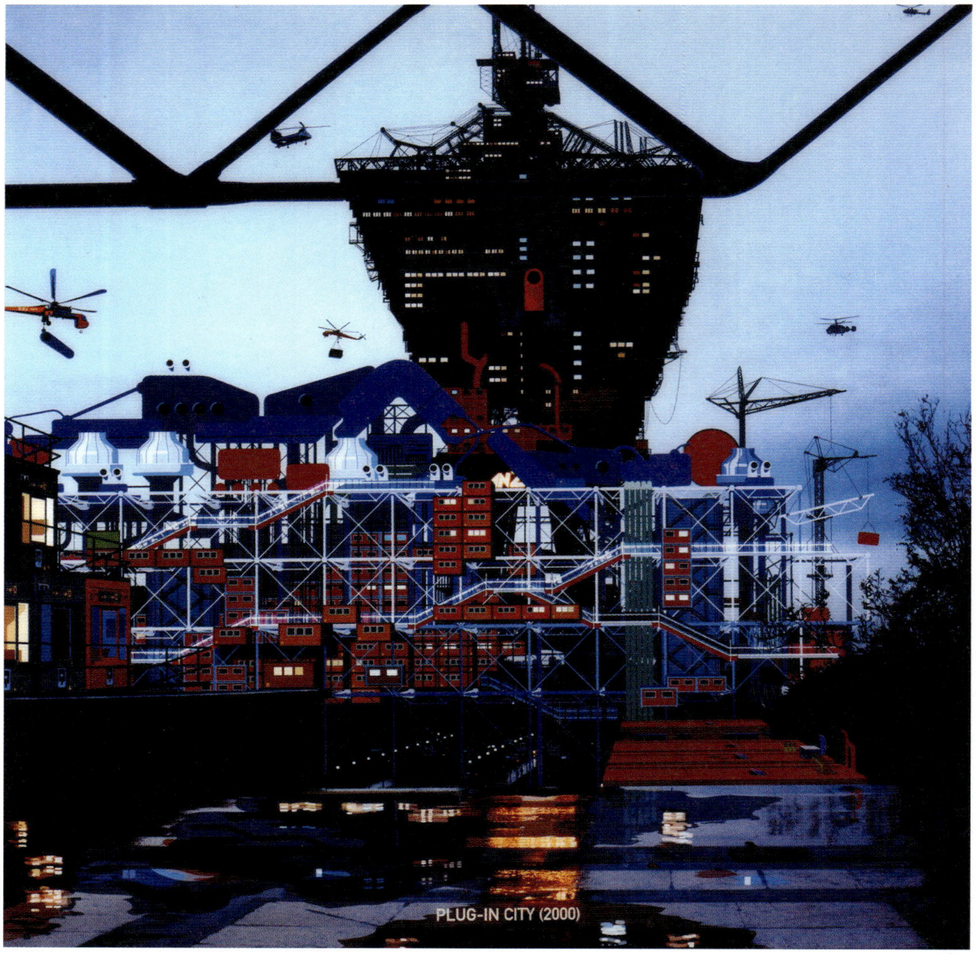

Alain Bublex, *Plug-in City (2000) – Expérience monumentale (Monumental Experience)*, 2003, triptych (detail: 2/3: Eiffel 3), Diasec chromogenic colour print, each photograph: 180 x 180 cm.
Gordon Matta-Clark, *Conical Intersect* (1975), chromogenic print, 99,7 x 105 cm.
François Schuiten and Benoît Peeters, "Les Mystères de Pâhri," in *Les Murailles de Samaris*, 2007 edition, p. 90. © Casterman

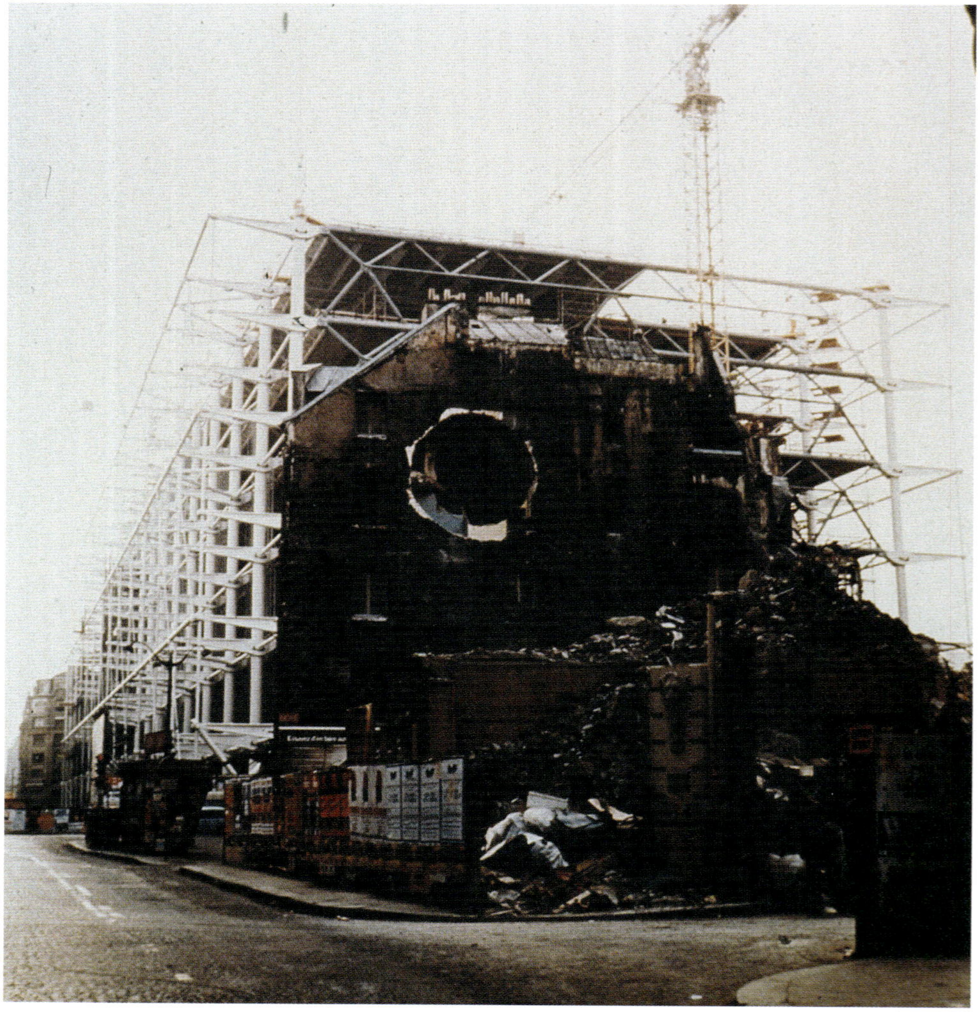

The Centre Pompidou inspires…

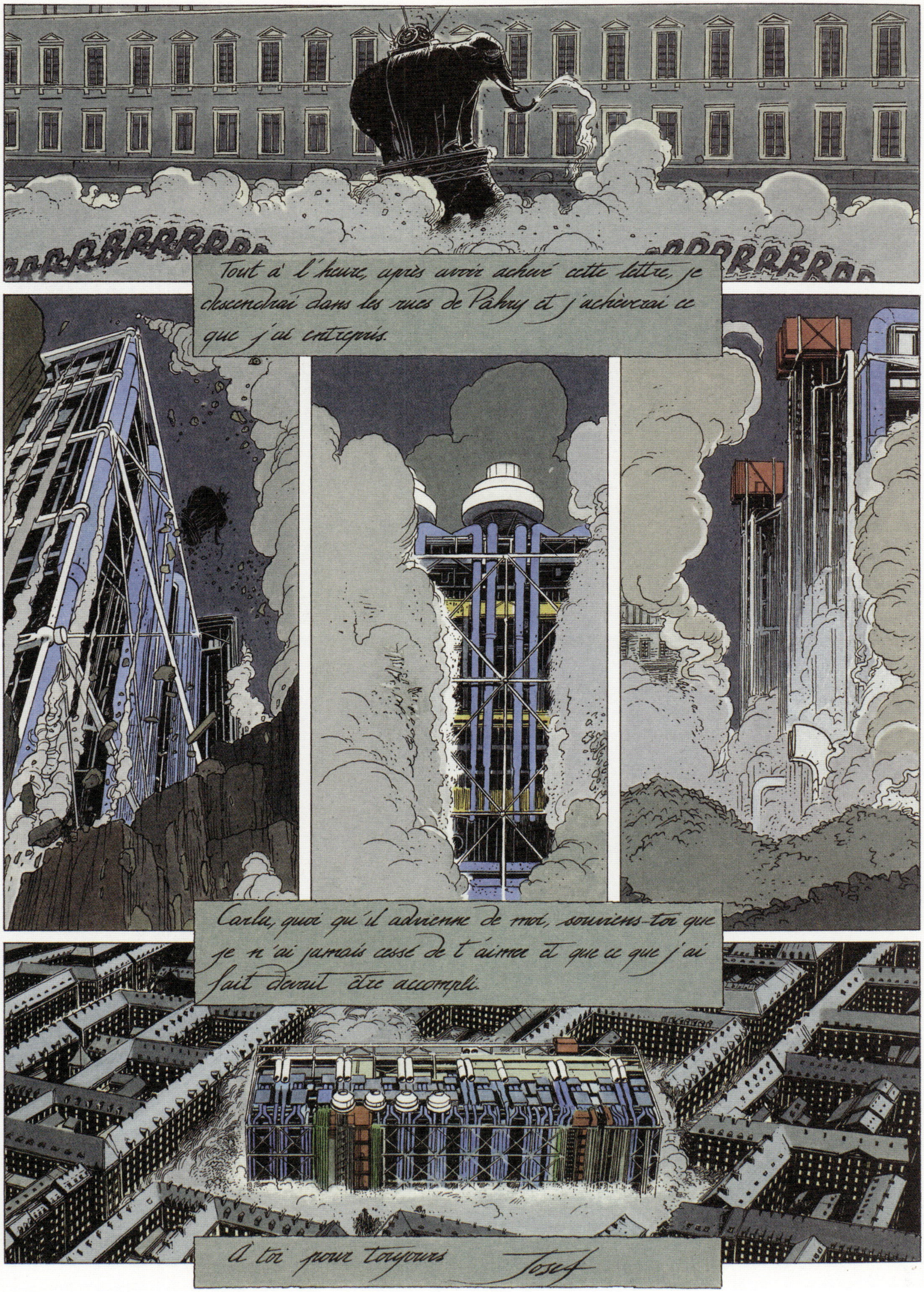
Tout à l'heure, après avoir achevé cette lettre, je descendrai dans les rues de Pâhry et j'achèverai ce que j'ai entrepris.
Carla, quoi qu'il advienne de moi, souviens-toi que je n'ai jamais cessé de t'aimer et que ce que j'ai fait devait être accompli.
A toi pour toujours Josef

Centre national d'art et de culture Georges Pompidou

The Centre national d'art et de culture Georges Pompidou is a national establishment under the supervision of the Ministry of culture (law no.75-1, 3 January 1975).

Alain Seban
President

Agnès Saal
Managing Director

Alfred Pacquement
Director of the Musée National d'Art Moderne – Centre de Création Industrielle

Bernard Blistène
Director of the Cultural Development Department

Jack Lang
President of the Association for the Development of the Centre Pompidou

Jacques Boissonnas
President of the Société des Amis du Musée National d'Art Moderne

Publication

Laurence Castany
Concept, Texts and Editing

Gammon Sharpley
Translation

les designers anonymes
Graphic Design and Layout

Danielle Fortier
Copy Editing

Patrice Henry
Production

Publication Department

Nicolas Roche
Director

Jean-Christophe Claude
Deputy Director, Head of Publishing

Françoise Marquet
Editorial Manager

Sales Department

Marie-Sandrine Cadudal
Department Head

Benoît Collier
Sales Manager

Francesca Baldi
Sales Officer

Josiane Peperty
Dispatch and Stock Control

Administrative and Finance

Nicole Parmentier
Payments

Matthias Battestini
Receipts

Administrative Assistants
Isabelle Charles-Planchet
Philippe Léonard
Danielle Malemanche

Image Management and Permissions

Claudine Guillon
Department Head

Mai-Lise Benedic
Iconography Documentation

Xavier Delamare
Assistant

Multimedia Department

Emmanuelle Bermès

Many thanks to

Patrick Bazin, Karine Bomel, Jean-Philippe Bonilli, Bernadette Borel-Lorie, Cécile Desauziers, Jean-Loup Guillaume, Stéphanie Hussonnois-Bouhayati, Nelly Jacquin, Martial Lhuillery, Alfred Pacquement, Vincent Poussou, Roger Rotmann, Didier Schulmann, Christine Sorin, Audrey Venet-Pasquier.

First printed in september 2011 by Artegrafica, Graphicom Group, in Verona, Italy